D1572244

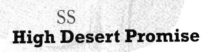

SS
High Desert Promise

SS

—*Kirt and Johanna Skinner*

High Desert Promise

The Skinner Family Legacy

SS

John Sackett Skinner

John A. Skinner

Robert H. Skinner

Christine Skinner Moore

Daniel H. Skinner

Johanna Skinner Owens

Publisher Skinner Family

SS

John Sackett Skinner is the fifth son of Kirt and Johanna. John and his four surviving brothers and sisters have inherited a love of historical preservation from their parents and all have worked tirelessly to compile information for this volume.

ISBN 978-0-6153366-8-8

Cover and jacket design by Sherry Green.
Jacket photo is of the Skinner Ranch gate.
Jacket inset photo: (left to right on horseback) brothers Kirt (Dad), Harold and Bill with their Dad Will

Text set in 11.5pt Adobe Caslon Pro.

Publisher Skinner Family
SS

10 9 8 7 6 5 4 3 2 1   09 10 11 12 13 14 15 16 17 18 19 20

Printed in the United States on acid-free paper.

To our Mom and Dad
and
Grandmother & Grandfather

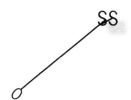

Out Where the
West Begins

Out where the handclasp's a little stronger,
Out where the smile dwells a little longer,
    That's where the West begins.
Out where the sun is a little brighter,
Where the snows that fall are a trifle whiter,
Where the bonds of home are a wee bit tighter,
    That's were the West begins.

Out where the skies are a trifle bluer,
Out where friendship's a little truer,
    That's where the West begins.
Out where a fresher breeze is blowing,
Where there's laughter in every streamlet flowing,
Where there's more of reaping and less of sowing,
    That's where the West begins.

Out where the world is in the making,
Where fewer hearts in despair are aching,
    That's where the West begins.
Where there's more of singing and less of sighing,
Where there's more of giving and less of buying,
And a man makes friends without half trying,
    That's where the West begins.

                              —Arthur Chapman
                              1911
            (Found in the old Skinner Cookbook)

SS

Contents

Contents Continued

SS

Acknowledgments

John Sackett Skinner, Writer

Over ten years ago our brother Bob Skinner and sister Joanne Skinner Owens looked at the mounds of papers, old letters, business documents, and bulging file drawers of information gathered over one hundred-forty-six years of history on the Skinner Ranch. These two folks vowed to make order out of chaos and began organizing the material into notebooks. This has helped my own research tremendously.

There have been many contributors to this work who deserve more credit than I can give here. First and foremost, I credit our mother, Johanna Skinner for her interest in the history of eastern Oregon and southwest Idaho, and her ability to record that history clearly and concisely. She was supported in that love of history by her husband, our dad, Kirtland Skinner, and her father-in-law William Skinner, who actually lived in, and was deeply involved with, the period our book covers. My brother Bob couldn't have been more co-operative. He was a great help to me by filling in the blanks, of which there were many. Thank goodness for his wonderful memory and his patience.

Another contributor was our sister Christine Skinner Moore, who was Managing Editor of the *Eastern Oregon Observer* for many years and who knows the history of eastern Oregon as well as anyone. Chris will never know how much help her historical articles and writings were to me.

There is our brother Dan who, like Bob, could describe every square inch of the ranch and whose brain I picked when I got mired down and needed the help he willingly provided.

I thank Joanne, our baby sister who, with Bob, got all this started when they started with their filing project. They filled four big boxes of historical documents into some semblance of order and she has spent months searching the Skinner archives for relevant pictures for our book. She also provided us lunch when it was necessary to meet.

Another important person is my wife Carole. Carole has been so patient and has willingly stepped up in support. She has taken over the household tasks allowing me more time with the manuscript. She has cleaned up after me, and she has been a Godsend. So have our kids, Mike and Sheryl, Becky and Art, Dan and Marie, and Diana and David and our terrific grandchildren. Their interest in this book and the support each one has provided has been heart warming and hugely appreciated.

Finally, I wish also to thank our Publisher, Sherry Green, of Golden Quill Publishing in Hillsboro, Oregon. Sherry has been beside me all the way, providing support, correcting my foibles, giving me the gentle push when I slacked off. My thanks go also to Linda Meyer, our editor. She is amazingly good at searching out the places I sort of slid over, or flat out made mistakes. She didn't let me get away with anything. Both of these ladies have been wonderful for me to work with.

To you all, to everyone who has provided documentation, encouragement and support, I give you my undying appreciation.

A Note from Joanne Skinner Owens

I first want to express gratitude to our parents Kirt and Johanna Skinner who instilled in us the importance of documenting and preserving regional and family history and artifacts. Without their intense interest in the southeast corner of Oregon this book would not have materialized.

Thanks: To my brother Bob who kept reams of material in safekeeping after our parents were gone and helped me assemble forty-three ring binders of material. To his wife Sara that never complained about the many times we covered every flat space in their home as we put the material in order. To my brother John for his three years of dedication to this writing and to Carole his wife for the support she gave him throughout the long process. To my sister Chris, brother Dan and wife Cathy for pictures and support. To my son Marty Owens for taking photos and supplying CDs. To my grandchildren Jake and Jessica Bertalotto who came to help when ever a computer problem arose. To my friend Bonnie Nester who put me in contact with Sherry Green at Golden Quill Publishing and Linda Meyer, Editor. To Eva Gibson, Portland Community College Instructor of "Write Your Life Story," for the guidance and encouragement she has given. Last but not least to my husband Duane for taking over many of the duties I usually do and advertising to many, "The Skinner's are writing a book!"

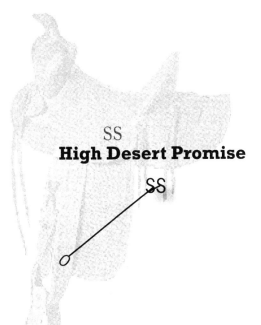

SS
High Desert Promise

Deep in the heart of a country kid is a longing; nay it is more than a longing. It is an addiction to wide open spaces, blue skies, the life of hard work, the serenity, the vistas, the sounds of silence, the song of the meadowlark or the eagle, the clean air, the smell of leather or new-mown hay or sagebrush after a rain. There is an old adage of the country:

   You can take the kid out of the sagebrush,
   You cannot take the sagebrush out of the kid.

   —The author, John, taking a moment deep in the heart of the country.

SS

Introduction

The little town of Jordan Valley lies in the southeast corner of Oregon, a few miles from the Idaho-Oregon border. Nestled snugly in among the mountains, peaks, and valleys, it lies on the eastern edge of Oregon's high desert. This is cattle country, and about thirteen miles west of the little town there is a cattle ranch. It was on this ranch, the Skinner Ranch beside Jordan Creek, that my six siblings and I grew up. We are the fourth of seven generations of the Skinner family in America who have lived, worked, and played in the wide-open spaces on this cattle ranch.

Out here the atmosphere is so clear one can stand outside at night, reach up, and almost touch the stars. The Milky Way carves an arc across the heavens like a white sash. The sun shines at least three hundred days a year. It gets hot in the summer and well below zero in the winter. Almost without fail in the summer, a cool breeze arrives in the early afternoon, and in winter the humidity is so low that even below-zero temperatures are easily tolerated.

It snows and sometimes the wind blows, but when spring arrives so does new life, and all kinds of God's creatures, wild and domestic, begin to make their appearance. Nothing warms the heart quicker than a just-born animal, whether it is a baby calf, a newborn colt, or a puppy out of a favorite cow dog. You would have to be pretty cynical and insensitive if a sight like that didn't warm your heart a bit.

When the sun warms the earth, grass begins to grow, trees begin to leaf out, and desert flowers begin to bloom. You cannot live in this country without being in awe of nature's annual rebirth. This is one of those rare places on Earth where Mother Nature teaches young and old alike the true meaning of life, liberty, and the pursuit of happiness. This is God's Country.

If you feel like going outside and yelling at the top of your lungs to let off a little steam, do it! Nobody is going to call you crazy or a nut case, because chances are, nobody will be close enough to hear you.

If you take the time, and you should, you can watch the distant mountains put on a fantastic show, changing colors almost by the hour, sometimes by the minute, as the sun caresses them from different angles. Steens Mountain and the Sheepshead Mountains about one hundred miles to the west put on a different type of show on clear, cold winter mornings as the sun rises. A mirage will form and the mountains will grow and recede, taking on odd shapes. As the sun warms the air, the mirage slowly disappears and the mountains return to their natural shape.

You might want to saddle a horse and take a ride around that old ranch for the sake of memories. If you do, you will see where the first man to settle here had his home, now just a hole in the ground where a cellar once was. Or take a moment and sit in the shade of the huge, old cottonwood trees that another settler planted well over one hundred years ago. On your way back to the barn, you will want to move off the trail about thirty yards to the west, to that special, slightly elevated point on Skinner's Ridge where you can see nearly the entire ranch. Then take a moment and think about the young lad you will read about in these pages, who while herding his father's horses, sat in this very spot and had a vision of the promise this land offered.

In later years, this same man, much older now, more fragile and no longer able to get on a horse, would slowly walk up Skinner's Ridge on a warm day and sit on a flat lava rock in that same spot. He'd light a cigarette and remember the promise that he believed this land held. He would remember with pride another promise, the one he'd made to turn this land into the best cattle ranch in the area.

While you are there, take a moment to remind yourself of the other folks you will read about in these pages, those who came later and who worked day and night putting their hearts and souls into this land, and then, on one occasion in 1931, with the ranch bankrupt and in receivership, nearly bid it good-bye. In these pages, you will read how it all worked out so they were able to stay. These people shed blood, sweat, and on many occasions, tears. But they hung in there. They stuck it out day by day, month by month, year by year, and eventually they were able to put it all back together again and make it the success it is today.

This can be a lonesome country too, eerily silent at times, especially at night. When coyotes out there in the sagebrush start howling at the moon, checking in and discussing the night's activities with their pals, they are only making plans to locate something to eat. You might hear an owl up in one of the trees, his big eyes peeled for a mouse for breakfast, telling everyone about it with his mournful call. In the quiet of the night, howling coyotes and that sudden mournful call of the owl can send a chill up the back of the uninitiated youngster.

If you check on the kids you will probably find the little ones snuggling just a bit deeper into their blankets, alarmed by these night sounds. Sometimes the silence is there in the daylight, too. And, that is good. If it is very quiet, you will hear the song of the meadowlark sitting on a fence post close by, or the scream of an eagle or a hawk circling overhead, like those coyotes and the owl, hunting for some lunch. When you see those things and hear those sounds, no matter how crazy and mixed up this old world is today, you know goodness still exists on this land—pure, God-given, natural goodness.

If it's crowds of people, bright lights, car horns and traffic noise, angry drivers and the hustle bustle of the city that you desire, this is definitely not the life for you. I suspect most folks who drive Highway 95 in this part of Oregon would consider it about the most boring, desolate stretch of road in America. We leave them to their thoughts, and wish them Godspeed. In our haste today, it is easy to miss the beauty and serenity of this wonderful land. For those people born and raised here, for those who have lived their lives here, and for others who sought the solitude, this is their Eden.

Life on this Ranch

Of the seven generations of Skinners in America, four generations live on Skinner Ranch today. Bob Sr. is a member of the fourth; his son Bob Jr., the fifth; his sons Silas (Si) and Mike, the sixth; and Silas's three children, and Mike's child, are the seventh. Si's younger brother recently married and makes his home on the ranch. Michael and his wife Kelsi have added another Skinner to the clan with the birth of a son they named Jayden.

There was a time not too many years ago when it required a workforce of thirty to forty hired men and even more teams of horses and mules to do the work on this ranch. With the efficiency provided by today's modern but very expensive equipment, it now takes only two or three Skinners to operate the ranch, with a hired hand or two in

Four-horse teams were a regular sight on the Skinner Ranch before the arrival of modern equipment. Here they are doing spring planting. Back row (L to R): Harold Skinner on disk, Tom Young in white shirt, and Kirt Skinner stand-

summer, and possibly one extra in winter. We must qualify that comment since the wives of the Skinner men often work alongside their husbands. The rewards offered by efficient equipment and a much smaller crew are a higher-quality harvest that serves to provide American consumers with the highest quality beef on their dinner tables.

Silas (great-great-great-grandson of the original Silas Skinner) and his wife Traci have added two boys and a girl to the crew. Kasen is nine; Regann, eight; and Cort, five. Kasen has already taken his place in a long line of Skinner Ranch kids who have contributed to the operation and success of this ranch. He has the genetic ability for horsemanship and an uncanny eye for matching a cow and calf pair in a big herd of cattle. That is not an easy task for even a more experienced cowman. Regann and Cort are just a bit too young yet, but it will not be long before they're equally involved.

ing on drill. Front row (L to R): Des Tibbits, Will Skinner standing in front of white horse, Hugh Skinner held by Willis Thompson (Tompy). Second from right: Bill Skinner on a white horse. Other men unidentified.

By the age of five or six, ranch kids begin learning the life of a rancher. They accompany adults in doing whatever sort of work is being done. They won't be expected to do the work, but they can observe and learn what to do as well as what not to do. Patience is a virtue, because that child, following along on a gentle horse, or watching his dad work on a piece of fence or equipment, will be asking a thousand questions. Why? How? When? How many? And so on. By school age a child will be fairly conversant and aware of what ranch life is like.

If a child born into a ranch family wishes to continue ranching as their life's work, they will be well prepared to take their place in line one day as owners and operators of a successful ranching operation.

Children born to these ranch families, along with their formal education, have a wonderful opportunity to learn independence early in life. Like generations before, in their early years these kids will

Left: Bob Sr. and his wife Sara. Below: Bob Jr. and his wife Karen. All live on the ranch. There are four houses on the compound.

begin taking their place in the ranch operation under the supervision and careful eye of their elders. Their formal schooling comes first, but they will be taught to do tasks geared to their ages, tasks that will provide them with a source of pride and accomplishment in themselves.

Home Again in Eastern Oregon

As a member of the Skinners' fourth generation, I spent the first twenty-three years of my life living and working on the Skinner Ranch. Several years ago, my wife Carole and I spent a few days visiting my oldest brother Bob and his wife Sara, my brother Dan and his wife Cathy, and their families at their homes on the Skinner Ranch in Jordan Valley. As one who adopted a different career, I still find it is a treat to go back home.

Family living on the ranch today include Bob's grandsons and their families. Above (left to right): Cort, Regann, Kasen, Tracy, and Silas. Left: Kelsi and Michael holding Jayden. (These are the sixth and seventh generations).

Others in the family who have not lived there feel that same need to visit, if only to pay homage to ancestry. There is, it seems, an inherent need to revisit family roots, renew family ties, and walk in the footprints of our elders.

For those of us who have lived there, every building, field, irrigation ditch, or gate in the fence—or even an old juniper post planted sixty years ago to hold up that fence—jars a memory.

The path up the trail to where the milk cow barn once stood is no longer used and now almost nonexistent, but I made my way through the sagebrush up to the old calf corral. At the top, I turned around to look back toward the houses, and back came the memory of the milk cart with two buggy wheels that we used to carry milk cans to and from the cow barn. With it came the memory of the day when in our youthful

John milking a cow. Dan is in the background. Joanne took the picture.

A cousin, Bert Palmer (seated), and Dan Skinner taking a break on the path back from the cow barn with the milk cart.

exuberance, my brother Dan, our cousin Bert Palmer, and I decided to race down that path pushing the cart with its cans full of milk. Of course there was a sudden stumble. When I close my eyes I can still see that cart somersaulting down the path ahead of us, scattering milk cans once full but no longer. We didn't have to run the milk through the separator that night. We did have to wash and dry the buckets and cans and do some heavy-duty explaining about why there was no milk.

The cow barn is gone and the willow calf corral is in tatters, but the barn's cement floor is still there, and so are some memories. I hated the job of milking cows then, and would now, but there was consolation in knowing that my older siblings also had to do that job before they were qualified for what the younger kids considered "real" work. Real work was buckarooing, driving a team of horses, working in the hayfields, irrigating, or doing whatever the "big guys" were doing.

Like it or not, there were a lot of cows milked in that barn. So why are there good memories? Maybe it was because of those big calves we tried to ride when our dad wasn't looking? There was the day my brother Dan got bucked off a calf and skinned his back on the willow fence. Three brothers never said a word until our mom found a little blood on his undershirt. Our parents admonished us never to ride the dairy calves again. But we did. I also think it was here at the cow barn that I tried my first cigarette. It was a "roll your own" out of a sack of Bull Durham tobacco. It was not well done and wouldn't stay lit. That was a good thing. But remember, we wanted to do and be just like the big guys.

During the Depression years, the cream checks sent weekly from the Swift & Co. Creamery in Caldwell, Idaho, came in real handy to buy school clothes, groceries, and, on occasion, to help a down-and-out neighbor or relative. I have strong nostalgia for the good times and the rough times, for the life I once lived.

Putting aside thoughts of the Great Depression, I left the site of the cow barn and walked out on that point where one can get near to a full view of this ranch. This was the exact point on Skinner's Ridge young William Silas Skinner had often visited when he herded his father's horses on this flat so many years ago. This story will tell how Will Skinner, when an old man and no longer able to mount a horse, would one day sit on that rock out here on the eastern edge of Oregon's high desert, light up a cigarette, and admire the product of his dreams.

*William Silas Skinner,
father of Kirt, on his
faithful mount, Bounder.*

For me, it was difficult that day to envision what Will saw from that vantage point as a small boy herding his father's horses. What he observed was an expanse of flat land covered with gray sagebrush. But in his mind's eye he saw what I saw that day, and it was not sagebrush. It was green fields almost as far as the eye could see, newly irrigated and highly productive. I saw barns and corrals and buildings necessary to the operation of a ranch, and homes both old and new. As a child, Will Skinner could not see those buildings, but through the years he had a hand in erecting most of those amenities on this land.

A day or so later I walked up Skinner's Ridge to a different location to get a different view of this marvelous valley of the Jordan. Skinner cattle were out on the range, and the fields would soon be dotted by huge round bales of hay. In the quietness, I heard the sound of a neighbor's tractor a mile or so away. I stood there for a moment and memories began to flow back. Over by the slough in a little cove, I saw a couple of mule deer grazing. I was easily fifteen years old before I saw my first deer. Now there are hundreds, and they have become a big problem to the ranchers on whose land they feed.

Pharmacy Hill.

From the elevation where I stood, I could see the more distant rolling hills to the north, east, and south where as kids, and then as young adults, we rode horseback and there and beyond with our dad and grandfather, brothers, and hired men, and in later years, by ourselves, working with cattle. It was fun then. Today, for me, it was only a nostalgic memory of a wonderful time gone by.

ooooo

The next morning we sat at Bob and Sara's breakfast table discussing Skinner family history and our relationship with the ranch and the country around it. Bob suggested we re-explore the community and the surrounding area. I was eager to accept his invitation.

We made our first visit to the cemetery in Jordan Valley. We spent a couple of hours there, reminiscing with the spirits. Some were relatives long since departed, among them little Sara Ellen Skinner, daughter of pioneers Silas and Anne Jane Skinner. Sara Ellen died at age two, most likely from diphtheria in 1883. It is a small cemetery, and not far away is her brother Thomas, one of Silas and Anne Jane's sons, born in 1877 at the Trout Creek Station. Thomas died in 1958 at age seventy-five. Beside him is his wife Violet (Glover) Skinner. Violet was a descendant of the Glover and Shea families, also prominent pioneers in the area. Nearby is the grave of Horatio (Ray), another son of Silas and Anne Jane. Ray was born on the Skinner Ranch and died in 1918 during the flu epidemic.

Many other folks I had known in their mortal lives are buried there, and even more whom I knew by family name and through local lore. So many of these people had a huge part in the formation and taming of this part of our great country, and in turning it into what it is today.

Later we drove up to the top of Pharmacy Hill, a rocky crag that stands guard over the town of Jordan Valley. Pharmacy Hill was named for a sign painted many years ago on the smooth face of a rock, advertising the local pharmacy owned by another icon of the community, Dr. W. W. Jones. "Doctor Walter W. Jones" is a name as prominent in Jordan Valley as the name "Jordan Valley." Dr. Jones was a highly trained, competent physician and a cherished friend of the family. Many people living in this community and elsewhere owe their lives to this respected and beloved physician. In the dead of winter, it was not unusual for him to ride many miles on horseback, or trudge through deep snow on foot to see to a sick or injured patient or to attend the birth of a baby. With the exception of our oldest brother Bill, who was born in Boise, Idaho, Dr. Jones attended the home births of nearly all of Will and Ella's grandchildren including the remaining six of my siblings.

During the years I lived in Jordan Valley, I had never taken time to make the trip to the summit of Pharmacy Hill. On this day we were rewarded with a three hundred and sixty degree, panoramic, bird's-eye view of the town of Jordan Valley, the surrounding community, the peaks, the valleys, and the mountains that provide a scenic backdrop to this valley of the Jordan. It was mid-April, and the view from the summit that day was spectacular. The atmosphere was crystal clear, typical of eastern Oregon in the spring. To the east and southeast, still covered with a blanket of snow, are the Owyhee Mountains and South Mountain with their rich histories of gold and silver mining. Further to the southeast and southwest, stand Parsnip Peak and Juniper Ridge. At the base of Juniper Ridge lies the Antelope Reservoir, responsible for converting thousands of acres of land from desert into productive farm and ranch land.

More than a hundred miles to the west stands the majestic Steens Mountain, each crevasse and canyon showing distinctly in the pristine air. Behind us to the north is Mahogany Mountain, another local icon. As residents we looked on these mountains daily, but we seldom took time to admire their beauty. On this day, these mountains were reaching out and beckoning to Bob and me like old friends.

If traveling through Jordan Valley, or if local and in the mood for ice cream or coffee, Skinners Rockhouse is a nice stopping place. 2006.

It was to this area of the West, to these mountains and valleys, that our Skinner ancestors first came. This is a country where untold generations of Native Americans, fur trappers, miners, and seven generations of Skinners have trod the same trails. It would be my guess that all of them, Native and invader alike, must have been equally as impressed as I was that day with the grandeur, stability, and beauty of this land. In the brilliant sunlight of that April morning, the mountains appeared completely unsullied in spite of the human invasion over the years, and in the face of this rapidly changing world.

As I admired this small corner of America, it reaffirmed why so many others and I have grown to love the Northwest as much as the original people must have. I could find no blame whatsoever in their desperate attempts to stem the tide of white invaders and preserve for themselves this land and their way of life.

The miniature mountain named Pharmacy Hill that we were atop that day is located on a ranch once owned by the late Thomas L. Skinner and his wife Violet. The ranch itself has been sold, but the home and buildings on this place are still owned by family members.

What remains of Inskeep Station on the Skinner Toll Road. Charbonneau's monument can be seen in the distance. Note: portholes are larger on the outside than inside to permit guns a larger area to swing back and forth sighting objects outside the building.

The oldest remaining house in Jordan Valley, constructed of locally quarried rock, is located here. It is now under the ownership of the descendants of Thomas and Violet. This later Skinner family has converted it into an increasingly well-known and fun stopping place called "Skinners Rockhouse." Bob and I hadn't had any coffee since breakfast, so we stopped in for a cup, and had a pleasant visit with some of the local folks. This gathering place features coffee, lattes, ice cream, souvenirs, old pictures of family and local events, and has many locally written historical books for sale.

The Sheep Ranch

The next day Bob and I drove to the neighboring community of Arock, located about midway between the Skinner Ranch and the Owyhee River. Our route followed Silas Skinner's historic toll road from the Skinner Ranch to three other historic places of interest on the toll road. We first visited the burial site of Jean Baptiste Charbonneau, infant son of Sacagawea, the young female guide who accompanied the Lewis and Clark Expedition. Then we visited the ruins of the historic

Inskeep Station at the Ruby Ranch. Our third and final destination that day was The Sheep Ranch, a historically important stagecoach station on the Skinner Toll Road. In its heyday this stage station provided eating facilities, comfortable amenities, and overnight sleeping quarters for stagecoach passengers and freighters.

This historic stone station has been partially restored by the Eiguren family, owners of the ranch on which it is located. The original builders built portholes in the building in order to repel attacks from hostile Indians and insure the safety of travelers. In a later chapter you will read that in 1868 Silas Skinner and his assistant David Shirk found it necessary to ward off an attacking band of Indians by firing their rifles from these portholes. As I looked out of those portholes that day and tried to imagine the situation Silas faced, I sincerely wondered how I, as Silas's great-grandson, would have reacted to the attack.

Having access to a telegraph system between Silver City and Winnemucca, Nevada, the Sheep Ranch also served as military headquarters for Captain Bernard, who served under the command of General O. H. Howard during the Bannock Indian Wars of 1878.

It was from here that Sarah Winnemucca, princess of the Paiute tribe, daughter of Chief Winnemucca, and granddaughter of Chief Truckee, volunteered to ride horseback to Steens Mountain to help the army locate the hostile Bannocks. Her service was at the request of Captain Bernard, in charge of the army contingent stationed at the Sheep Ranch. Bernard sent word ahead by telegraph to army units to provide Sarah's group with anything she might need, including fresh horses to complete her mission. Sarah was accompanied by two other Paiute Indians, and over the period of three days, they rode horseback well over two hundred miles to Steens Mountain and back in an attempt to locate the hostile Bannocks for the army. At the same time, she was able to free her own tribe, the Paiutes, from the Bannocks. Under the leadership of Chief Buffalo Horn, the Bannocks had taken the Paiutes hostage in an attempt to force them to join the battle against the settlers.

South Mountain

The next day, a Sunday, I felt a bit guilty about taking Bob away from his family again so I picked up my brother Dan. We were both at loose ends so we decided to drive up to South Mountain. We never did get there because we stopped so many times, at so many historical places along the way, that we ran out of daylight. We spent most of our time near the foot of what is known locally as the Trout Creek Grade that Silas Skinner constructed for his toll road, and is also near the site of Silas and Anne Jane Skinner's Trout Creek Station on the toll road.

It gives one an eerie feeling to tread in the dust of ancestors, to see the same terrain their eyes saw, and to then realize how much has changed since they walked this Earth, and yet so little. Slight evidence remains of the bustling activity of days gone by, but we found the original well, the home's lava rock foundation and that of the hostler's living quarters—and that was about all. The station house itself burned down many years ago.

Silas Skinner, my great-grandfather, decided this would be an ideal place to build a home. He located it near the foot of Trout Creek grade approximately halfway between Silver City and the next station, the Sheep Ranch. In addition to being his family home, he made it an eating stop for stagecoach passengers and freighters, possibly with limited overnight accommodations for stagecoach passengers. With the long and steep grade ahead of them, he guessed that by locating his station near the foot of the grade, teamsters would stop for a meal and to rest their teams before going on. Silas, always the businessman, was prepared to provide—for a fee of course—more horse, oxen, or mule power if needed by the teamsters to negotiate the grade. He was right on all counts.

Recording History for This Part of Oregon

During those few hours and days reacquainting myself with this country I grew up in, I began to ask myself some questions. Besides mining, what was it about this rather remote, mountainous, sagebrush covered land that grabbed the heart and soul of people who migrated to this area? Why did they decide to stay here when the mining ended, and then to make it their home? And then, what is it that makes their descendants so fiercely love and respect this land?

With the rapid advancements in technology, we may one day be able to open a cyber-window on our television sets through which we can follow the progression of history as it unfolded. Until that day arrives, all we have is family lore and recorded history available to us, and in addition to it, I believe the answers to the above questions may have been revealed in the first few pages of this book.

Unfortunately, in their attempts to record history, some historians have distorted it. Others have altered history intentionally for their

Always dressed in a tie and vest, Will Skiner is on a family camping trip with Trout Creek a few feet away.

own benefit. Slight distortions are nearly unavoidable and can happen due to lack of knowledge or from speculation about historical events that have taken place.

With that in mind, we have made this attempt to record as accurately as possible the history of our family line from 1862, when Silas Skinner, or "Sam" as he became known, arrived in America.

Most of the knowledge of the Skinner family has been passed down orally from generation to generation, enhancing and supplementing historical records about our family. We understand that one person will hear and remember something differently than another hears and remembers, so in later years some family members have taken the initiative and recorded much of the oral history as it was told, or soon thereafter. Slight distortions of events are nearly unavoidable, but since the stories being told and retold were changed but little—some nearly verbatim each time—we believe we have provided herein a reasonably accurate record of the Skinner family in America.

Our family's link to the historical era following Silas Skinner's arrival in Silver City in 1863 through the 1960s, was Silas and Anne Jane's son, Will Skinner. Will was my grandfather and an excellent storyteller with a superb memory.

A great deal of the information herein comes from Will Skinner's writings. He had an uncanny ability to recall historical events accuratly, and then describe them on paper. That which he did not write about but often discussed was diligently recorded by his daughter-in-law, my mother Johanna Murray Skinner. When Will began reminiscing, she grabbed whatever was available to write on, from the backs of envelopes to the backs of calendars to a crumpled piece of scrap paper, onto which she recorded his words. She haunted libraries, searching for anything that even hinted of local history. She read and compared history books. She spent hour after hour making notes from every historical bit of information she could find in order to check and double-check the information she gleaned and recorded.

Ample evidence indicates it was she who first intended to write this book. Her life was cut short before she could complete her task, so we have combined our mother's careful work with the superb memory of our father, whose life covered most of the history herein, and our grandfather, to whom we are also indebted. We therefore dedicate this book to the memory of our parents Johanna Murray Skinner, her husband Silas Kirtland Skinner, and our grandparents William Silas Skinner and Ella Sackett Skinner.

Rather than mine alone, this effort to record the Skinner history is the work of many. Others who have contributed to the abundance of historical information are Will's son Kirtland and a number of Will's grandchildren. Chris Skinner Moore, Will's granddaughter and retired editor of the *Ontario Argus* newspaper, is another, as is his grandson Robert Skinner, and another of Will's granddaughters, my sister Joanne Skinner Owens. Many of Will's grandchildren and great-grandchildren have inherited the thirst for knowledge of family and the history of the area surrounding this corner of Oregon and the Skinner Ranch.

Occasionally the dates of events which Will Skinner recalled are a bit different from the actual. He may also have added some embellishment to add color, but even with those liberties taken, his memories did not clash greatly with other historical writers. He was a proud man and he suffered some hard knocks in his life, but he was, in every sense of the word, a pioneer who made significant contributions to the history of southeastern Oregon, southwest Idaho, and the Skinner Ranch.

SS

1

SS

Our Beginnings in America

The Skinner family heritage begins on the Isle of Man and dates back to about 1600, the approximate birth year of Ewan Skinner, the first recorded member of our branch on the Skinner family tree.

The Isle of Man is a tiny landmass approximately twenty-five miles long and twelve miles wide, located in the Irish Sea between Ireland and the coasts of England and Scotland. Known as "Manxmen," most of these islanders historically occupied small farms called "crofts." Anne Hampton Humphries, a granddaughter of Silas Skinner, was born and raised on the Isle of Man. She wrote in a short essay that primarily women and children planted and harvested their meager crops and tended to their few animals—typically a pig, a cow, and for the more well off, a horse. Because of the closeness of the sea, most able-bodied Manxmen were seafarers or were otherwise involved in the maritime industry.

According to the obituary of his wife, Anne Jane Callow, Silas Skinner followed the sailing tradition of his elders and went to sea at the tender age of about nine. We suspect he accompanied his elders on short sailing trips to England, Ireland, and Scotland at an even earlier age. At about twelve, he became a full-time sailor, a profession he would follow until he was twenty-eight years of age.

On at least one of the occasions we are aware of during his sailing career, Silas made a trip to visit friends and relatives in Ashtabula, Ohio. Ashtabula had become the new home to a large number of Manx families. The first recorded Callow in our family was Robert Callow, born in 1630 on the Isle of Man. The Skinner and Callow families had been neighbors and close friends on the Isle of Man. When Silas was about twelve, his parents sent him to fetch a midwife to attend the birth of an infant being born into the Callow family. That child, born

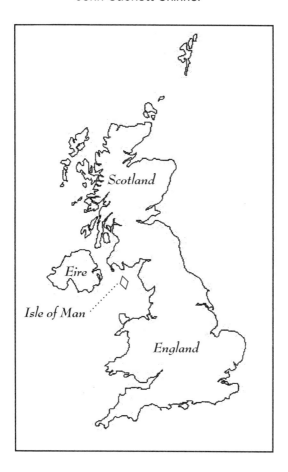

in January 1846, was christened Anne Jane and would one day become the bride of Silas Skinner.

In 1865, traveling with her grandfather who lived in Ashtabula, Ohio and was visiting family on the Isle of Man, eighteen-year-old Anne Jane left the family home of Balla Callum (home of the Callows) and migrated to America to live with her grandparents.

Under the tutelage of an aunt who also had previously migrated to America, Anne Jane soon became an accomplished seamstress and dressmaker. Along with her sewing, she opened and operated a millinery shop and became a successful business person in Ashtabula, often sought out for her knowledge of business affairs.

When Silas Skinner made a visit to Ashtabula, he quickly became aware that his ex-neighbor from the Isle of Man had grown into an at-

Left: Anne Jane Callow as a young girl on the Isle of Man. Right: Silas Skinner, man of many talents and interests.

tractive and ambitious young woman. There is no question that on that visit to Ashtabula, Silas was smitten by the charming Anne Jane. Silas, however, heard the call of the sea and for whatever the reason, possibly contractual, he returned to his ship and his sailing career.

Silas Skinner

Silas did not leave a diary of his world travels as a mariner. We don't know where he traveled or the name of the ship he sailed on. While none of his personal writings remain, we know he communicated with Anne Jane on a number of occasions. Silas was a capable man and an intelligent, astute businessman. With the many successful business affairs he was to become involved in, there is no doubt that he could read and understand legal documents clearly.

But why did Silas decide to leave the sea? What convinced him to leave the mariner's life he'd led for sixteen years? He was in his twenty-eighth year and might well have decided to explore other avenues to success.

I put myself in Silas's shoes for a moment and attempted to understand the workings of his mind as he reached the decision to give up sailing, in reality not dissimilar to the same processes most young people must work through in choosing professions. Not one to leap to conclusions, Silas probably worked his way through his options. He likely realized that major changes in one's professional life should not be made without a great deal of thought.

The story of our family in America begins with Silas Skinner. Silas the mariner arrived in America in 1862 at age twenty-eight. We have only a little knowledge of his life before that time so when we started this history of the Skinner family in America, I knew we were going to need help. We had to find a way to get Silas off the boat and onto land to entice him to make his life in America. I turned to a picture of Silas that hangs in my office said to myself, "I wish you could tell me how you came to make your decision."

The following fictional section—not historically documented— makes an attempt to draw a mental picture of Silas's mind-set during that period in his life. If Silas heard my pleas for help, the following is his response.

The tall bearded Manxman stood on the ship's deck, his hands clasped casually behind his back. Almost unconsciously, he watched the bow nodding into the ocean swells as the ship approached the Golden Gate passageway into San Francisco Bay. Except for his very early years on the Isle of Man, ships and the seas they sailed on represented the only home Silas Skinner had ever known. Over the last several months, however, he had become increasingly restless. It was 1862 and he was in his twenty-eighth year. He recognized that sailing need not be his sole profession, and the thought of owning land now occupied his mind, among other things. If a change was to be made, perhaps this was the time to make it.

The sea roughened a bit as the ship crossed the bar into the bay, and it reminded him of his dilemma. He smiled to himself thinking, "The sea and I both seem to be a bit restless, but while the sea cannot control its destiny, I can control mine."

As the ship moved slowly toward its mooring, Silas's mind turned to the many ports and harbors around the world that he had entered during his sailing career. Each had its own charm, its own exotic people and intoxicating smells. To each its own personality.

The Bay Area of California, however, had always been the most exciting, and the one most sailors looked forward to visiting of any port he knew.

Where else in the world could a person find such thriving industry, bustling activity, and unbridled wealth, long after the end of the gold rush? The area was continuing to grow rapidly, attracting more and bigger industries and the hoards of people to support them.

Silas promised himself he would at least investigate some other opportunities while ashore. He was so deeply involved with his thoughts that he did not hear the approaching footsteps come to a stop beside him.

"Silas, m'lad," remarked the ship's captain, "ye seem a wee bit pensive these days. Is there a problem t'be solved?"

Silas turned to face his captain. "Aye sir, t' be sure, I've been doing a bit o' thinkin' lately about takin' a long look at this New World called America."

The captain's retort was direct. "And what do ye have in mind as a manner o' makin' a living, Silas Skinner? What do ye know besides sailin'? Ye be a smart lad, but ye'll go out there and find some lassie just a waitin' for the likes o' ye. A comely lad ye are, m'boy, and ye must have a fair sum in yer boot from yer years a sailin', if ye haven't been foolish with it. I'll give ye some good advice, lad. Stay with the sea. She's a mighty fickle mistress, but she's nary as fickle as any o' the women ye'll find a walkin' the streets o' the city."

Silas's answer was meant to put the old Captain at ease. "Tis not in me plans, sir, to be hasty. I've not yet had the opportunity to investigate another profession. Tis always possible I shall return to the sea. As for the ladies, well, I've a dear friend in Ohio for whom I hold strong feelings." Hoping to end the conversation, Silas added, "Beggin' yer pardon, sir, but tis near time to moor the ship, and I must return to my duties."

As the captain dismissed him with a "hmmmph" and spun on his heel, Silas called after him. "Sir, I thank ye kindly for yer good advice."

But the old sailor acted as if he hadn't heard. Silas did not let the Captain see his quick smile. The captain's advice carried merit. However, it was not women Silas was seeking, but land and opportunity.

Before taking his leave from the ship the next morning Silas packed his seabag with his personal possessions and stepped onto the dock. He located a small hotel nearby, rented a room for the night, and stowed his seabag in the room. He locked the door and went for a slow walk through the streets of the city. The day was bright and sunny, and the crowds of people were in a festive mood. He was intrigued by the clatter of horse hooves on the streets, the laughter and conversations of couples walking arm in arm, and the bustling crowds.

He was amused by the sidelong glances he received from some of the ladies as he passed by. He smiled to himself as he remembered the Captain's admonitions from the previous day.

Moving along with the flow of activity, Silas concluded that life at sea was quiet, lonely, and unexciting compared to life ashore. He ate his lunch in a small café, savoring food that was nicely prepared and tasted far better than the shipboard fare he was used to. When he finished his lunch he continued walking slowly, hands clasped behind his back, taking in the sights of the city He found a small park where he took a seat on a shaded park bench and pondered his future. He continued his walk as the afternoon turned to evening and he returned to his hotel.

Not yet ready to retire for the evening, he found an eating-house close by and enjoyed another peaceful meal. For the second time that day he realized the ship's galley could not compete. Silas had about decided that life on shore was good.

With twilight approaching, he returned to the hotel and took a seat in the lobby for a time, watching people come and go. Two men seated nearby discussed the considerable success of gold and silver mines operating in Nevada, and the wealth being generated in the mining industry. Without being overtly intrusive, Silas listened carefully to every word said.

The more he heard, the more interested he became. Could it be? Was gold mining the catalyst that would entice him away from the *sea and the big ships? By morning Silas Skinner had made up his mind. He had decided to seek adventure and wealth in the Comstock gold fields of Nevada rather than return to his ship.*

The Search for Gold

We have no record of how Silas Skinner traveled to the Nevada gold and silver mines, but travel there he did. He went to work in the mines as a laborer until late in the fall of 1862. Word then reached the Nevada miners that significant gold strikes had been discovered in the Boise Basin area in the southern mountains of the Territory of Idaho. Silas Skinner, excited by this news, teamed up with another man whose name has now been lost to history. Each with a mule to carry their meager belongings, the two men started north on foot.

It has been speculated that Silas's companion on this trek may have been a man named James Donnelly, who later partnered with Silas and the Jordan brothers on the construction of the first toll road in the Territory of Idaho.

The two men wintered in Carson City, Nevada, and in the early spring of 1863 continued their walk through northern Nevada, eastern Oregon, and southern Idaho. Later that spring they arrived in Idaho City, in the south central Territory of Idaho. Idaho City was rapidly becoming the epicenter of Boise Basin gold mining.

Golden Friendships

Almost concurrently with Silas Skinner's arrival in Idaho City in the spring of 1863, a local gold prospector named Michael Jordan led a group of twenty-nine prospectors with some sixty horses and mules out of the Boise Basin on a gold prospecting expedition into the Owyhee Mountains of southwestern Idaho. It is likely they were searching for the famed and fabled Blue Bucket Gold Mine.

Rumors held that The Blue Bucket mine was a fabulous gold field discovered by immigrant travelers heading west. Following the discovery, and in their haste to move on, the travelers had marked their find with a blue bucket. Upon their return to the area, they were unable to relocate the blue bucket marker or the gold field.

Neither did Jordan's group of prospectors locate The Blue Bucket Mine, but on May 18, 1863, they arrived at a small creek in the mountainous area where they decided to camp for the evening. Prior to removing the saddle from his horse, one member of the group, a physician by the name of Ruud, took a pan and shovel and scooped up some gravel. In just minutes, his pan showed in excess of a hundred "colors" (gold).

Almost immediately the entire group was excitedly panning for gold, and all had outstanding results. Over the next few days, the prospectors staked their claims and drew up laws. They named the area "Discovery Bar," and the creek they were on, "Jordan Creek" in honor of the group's leader, Michael Jordan. The prospectors then moved further up the creek and established another camp they named "Happy Camp," later changed to Ruby City, which, even later, would be encompassed by Silver City. Several other small mining communities were eventually established in the area, including Booneville and Wagontown, and much later, Delamar and Dewey.

We know from family accounts that when Michael Jordan returned to Idaho City with news of his rich gold strike and his newly acquired mining claims, he and Silas Skinner somehow became acquainted. When Michael Jordan returned to the place the miners had named Happy Camp, Silas Skinner accompanied him.

Over the next year Michael, his brother James Jordan, and Silas or "Sam," as he was known, became heavily involved in a number of business dealings involving the mining industry. The three men became fast friends. Michael Jordan's diary, now located in the Owyhee County Historical Society in Murphy, Idaho, contains many entries of business affairs primarily related to the mining industry, in which the Jordans and Silas Skinner were involved.

SS

2

SS

Mining and Transport

With the rapid expansion of the mining industry, Silver City soon encompassed Ruby City, and became the major center of the mining operations in the Owyhee Mountains. Because of the rapid growth and increasing importance of the mining industry, Silver City was soon named the County Seat of Owyhee County in the Territory of Idaho. Silver City's population during the buildup of the mining industry eventually approached and probably exceeded five thousand residents, including the surrounding communities.

The early extraction of gold and silver in the Owyhee Mountains was done by placer mining, a method that required miners to run water through sluice boxes to extract the heavier gold and silver from stream beds and nearby topsoil. It was not long before placer mining was replaced by mine shafts that followed veins of precious metal deep into the earth. As production increased, so did the problems of providing supplies for the mines and the arriving hordes of miners. Following the extraction and smelting of precious metals, there were also problems transporting the precious metals out of Idaho to refineries in California.

During the 1860s, the United States was attempting to retire the huge debt resulting from the Civil War. The millions of dollars being generated by the Idaho mines were having a positive effect on restoring the economy and attracting money from many foreign investors.

The names of some of the more prominent mines were "War Eagle," "Morning Star," "Ida Elmore," and "The Golden Chariot." These were destined to become household names, famous both nationally and internationally for their high production of gold and silver.

At one time, the United States government considered building a mint near Boise, Idaho, but politics intervened and the mint went to San Francisco. Smelting of the ore took place in Silver City, but other facilities were inadequate for the volume of ore produced by the mines.

Problems with the Old Trails

All was not well with the mining operations, however. The industry faced extreme problems with transportation into and out of the mining area. Located in a rugged and mountainous area, horse and mule pack-strings transported supplies and equipment into the area, and conversely transported the smelted ore to the Bay Area refineries in California. This transportation method was slow and inadequate for the volume of ore produced by the mines. During the winter months, snow was so deep that almost every kind of movement in or out of the mining area ceased.

After snowmelt, packstrings made up of horses and mules numbering in the hundreds traveled on ancient trails established by animal migrations and native trading and hunting expeditions. These trails were later followed by fur traders. In time the packers used three primary trails.

The most prominent was the Overland Trail that originated near Chico, California. Ships navigated the Sacramento River as far north as Chico and Redding where they were met by packstrings. As the trail became better established they were eventually met by wagons. The Humboldt Trail was also used by packstrings and by wagons traveling north through Nevada to Winnemucca, and merged with the Overland Trail at Duncan's Ferry at the Owyhee River crossing. The Overland and Humboldt trails continued east from the Owyhee River up Jordan Creek to near the community of Baxterville, later to be renamed Jordan Valley. The trail then turned northwest toward the location of Cow Creek. Cow Creek also originated in the Owyhee Mountains, flowing southwest from near Wagon Town and drained an area to the west of Jordan Creek drainage. The trail then turned northeast and followed the Cow Creek drainage to near the settlement of Wagon Town, and from there into Silver City.

During the winter months the trails into the mining area were all but impassable, and all traffic stopped at Baxterville, later to become known as Jordan Valley.

An alternative access to the Owyhee mines was The Blue Mountain Trail that originated at The Dalles on the Columbia River. Ships sailing from San Francisco brought supplies up the river to The Dalles where they were met by packstrings and eventually by freight wagons. The Blue Mountain Trail followed east through the Blue Mountains of Oregon

Jordan Valley, early 1900s.

and up the Snake River into Central Idaho. At approximately the same time Silas Skinner was building his toll road from Silver City to the Owyhee River, a man by the name of Carson was constructing a toll road from the Blue Mountain trail on the Snake River up Reynolds Creek into the mining area. Carson's toll road joined Skinner's Toll Road near the settlement of Wagontown. Carson did not keep the road in good repair, so it was used almost entirely by pack strings; although, apparently, some freight wagons were able to negotiate the road in good weather. In the winter this road was closed due to deep snow. Silas Skinner and his partners eventually bought the Carson Toll Road, repaired it, and put it into good condition. They also constructed a toll gate near where the two roads came together below Silver City.

All three of these trails were very rough, subject to bad weather conditions, and attacks from roaming bands of hostile Indians and highwaymen. The weather conditions generally dictated the route the packstrings and, eventually, wagons followed. In summer months, it was necessary to stay close to water. If rainy, muddy trails often caused the traffic to divert to drier ground. In the winter, the routes were controlled by snow depth.

The Town of Jordan Valley

In late fall and winter the packstrings and travelers seeking work in the mines congregated at a place that would later be named Jordan Valley because they could go no further due to deep snow. A small community developed and rapidly expanded. The settlement first became known as String Town due to the number of camps and shanties that spread out along the trail. Later it became known as Dog Town because the number of dogs that arrived with the travelers.

John Baxter, who owned a small ranch in the area, recognized an opportunity to make some money and built a store, and hotel to provide for the people trying to get to the mining area to seek work. Freighters also gathered here awaiting the spring thaw that would allow them to proceed up the Cow Creek trail to the mining area. The settlement at that time became known as Baxterville. Much later the town would become known as Jordan Valley, named for Michael Jordan, and for the creek that was named in his honor.

SS

3

The Skinner Toll Road

It is important to fully understand the problems faced by the mining industry in southern Idaho during the 1860s, and those individuals, and companies, who operated and worked the earth to develop the potential wealth that was available.

The Owyhee Mountains in southern Idaho held a bonanza in precious metals. The tremendous wealth the earth held affected the welfare of the entire nation. Yet, the mining industry was hamstrung. It was impossible to maintain the extraction, and delivery of smelted ore to the processing operations in San Francisco for further refining because transportation into and out of the mining area was snail paced in summer months and almost non-existent in the winter.

By the early 1860s, transportation problems in the mining area were reaching a critical point. The mining industry and companies who operated and worked the earth to develop the potential wealth that was available could no longer depend on current methods to sustain their operations.

It was into this far from perfect situation that Silas Skinner arrived in the spring of 1863. He filed for and worked several mining claims that he worked on his own that summer, and he also worked with his newfound friends and associates, Michael and James Jordan in their mining operations.

Silas apparently did quite well with his own mining endeavors through the summer, but he quickly realized there was a business venture that would be far more rewarding financially than the search for gold. Like many others, Silas had become painfully aware of the problems with moving people, supplies, and mining equipment into the mines and mine products out of the mines for processing in San Francisco.

Silas believed he could provide a far better and shorter way. In the fall of 1863, following a visual survey of the area, he settled on the most convenient route to construct a road. His chosen route followed a historic trail previously established by wild animals and Native Americans over the centuries and later by fur trappers. It was considerably shorter than the distance traveled using the current access to the mining area through the Cow Creek drainage. The route Silas designed began at Ruby City and followed down Jordan Creek canyon westward for about twenty miles to the settlement of Baxterville, and eventually some fifty miles beyond to the Owyhee River. Surveys of the country had not yet been completed and, at that time in history, the Owyhee River was considered the state line dividing Oregon and Idaho.

Skinner realized that to be profitable on this venture, it would be necessary to build a road that could be maintained, and remain open and passable year round. After he made his decision on the location of his road he, with brothers Michael and James Jordan and Peter Donnelly, formed a partnership and construction on the toll road began in the fall of 1863.

Building a Road

As one of his first projects setting up for construction, Skinner hired an acquaintance and fellow Manxman named Phillip Clegg. Silas had known Clegg previously and knew that he had no fear of hard work. Silas advised his partners, Clegg could do the work of two men, and so was paid quite handsomely because of his ability and ambition. A number of Clegg's descendants also continue to live in southwestern Idaho and southeastern Oregon today.

The construction tools available to the road builders in the 1863 were primarily mining tools. They consisted of picks, shovels, dynamite, log chains, and manpower. A yoke of oxen owned by Silas provided the power necessary for the heavy work. As work on the toll road progressed the first miles down Jordan Creek from Ruby City, the partners encountered some very rough going. The area was mountainous, and in following Jordan Creek it was necessary to negotiate a number of hairpin turns in steep and rocky terrain. Dynamite was necessary to break up rocky ledges to allow widening of the roadbed. Aware the sharp turns would be especially difficult for the large teams of horses and

Workers toiling on the toll road. Picture courtesy of Ontario Argus Observer.

mules to negotiate, and aware it would be disastrous for teams arriving from opposite directions at the same time at a sharp turn, Skinner, in these places, made the road wide enough to allow room for two teams to pass. It was also the practice of the teamsters to attach bells to the hames on the harness of their lead teams to warn teamsters coming from the other direction.

Freight teams pulling two to three wagons required special training in negotiating these turns in the road. The teamsters had to know how to handle twelve or more horses or mules, usually pulling two wagons around a sharp curve in the road. In this situation, the lead teams could be and most likely were out of the teamsters' sight while they made the turn. The following horses continued on a straight line because they had not yet reached the corner and needed to keep the wagons on the road.

These long teams were controlled by just one line, known as the jerk line that ran to the left horse on the lead team. A jerk on the line meant a turn to the right. A steady pull on the line meant a turn to the left. The rest of the teams of horses or mules were controlled by the voice of the teamster. If we complicate this situation by adding another team and wagon coming from the other direction meeting on a curve, we can begin to appreciate the expertise of these men and their ability to handle horses and mules.

In order to make the road accessible year-round for freight wagons and stagecoaches, Silas placed his road on the north side of the creek to take full advantage of the sun during the winter months. He also provided width enough on the roadbed to allow teamsters to vary their path through troublesome boggy areas in inclement weather.

The partners blasted their way through rock ledges with dynamite and used the oxen to remove the rocks, some weighing more than a ton. They pulled the rocks off the road's right-of-way to the side of the road, and in many places used the rocks to build up a solid roadbed. Where rocks were not a problem, the oxen pulled heavy timbers to remove brush and small rocks from the right-of-way, and to smooth the surface.

The method of estimating the distance between two points during this era was ingenious. Mileage was calculated by first measuring the circumference of a buggy wheel to determine the number of feet around its rim. A flag was tied to an outer spoke of the wheel, and as one man drove the buggy, another man counted the revolutions of the buggy wheel.

At a point where the approximate distance of a mile was reached, a stone was engraved with the mileage from a certain starting point. Take a moment to consider how challenging it would have been to accurately count the revolutions of the buggy wheel. The day could have been very warm, and the counter might have partied a bit too much the night before…and then think about how boring the job would be—to sit and watch the wheel go around. Surprisingly, it really was a quite accurate method of recording mileage. Surveys of the country would soon be made that corrected errors in property lines, state boundaries, and mileages. Several of these "mile stones" have been found and have been preserved for posterity.

The road continued down Jordan Creek, to a point where Jordan Creek entered a long, looping gorge that would, with its extremely rocky and rugged terrain, add many miles and sharp curves to the road construction.

To avoid this obstacle, Skinner diverted the road away from Jordan Creek, and followed a westerly route up over Long Ridge. The diversion required the road builders to construct a long and steep grade that became known locally as the Trout Creek Grade near the confluence of Trout Creek and Jordan Creek. The grade, though steep and difficult

A mile marker from the Skinner Toll Road—13M is chipped out of lava rock. Here it is lightly lined with chalk to show up better for the photo.

to negotiate in inclement weather, eliminated many hazardous miles, as well as some very difficult engineering and construction problems. The road builders considered the long, steep grade to be a worthy alternative rather than to try to construct the road through the gorge.

Once the construction on the road emerged from the mountainous area between the Jordan Valley and Silver City, the construction work became much less difficult, and less steep and rocky. The work continued down Jordan Creek, and on westward through the Jordan Valley toward the Owyhee River. For the most part, all that was required was the heavy log chain, with the oxen pulling heavy timbers. The roadwork continued through the settlement of Jordan Valley and for about five or six miles where it joined the trails earlier established by packstrings and some wagon freighters. Silas improved the road from that point on westward to where the Inskeep Station would soon be built, near where Jordan Creek and Lower Cow Creek joined.

The Inskeep Station

In 1863, Edward (Doc) Inskeep and Frank Osgood were on their way to the Owyhee mining area and camped near the point where Jordan

Creek and Cow Creek merged. They noted the abundance of grass available for livestock feed, and the availability of water. With Skinner's road soon to be a reality, the two men recalled their old campsite, gave up mining, and decided to build a stage station at this ideal location.

Ruth Inskeep, a descendant of Edward Inskeep, in a ten-page undated history of the Inskeep family, described the construction of the station:

They built a six-room house out of lava rock put together with mud mortar. In front was a large men's room with a bar, office, and a huge fireplace. The bar was a cupboard built along the wall. Behind the large room for men, was a smaller parlor for the ladies, also with a fireplace. Off these rooms to the east opened three bedrooms. On the west, a room with a lean-to roof served as the kitchen. Portholes for defense were built in the walls. Near the kitchen on the west, there was a cellar for storing supplies and a well for water. Directly in front of the house and across the road was a large enclosure complete with a well and other facilities for the care of work cattle, horses, and mules. A high rock fence surrounded it, with only one gate, directly opposite the house.

The defense of the station was tested on several occasions by hostile bands of Indians, but usually the attacks were repelled successfully. On one occasion however, a band of hostile Indians fired on the station and successfully opened the gate to the corral. They set fire to a wagonload of hay and drove off a bunch of oxen belonging to a man named Sim Glass, a close friend of the Skinners. Glass was using the oxen to haul hay from the Jordan Valley to Silver City, and was staying at the Inskeep Station. While the Indians did little damage to the station itself, they drove Mr. Glass's oxen over the Owyhee River canyon rim to their deaths.

Inskeep Station, also known as Ruby Fort. The only identified people are Will Skinner with the pipe, his son, Bill Skinner, with his back to the camera, and Sim Glass, last on the right.

Many years later in the early 1960s, the Inskeep Station, now known as the Ruby Ranch, would again become historically famous following the discovery that it was here that the death and burial of Jean Baptiste Charbonneau had taken place in 1866. Charbonneau had originally gained fame in 1805 as the infant son of Sacagawea, guide for the Lewis and Clark Expedition, and her husband Toussaint Charbonneau.

The tiny graveyard has been designated as an Oregon State Park. A later chapter will provide a comprehensive discussion of the investigation and discovery of the Charbonneau gravesite that was conducted in the late 1960s by my parents, Johanna and Kirt Skinner.

Toll Road Franchises

In 1865, with his toll road nearly completed, Silas Skinner and a man named H. Laughlan formed another partnership and bought The Reynolds Creek Toll Road from Thomas Carson and completed necessary repairs

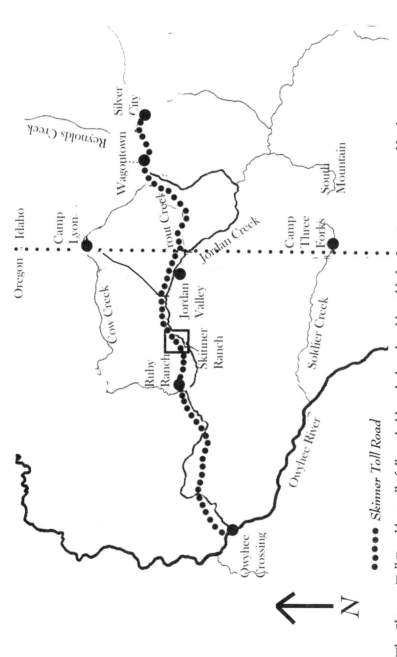

The Skinner Toll Road basically followed old trails, but the old trail led up to Camp Lyon and back up to near Wagontown following the creeks. Skinners Toll Road was more direct reducing travel time.

Hill Beachey barn and corral at Ruby Ranch (Inskeep Station). The rock corral held oxen and other animals.

that made it passable year round to wagons and stagecoaches. Carson had connected this toll road with the Blue Mountain Trail that originated at The Dalles on the Columbia River and ran east to the Snake River and into Central Idaho.

It is unclear why Skinner waited to apply for these franchises for his toll roads until they were nearly completed. With both roads leading into Silver City now under his control, Skinner made application in late 1865 to the Third Idaho Legislature for franchises to construct and operate a toll road from Ruby City to the Owyhee River and operate the Reynolds Creek Toll Road. The Legislature granted both franchises on January 3, 1866. Under "New Advertisements" on September 30, 1865, the *Owyhee Avalanche*, carried the following advertisement:

> The undersigned have purchased the entire interest of Thomas Carson in the Booneville and Reynolds Creek Toll Road. The road will hereafter be under

> the control and management of Skinner
> and Laughlin. The public can rely upon
> this Road being kept in thorough repair
> at all seasons of the year.
> Silas Skinner
> H. Laughlin
> September 30, 1865

Silas Skinner's new toll road was now completed from east to west. Continuing west beyond the small community of Booneville, the toll road joined the more or less established Humboldt and Red Bluff trails approximately seven miles east of the Inskeep Station. The franchise Silas Skinner was granted by the State of Idaho, however, required that the partners also construct and maintain the existing wagon road from that point west, past the Inskeep Station to the original trail's terminus at Duncan's Ferry on the Owyhee River.

West of the Sheep Ranch it was necessary for road builders to construct a new grade out of the valley in which the Sheep Ranch was located. It was on this section of the toll road that Silas Skinner and David Shirk were conducting maintenance when they were attacked by hostile Indians at the Sheep Ranch.

Because this part of the road had been previously established by freighters, the terrain to the west, toward the Owyhee River, required little construction beyond dragging large timbers to widen the roadway, clear the brush, and remove smaller rocks from the right-of-way.

At the point where Silas Skinner's Toll Road entered the Owyhee River Canyon near Duncan's Ferry, it was necessary to construct a long and arduous ten-percent grade for access into the canyon and Duncan's Ferry. Once again, it was necessary to use picks, shovels, dynamite, and oxen power to move huge rocks into place to construct the roadbed. With the completion of the grade, the Skinner Toll Road from Ruby City, Idaho, to the Owyhee River was at last completed.

Toll charges were established by the Idaho Legislature for the Reynolds Creek Toll Road as follows:

Loaded wagon and team (two horses,
mules or oxen) $3.00
Each additional team or yoke $1.00
Man on horseback 50¢
Cattle or horses (loose) 12.5¢
Swine or sheep (per head) 10¢
Team and Empty wagon $1.50

The second franchise granted by the Third Idaho Legislature to the partnership of Silas Skinner, the Jordan brothers, and Peter Donnelly, was the right to construct a toll road from Ruby City in the Owyhee Mountains, southwest down Jordan Creek some seventy miles to Duncan's Ferry on the Owyhee River. Surveys of the country were yet to be completed, and at that time the Owyhee River was considered the boundary between the Territory of Idaho and the State of Oregon. The toll fees established by the State of Idaho for the toll road from Ruby City were approximately double those set by the Legislature for the Reynolds Creek Toll Road.

With construction completed, the Skinner Toll Road rapidly became one of the most important in the West, according to California newspapers. Soon after his arrival in Idaho, Silas Skinner had recognized the extreme need for a way to provide relief from the current system of snail-paced transportation. His new road became an extremely important link between the supply points in California and the mining district of the Owyhees.

With the passage of years, the road has added to the rich early history of mining, Indian wars, and the settling and civilization of the Jordan Valley. Although mining is no longer the big industry in the area, portions of the Skinner Toll Road remain in use by ranchers and historians, and to this day the road remains an icon of historical interest in the area.

The Journey of the Teamster

Even with Silas Skinner's road completed, which provided a much easier access to the mining area, it was still a difficult journey. We can only guess at the hardships experienced by both man and animal during this period in our history. Trains had yet to connect from east to west. The airplane was the dream of a child lying on his back watching an eagle circle in the sky.

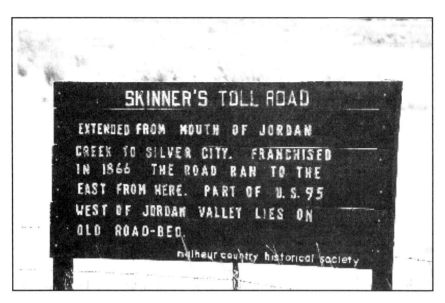

Above: modern sign marks the historic Skinner Toll Road.

Left: Nearly 150 years later, near the Skinner Ranch Headquarters, one can still see where wheels have rolled on the Skinner Toll Road. Silas's descendants walk the road in 2003.

Imagine, a teamster driving a team of eight, ten, or more horses or mules, usually pulling two and sometimes three heavily loaded wagons in tandem approaching a long, crooked, sometimes muddy grade. The teamster had to unhook the rear wagon, and leave it at the bottom of the grade.

Going up the grade with one wagon the teamster had to give his team frequent chances to get their breath. When he stopped, he dropped a "rough lock" under the wheels to relieve the strain on his team of holding the wagon from rolling backward. (Roughlocks were heavy iron skids the driver could drop under the wheels of the wagon.) Once the team had rested a bit, the teamster continued, eventually making it to the top of the grade with one wagon. Leaving that wagon at the top, he returned to the bottom for the other wagon. Depending on the length of the grade and the weather conditions, it might take a full day or more to move the wagons to the top of the grade before he could continue.

The descent of these grades was equally as difficult, but the problem faced by the teamsters, was quite a different one. Going down the grade it was necessary to hold the wagons back so that they would not overtake and run over the teams. The driver solved this problem, again with the use of the roughlocks. The teams and wagons usually traveled in a group for protection and in cooperation, all having to face the same conditions. These men were hardy souls and superb teamsters as well. Travel conditions were only a little less difficult during the summer months with the heat and dust, often lacking water along the route, and always the threat of being attacked by hostile Indians. Indeed, it is not difficult to realize why the extreme inflation of prices existed in the mining area.

Stagecoaches eventually traveled these trails, but it was not until the Skinner Toll Road was finished and in operation that coach travel became prominent. The coaches primarily carried passengers, mail, and critical documents relating to the mines and payrolls. The standard size team on stagecoaches during the summer months was four horses, and in the winter, six. Fresh horses were available at the stage stations every six to eight miles.

City Growth Invites Trouble

Will Skinner related the following story that took place in early Silver City. There had been a fight in which a man was killed. A trial was held and the killer was sentenced to die by the hangman's noose. Gallows were constructed and the date set for the hanging. On that day the killer was being transported to the gallows by wagon. He was sitting on his coffin, tied securely with ropes. A number of young men and boys were running to get ahead of the wagon, as the event was to be public. The prisoner, obviously a callous fellow, yelled out, "There ain't no reason to hurry, fellows. Ain't nothing going to happen 'til I get there."

With mining operations growing and requiring more workers, other businesses followed. General stores, butcher shops, eating-houses, saloons, and hotels appeared. The mine operators built nice homes, and churches arose soon after. Along with the niceties of the city, a seedier side came with the growth. There was gambling, there were gunfights, and there were people killed. A red-light district came into existence, following the money and the crowds. If there was law, it was the law of the frontier. In most cases, life was cheap and justice was quick.

Commerce in the West was booming at this time, and the Skinner Toll Road was gaining more and more importance as the need for moving supplies and people continued to grow. On May 19, 1865, the *Owyhee Avalanche* reported that,

> The Ruby City and Jordan Valley road is now in good order for teams—empty or loaded. By this road, it is just twenty miles to Baxter's Ranch, and the only direct or even passable one to the valley, and the Owyhee crossing on the Nevada and California roads. It is built on the north side of the creek, thus giving it the full benefit of the sun to keep it dry. Mr. Skinner informs us that the Company will keep it in good traveling order the entire year.

The partners set up a tollgate just below Ruby City near the junction of the Reynolds Creek Toll Road and the Skinner Toll Road. Thus, Silas Skinner and his partners were assured that they controlled all travel on both roads coming into and going out of the Silver City mining area, and further, that all traffic would be subject to paying the toll charge to use either or both roads.

Problems on the Toll Road

Even with improvements it was not long before operational headaches began to plague the road partners. Complaints began to surface in the press and elsewhere pointing out the lack of adequate upkeep on both of Skinner's toll roads. Inclement weather, melting snow, and muddy roads on occasion caused stagecoach passengers to have to walk alongside or to help lift the coaches over deep water. To make matters even more difficult for the partners, it was reported that the gatekeeper at the tollgate appeared unconcerned about bad road conditions on the toll road, and kept the gate closed, opening it only after payment of full toll charges.

With continued complaints and increasing traffic on the toll roads, the partners found it necessary to establish rules for conducting maintenance and repair on the roads. One of the rules they immediately decided upon to quell complaints required that one of the partners go over the road at least once a week to make repairs, and, if necessary, to provide general supervision.

It was also a practice during the winter for a man and a team of horses to go ahead of the stagecoaches to make sure the road was open and in good repair. When snow became deep, the partners started a maintenance man and a team from Silver City, and another from the Trout Creek Station each day to ensure the road would be clear and passable.

Train Tracks Span the Country

With Silas Skinner's Toll Road completed and in use, another transportation system was starting to become an important factor in the West. The Central Pacific Railroad had started extending their tracks from west to east. Central Pacific Railroad and California Steam Navigation Company teamed up to romance the Idaho trade by moving freight from Sacramento via Truckee, California, for delivery over the Skinner Toll Road into Silver City at reduced rates. Along with the CSNC and the CPR, the Teamsters Association of San Francisco offered special rates in favor of goods being shipped to the Owyhee mines by way of Susanville, and the Skinner Toll Road.

As the Central Pacific Railroad extended their tracks further eastward, stagecoaches and freight teams pulling two wagons began meet-

Hill Beachey Barn at Inskeep Station. Photo by Chris Skinner Moore.

ing the trains at the advancing eastern end of the railway construction. The positive result was that traffic was beginning to move far more rapidly between supply points into and out of Silver City, with the only access being over the Skinner Toll Road. Travel time between California supply points and the mining area in Silver City was reduced from months to just over a week.

When the Central Pacific Railroad tracks reached northern Nevada, the town of Winnemucca became the main shipping terminal for the Owyhee mines. Travel time was cut immensely. The first transcontinental railway became a reality in 1869 when the Union Pacific Railroad tracks and the Central Pacific Railroad tracks came together at Promontory Point in the Utah Territory. With the nailing of the Golden Spike, the railroads had essentially opened up marketing and trading opportunities coast to coast, and both were to become competitive markets for the booming mining industry in Idaho.

Stagecoaches

Silas Skinner and his partners benefited quite handsomely because every pound of freight, and the faster-moving stagecoaches going into the

Owyhee mining areas and on to the Boise Basin and Idaho City, traveled on and paid toll charges on their toll roads. Of equal importance, products of the mining industry and travelers destined for California traveled over one or the other or both of their toll roads.

With the coming of the railroads, Hill Beachey, who owned and was an experienced operator of a stagecoach line, secured a lucrative contract to deliver mail and travelers from Winnemucca, Nevada, over the Skinner Toll Road to Silver City, the Boise Basin, and beyond.

Hill Beachey built stations along the road where replacement horses were available. He also built barns for his coach horses, one of which he placed at the Inskeep Station. That historic barn stood for many years, an icon of a historic period in the West. The barn was on the Ruby Ranch property, and hence was owned by the Beers family for some time. The Ruby Ranch was sold several times in later years. Over those years, the old Hill Beachey barn fell into disrepair and was ultimately torn down because of its dangerous condition.

The Hill Beachey Stagecoach Company established stations along the Skinner Toll Road at intervals of about six to eight miles to provide replacement teams that would accommodate faster-paced stagecoaches. These stations varied from small one-room houses, to larger and more comfortable stops that provided food. Some stops provided comfortable overnight facilities for travelers who wished to lay over. With renegade bands of Indians roaming through the area, often conducting raids on settlers, a telegraph line was built between Silver City, Trout Creek, and Winnemucca, making travel on the road a bit more secure.

One of the more comfortable and elaborate way stations was at the Sheep Ranch approximately halfway between the Inskeep Station on Lower Cow Creek, and the Owyhee River. "The Sheep Ranch" became known by that name after a band of sheep being trailed from Humboldt County, Nevada, to the meat markets in Silver City, got caught in an early winter snowstorm. The herder built a sagebrush corral to keep his sheep safe from coyotes and wintered them near the station. The sheep never made it to the mining area, however. A band of hostile Indians stole them, and hid them in a secluded canyon where they eventually were found. The Indians had killed the sheep and used the pelts for clothing and as saddles. The name "Sheep Ranch" stuck, and the historic stage stop will forevermore be known as "The Sheep Ranch."

The next stagecoach station going east was the Inskeep Station, followed about eight miles east by the Company Station, but still west of Jordan Valley. It was owned by the stage company, and only provided replacement horses for the fast-moving stagecoaches. It had no accommodations for travelers. The next station was Skinner's Trout Creek Station, about halfway between the Company Station and Silver City.

Even with the continued sporadic harassment from the Indians, rapid economic progress continued to be made with production increasing in the mines of Idaho, and in other industries in all areas of the Northwest. With the ability to provide faster movement of freight and to bring more people into this new land, life appeared to be good.

SS

4

SS

Dark Clouds of War

In the mid 1860s, a threatening storm of war had begun to form over the Northwest. Indigenous Indian tribes who had occupied these lands for untold centuries were increasingly alarmed by the invasion of white settlers into their hunting grounds, fishing streams and lakes, and food-gathering areas. Settlers flooded into the region, settling on choice land and pushing the tribes from their territories.

It was to be expected that the Indians had begun to push back. While they were disorganized at that time, and with no specific leader, they conducted raids on homesteaders, burning down their buildings, stealing and killing livestock, and harassing freighters. The Indians had no interest in the precious metals coming from the mines. They had, however, become very concerned about settlers squeezing them out of their homes and their homeland.

Unlike the settlers, the Indians did not share the white man's concept of personal ownership of land at that time in their history. Each tribe ranged over areas within their own geographical territory. These areas were now significantly diminished as settlers homesteaded on land favored for hundreds, perhaps even thousands, of years by the Indians for their winter food supply.

The Paiute Indian tribe that had occupied southwestern Idaho, eastern Oregon, and Nevada for thousands of years was not a warlike tribe. Their leaders made extensive attempts to befriend the settlers, but were rebuffed. In her book, *Life Among The Piutes: Their Wrongs and Claims*, Sarah Winnemucca writes that her grandfather Chief Truckee, and her father, Chief Winnemucca had tried very hard to befriend "their white brothers," but had little, or no success.

There were occasions, in which the Indians taught the settlers methods of living off the land when weather or famine conditions would have ended the settlers' existence. Still, the Indians were distrusted and even despised. The settlers continued to resist their overtures, considering them to be savages and, because of their lifestyle, more animal than human.

Raids on settlers usually were conducted by renegade Indians but included a few Paiutes as well white outlaws who ran with the war parties. These outlaws often provided weapons to the Indians and helped to keep the settlers stirred up.

It would not, however, be appropriate in this forum to have a philosophical discussion regarding rightness or wrongness of the actions of either Indians or invaders. Unfortunately, the history of the human race is also the history of wars, usually over territory and the ownership of land. Historically, the strong prevail and the weak are vanquished. It is a sad and unfortunate fact, however, that when the Indians finally did give up, the government forced them onto reservations where they were treated as captives, and then made little or no provision for supplying their food and clothing needs. Consequently, thousands died of starvation and disease during the winter months.

Some corrupt government Indian agents on the reservations can be blamed for much of the hostilities that existed and for the many deaths of both Indians and settlers. Many of these agents lined their pockets with government money meant to buy food and clothing for the vanquished and starving Indians. That, however, is the subject of another book.

Indian Attack at the Sheep Ranch

Silas Skinner was involved in at least one altercation with Indians when he and a man named David Shirk were attacked at the Sheep Ranch. Shirk had been hired to accompany Silas on a road-maintenance trip. In *The Cattle Drives of David Shirk from Texas to the Idaho Mines, 1871 and 1873*, Editor Martin F. Schmitt related Shirk's account of the attack. Skinner was conducting maintenance on the toll road and had hired a man named David Shirk to help him. The two men left Silver City on horseback, and planned to stay at the Sheep Ranch overnight. After they retired, they became aware that Indians were around. In his book, Shirk gives a firsthand account of the attack. The following is as it was copied by our father.

On November 15, 1867, on horseback and leading one pack horse to carry our provisions, we made the Sheep Ranch about lunchtime. This place consisted of a rock house covered with rye grass and dirt, and a little shed that answered as a stable. We observed portholes had been cut into four sides of the cabin. We spent the rest of the day throwing rocks out of the road and we returned to the house about sundown. Mr. Skinner being more experienced than I, took the lead in making arrangements for any contingencies that might arise, and as we were in dangerous country, nothing was omitted.

After our evening meal, we made such other arrangements as prudence and safety could suggest in the event we were attacked by the Indians, then unrolled our blankets and went to bed. While I couldn't sleep, Mr. Skinner appeared to be resting easier than I, but I soon discovered he too was alert and wakeful. When one of the horses began to snort, we got up to investigate and soon discovered that the Indians were around. We realized the peril of our situation yet we remained calm, and determined not to open fire unless driven to do so in self defense.

The Indians soon made us realize that it was a fight to the death, as they made attempt after attempt to fire the grass roof with torches made of sagebrush and other material. We opened fire and compelled them to keep at a safe distance. We fired through the portholes first from one side of the cabin then from another.

They then fired the dry grass in back of the cabin, but we were able to put it out with water we had stored the previous evening. From the looks of the ground the following morning, I am satisfied we sent more than one of the savage devils to their happy hunting grounds. Silas Skinner was a fearless and resourceful man, and was well liked by all who knew him.

Mr. Shirk further wrote that the Indians had stolen their horses during the skirmish, and that he and Skinner were forced to walk back to Silver City. On the way, near the Gusman Ranch on Jordan Creek, a few miles east of the town of Jordan Valley, they discovered and buried the mutilated bodies of James and Michael Jordan, Silas Skinner's close friends and business partners. Skinner and Shirk determined the two brothers had been ambushed and killed by the same Indian raiding party that had attacked them the night before at the Sheep Ranch.

Following the death of the Jordan brothers, one of their relatives came from the East to settle their estates. The Jordan's shares of the toll road partnership with Silas Skinner, and their mining interests were sold to E. H. Clinton, who became Silas Skinner's partner. Clinton was heavily involved in the mining industry in the area.

An Uneasy Peace

In 1868, despite being rounded up by the army and put back on the reservations, the Indians' restlessness continued. Bands of renegade Indians, often accompanied by renegade whites, continued their sporadic harassment of settlers and freighters. After many complaints, the United States government finally established a number of army posts along the Sacramento–Silver City road to protect travelers and freighters. One of those army posts was established on Upper Cow Creek and was named Camp Lyons in honor of the territorial governor of Idaho.

It was garrisoned by three companies of soldiers. Nothing remains of Camp Lyons today.

Most of these soldiers were veterans of the Civil War, and had little stomach for more fighting, and even less when it came to fighting the Indians. Few were well-trained for the sort of battle the Indians fought, and were not overly ambitious about their duties to protect the settlers. It was usually up to volunteers to defend their families and their properties. Slow freight wagons traveling in groups continued to circle their wagons when they stopped for the day. They enclosed their livestock in the circle, and posted guards to protect themselves and their cargo from raiding Indians and the highwaymen who often joined Indian war parties.

The Indian skirmishes and raids continued to rage up and down the valley until 1868, when the army brought the Indians under government control and moved them back onto their reservations. There followed a period of uneasy peace between the Indians and the settlers.

SS

—Wedding picture of Anne Jane Callow and Silas Skinner, February 24, 1870.

5

SS

Silas Takes a Bride—A Family Begins

Anne Jane Callow, who was to become the wife of Silas and mother of Will, was born in 1846, in Parish Andreas, Isle of Man. Her family was close neighbors to the Skinner family. At eighteen years of age in 1864, Anne Jane, traveling under her grandfather's protective wing, left her family home of Balla Callum (home of the Callows) and migrated to America to live with her grandparents in Ashtabula, Ohio.

Under the tutelage of an aunt, Anne Jane soon became an accomplished seamstress. Along with her sewing, she opened and operated a millinery shop and became a successful businessperson in Ashtabula, often sought out for her good business sense. At the time of Silas's visit to Ashtabula, his former neighbor had grown into an attractive and ambitious young lady.

History, handed down from Will Skinner, firstborn son of Silas and Anne Jane, through Silas Kirtland Skinner, firstborn son of Will and his wife Ella, tells us that, while Silas was visiting Ashtabula, a romance developed between these two young people. Clearly, Anne Jane would be his chosen partner for life. But for whatever reason, possibly contractual, Silas heard the call of the sea and returned to his ship. Silas Skinner loved sailing; he also on his visit had developed some very warm feelings for Anne Jane, and she for him. Yet, if there was ongoing correspondence between the two, our family has no record of it.

A Wedding

In 1868, Silas felt comfortable enough with the toll road operation to turn the management over to his partners and book passage from San Francisco to the Isle of Man to visit relatives and friends. If the purpose

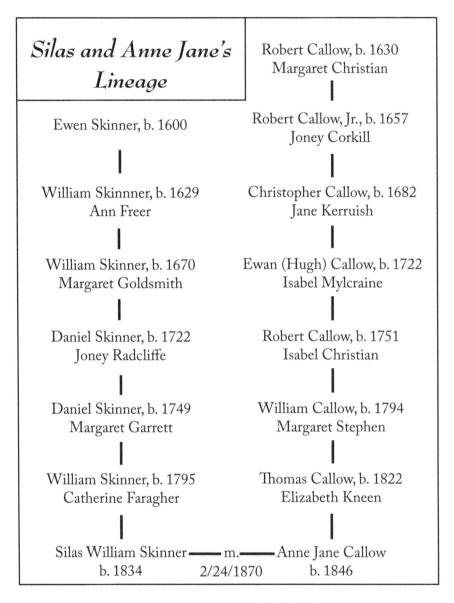

Silas and Anne Jane's Lineage

Robert Callow, b. 1630
Margaret Christian
|

Ewen Skinner, b. 1600
|

Robert Callow, Jr., b. 1657
Joney Corkill
|

William Skinnner, b. 1629
Ann Freer
|

Christopher Callow, b. 1682
Jane Kerruish
|

William Skinner, b. 1670
Margaret Goldsmith
|

Ewan (Hugh) Callow, b. 1722
Isabel Mylcraine
|

Daniel Skinner, b. 1722
Joney Radcliffe
|

Robert Callow, b. 1751
Isabel Christian
|

Daniel Skinner, b. 1749
Margaret Garrett
|

William Callow, b. 1794
Margaret Stephen
|

William Skinner, b. 1795
Catherine Faragher
|

Thomas Callow, b. 1822
Elizabeth Kneen
|

Silas William Skinner——— m.———Anne Jane Callow
b. 1834   2/24/1870   b. 1846

of the trip was to visit Anne Jane and ask for her hand in marriage, he was disappointed. It seems more probable that she was in Ashtabula, Ohio, at this time.

Inevitably, stories will vary in the way they are told, possibly embellished or glamorized to add interest. So it was with the romance of Silas and Anne Jane Callow. The first story, from the memory of their son Will, leads us to believe that in his haste to get his toll road completed and in operation, Silas had severely neglected his lady friend, Anne Jane in Ashtabula. She on the other hand, had grown tired of waiting and had decided to send Silas a letter in which she rather pointedly asked him to advise her as to what exactly his plans were for their continued relationship. In fact, she informed him she had another attractive opportunity available to her with a young attorney.

Will's story goes on to say that Silas prevailed, and Anne Jane agreed to marry him. Silas made immediate plans and booked passage for them both to return to The Isle of Man, where they were married in 1870.

Will Skinner and his sister Carrie were both good storytellers, and even when they were quite elderly, both were remarkable in their ability to clearly recall historic events surrounding their childhood at the Trout Creek Station. When Will recalled events of their childhood, however, it was obvious that he added color and embellished his stories.

His sister Carrie was ladylike, soft-spoken, and genteel. When the two were together, the history of their early lives would invariably come up, usually at the request of a younger family member. Each remembered many of these events quite differently. When Carrie told a story the way she remembered it, Will constantly interrupted her, and would begin telling the story the way he remembered the same event. After several of these interruptions, Carrie would put her hand on Will's knee, and very gently and very sweetly would say, "Now, Will dear, may I tell the story the way I remember it?"

Carrie's version of the events leading up to Silas and Anne Jane's wedding must have been told at a time when Will was not present, or at a time when she prevailed over his interruptions. In Carrie's version, Silas returned to the Isle of Man for the purpose of marrying "his girlfriend," but found Anne Jane had migrated to America. He quickly returned to New York, with plans to visit her in Ashtabula. However, a letter from his partner E. H. Clinton awaited him in New York, advising him to come to Idaho immediately because of troubles developing in one of their partnership businesses. Silas changed his plans and returned to Idaho, but he also sent a letter to Anne Jane in Ashtabula asking her to marry him.

According to Carrie, the answer Annie sent back to Silas was an emphatic no, and she further informed him that she was now engaged to another young man. Silas reportedly sent back word saying that simply could not be, that he had considered her to be his girl since he had held her on his knee as a child.

Silas was not one to be spurned. He refused to take her no for an answer. It was only after much correspondence that he was eventually successful in convincing her to marry him.

With her plans now including Silas, Anne Jane closed her business affairs in Ashtabula and returned to her family's home on the Isle of Man to complete preparations for their wedding. Several months later Silas followed.

Their wedding, solemnized on February 24,1870, was attended by their many relatives and friends, according to their daughter Carrie. The big event took place in Kirk (church) Andreas in the Parish of Andreas, with Silas's cousin John as his best man. The identity of Anne Jane's attendant is no longer known.

Carrie described the bride as "beautiful in a flowing white wedding gown." Silas, to show his new bride and those attending the wedding how pleased he was to have married his true love, had a red carpet laid from the church door to a carriage that was drawn by four horses.

As they left the church in the carriage following their wedding ceremony, Silas gleefully celebrated by throwing coins to schoolchildren being shepherded along the road by their teachers. The chaos that developed from children scrambling to pick up the coins caused a great deal of consternation for the teachers, who were attempting to maintain decorum.

Several of the teachers were observed pocketing a few of the coins for themselves. Silas was quite amused by the event, and apparently was not too severely chastised by his new bride. Following their wedding, the couple honeymooned in London, after which they boarded a ship and traveled to Ruby City, Idaho.

Who is to say which story is the correct one? They are not that far apart, but Carrie's version would appear to be the more factual one, and definitely the more interesting. After his returning to Ruby City, Silas and Anne Jane proceeded to set up housekeeping, along with the continued management of the toll road and Silas's mining interests.

A Pioneer is Born

On May 8, 1871, a son was born to Anne Jane and Silas. Following a longstanding family tradition, they named him William Silas in honor

Young Will in a red velvet suit.

of his paternal grandfather and his father. In 1872 Silas, Anne Jane, and their one-year-old son moved from Ruby City down Jordan Creek to near the foot of the Trout Creek Grade where Silas had built a new stage station. Approximately halfway between Silver City and the Sheep Ranch Station, the new station became a popular eating stop on the toll road. The home was built to be large enough to accommodate the family as well as their visiting guests.

In later years Will recalled that his parents hosted many social events for their friends, some of whom arrived from many miles away, in buggies, wagons, or on horseback. Anne Jane, with the assistance of their Chinese cook, prepared meals for the group. The dancing stopped at midnight for a feast, and then would continue on through the night, occasionally into the next day. Anne Jane and Silas took great pride in their new home and in their friends. In addition to feeding them several meals during these events, arrangements were made to accommodate some guests overnight.

Three more children were to join the family while they lived at the Trout Creek Station. Of these, Catherine (Carrie), was born March 31, 1873; Annabel, February 19, 1875; and Thomas Lewis, February 12, 1877.

The Trout Creek Station was not designed to provide overnight facilities for stage passengers, but it was a premier "eating house" on the Skinner Toll Road. It was located approximately midway between Silver City and The Sheep Ranch. The Sheep Ranch was a full-service station stop that provided overnight facilities for stagecoach passengers who wanted to layover.

Anne Jane obviously put her expertise in management and her organizational strengths to use in making the Trout Creek Station one of the nicest stopping places on the toll road. On May 18, 1878, the *Owyhee Avalanche* reported as follows, "The Skinner Mansion at Trout Creek is one of the most hospitable, and homelike resorts to be found in the country. The ladies there are always in a cheerful mood, and guests are the recipients of such courtesies & attention as always inspire a desire to call again."

The Skinners also maintained a large garden near the station to provide fruits and vegetables for their guests' meals. On at least one occasion, a swarm of locusts descended on the plot. Everyone available—including the Chinese cook, an Indian hired man, and the children—was recruited to keep the locusts moving by using tin cans, aprons, sticks, and whatever else was available and effective. No sooner had the locusts moved on, than a huge cloud of grasshoppers arrived and stripped the garden clean. The next few dinner meals may have been more than a little short on fruits and vegetables.

SS

6

SS

Horses and Cattle

The lifeblood of a ranch is in its livestock. Silas was a lover of fine horses. He obviously carried a dominant gene he passed down to many of his descendants. We each carry a spark in our eye for a good horse and appreciate its work out on the ranch.

The Standardbred Trotters

In the mid-1870s Silas traveled to Kentucky and brought back a small herd of top-of-the-line Standardbred trotting horses. Included were a well-known stallion and five or six Standardbred mares. We assume he brought the horses west by train to Winnemucca, Nevada, and then trailed or led them to Trout Creek. Standardbred horses were well known in the eastern and southeastern United States racetracks as trotting horses, and were very well known for their stamina. Silas had more than racing in mind for his horses, but from this small nucleus, he did develop and train some high-class trotters that later competed and became quite famous in California racing circles for their speed.

Silas also began the process of upgrading his large herd of range horses in eastern Oregon by introducing the trotting blood into his grade mares. The result was very successful. His horses became popular in the community as light draft horses, fast-paced buggy horses, and riding stock.

A Family of Horse Lovers

Silas Skinner's son, Will, inherited his love of horses from his father, and in later years he told of a scene he observed at about age seven, when soldiers were preparing to leave the Trout Creek Station after subduing renegade Indians. He wrote the following story of an experience he had after an army officer invited him to watch the camp's early-morning activities.

One lovely sight to me I remember seeing at the Trout Creek Station when the soldiers were returning after the Indians were put back on their reservations. Two companies of soldiers, mounted and [with] their equipment, had camped all night at Trout Creek Station. I was much interested in their horses, watching them unsaddle and put nosebags on the horses with grain. Each wagon had grain boxes on each side for the mules. They were tied to the wagon and grained there. The Captain and two other officers were quartered in our house.

The Captain had noticed me watching the horses and he said to me, "Young fellow you like horses, don't you? Now if you want to see something pretty get up early, anyway by four a.m. These horses and mules will all be out there in that basin (which is southeast of the station). They will get a bugle call at 4:15 a.m. and a second call shortly after that will mean to come. There will be the two guards out there with them who will bring them if they do not come, but I believe you will see them on the first call start to bunch up and on second call they will file right into camp for their grain."

So, I was up a little before four a.m. The horses were all scattered over the basin, some grazing, some sleeping, and in many little bunches. The first bugle call went out. The guards were above them on the hill. By the time they got on their horses, most all the horses and mules came together. On the second bugle call, they came right into camp. Was the prettiest sight I had ever seen. The guards just followed them in. Some two hundred and fifty horses and mules knew just what those bugle calls were for.

Will Skinner on Bounder (left) and Virginia Fleming (right). Virginia is riding Buck, the last of the Skinners' Standardbred Trotters.

He went on to recall that the horses and mules were brushed and combed, given their grain, saddled and harnessed. After breakfast the soldiers loaded their gear in the wagons and left the station with mounted soldiers first, followed by the wagons pulled by mules, and then the extra horses.

This was also a period in which both the mining companies, and Silas Skinner and his partners prospered. The already heavy traffic on both toll roads was increasing in both directions into and out of Silver City. For the partners on the toll roads, times were good.

The Emergence of the Cattle Industry

In 1869, cattle ranching had begun to arrive in southwest Idaho and eastern Oregon. This new industry had a tremendous economic impact on this area of the northwestern United States and soon eclipsed mining as the main industry in the area. Cattle ranching would eventually have a tremendous economic impact on the whole northwestern United States. Today it is the number one industry in the area. The need for meat to feed the miners first sparked the cattle industry.

Three men, John Catlow, Cornelius "Con" Shea, and David Shirk were primarily responsible for introducing cattle into the Northwest.

The meat market in Silver City. The bath house is to the far right. A barber shop is just this side of the bath house.

Con Shea arrived in Silver City in 1863. He had worked as a blacksmith and had accumulated a rather large sum of money for that time. Fate however, apparently did not smile favorably on Shea, and due to unknown circumstances, he had lost most of his money. An acquaintance, John Catlow came to Shea with an offer. Catlow was involved in a number of businesses in the area, among them a butcher shop that supplied meat for the miners. There were very few beef cattle in Oregon and Idaho, and meat was an expensive commodity. In comparison, cattle in Texas were plentiful and inexpensive.

John Catlow made a deal with Shea; he would provide the financial backing if Shea would go to Texas, buy a large bunch of cattle, and hire the necessary crew to help him trail the herd over sixteen hundred miles to Idaho through desolate and largely unsettled country. Shea took Catlow's offer and started for Texas. He made it only as far as the Raft River in the south-central Territory of Idaho where he encountered a large herd that had just been trailed from Texas. He bought

Wedding picture of Violet Glover and Thomas L. Skinner (Will's brother).

these cattle and drove them to the Bruneau area in southwest Idaho where he wintered them on the abundant feed.

Con Shea's herd of cattle was the first herd of any size to come into the Territory of Idaho. Shea, along with several others, including David Shirk, made a number of cattle drives from Texas during the following years. Shea eventually owned and operated the biggest cattle operation in southwest Idaho and southeast Oregon.

Shea's widowed niece and two of her daughters came from eastern Canada to stay with him. She later married Gardner B. Glover, another pioneer in the area. Their daughter, Violet, later became the wife of Thomas L. Skinner, and with their offspring, thereby established another branch on the Skinner family tree. Thomas was the son of Silas and Anne Jane Skinner. A number of Shea's descendants continue to live in Idaho and Oregon today. Shea eventually sold all his cattle and moved to California, where he went into the real estate business.

With the abundance of grass on the range at that time, cattle could winter very nicely without being fed hay. In the 1870s, several ranches that cut hay had started operating along Jordan Creek. The hay was taken to a local stationary baler and then freighted into Silver City for use by the livery stables. The first rancher in the area cut hay by hand with a scythe and raked the hay into piles with forked sticks cut from willow trees.

More modern methods would arrive in later years when a rancher purchased a horse-drawn mowing machine. The gathering process with forked sticks continued until the pitchfork finally arrived. The pitchfork was eventually followed by the horse-drawn dump rake. With necessity being the mother of invention, the methods employed to process hay and preserve it for use have become more sophisticated over the years.

SS

7

Rough Years

The economy in these declining years had an effect on industry around the toll road. Then Silas became injured in an accident. It seemed hard times were upon the mining industry and the family.

Declining Revenues

In the early 1870s, word reached the Owyhee mines that the nation's economy was in decline. The Bank of California had closed its doors and was no longer supporting the mining industry. With little financial backing, mining throughout the Northwest went into slow, steady decline and finally met its demise in the Owyhee Mountains area in the 1930s. That precipitous decline naturally had an effect on the business of the Skinner Toll Road.

In 1863, Owyhee County had granted Silas Skinner franchises to construct the toll roads over five-year periods. In 1878 the third five-year period was coming to an end, at which time the county elected to rescind the franchises in order to take over and maintain all roads in the county.

With the mining industry in decline, and faced with the loss of their toll road, in 1878 Silas Skinner and E. H. Clinton traded the Trout Creek Station and road equipment to C. D. Bachelor for land he owned on Jordan Creek, about thirteen miles west of Jordan Valley. C. D. Bachelor continued to own and operate the Trout Creek Station for a number of years. When the trade was made, Clinton sold his interest in the Morning Star Mine to an eastern mining company for $450,000. Almost immediately the mine flooded. Clinton was unable to collect even a penny from that particular property.

Silas Gets Injured

In 1874 or 1875, Silas was the victim of a serious accident while on horseback working with his livestock. The horse he was riding stepped in a badger hole and fell. As a result, Silas suffered several broken ribs. The doctor in Silver City advised him one of the broken ribs had punctured his lung. The doctor, however, did not feel capable of caring for a broken rib. Several trips were made to California to see doctors who had more training. None could offer much help. Hemorrhaging occurred, and Anne Jane made the decision to take him to Liverpool, England, for care from more highly trained physicians in more qualified medical facilities.

What follows is a letter written to our parents in 1958 by Silas and Anne Jane's daughter, Annabel (Skinner) Hampton. She graphically describes the family's efforts and their attempts to bring healing to Silas. The letter is a fascinating account of life, tragedy, early medical care, and travel in the last century, but even more about the love and dedication of a young wife to her seriously injured husband.

Dear Kirt and Johanna:

Strong hearted mother said she would take daddy to Liverpool where doctors could set broken ribs. So with poor sick daddy and two small children, Will age four, and Carrie, age two, she started out from Jordan Valley for the nearest railway in Winnemucca, Nevada. It was necessary to take Daddy on a mattress in a wagon. It was a long journey for a sick man, and roads then were not too good.

I believe she took the mattress on board the train also. There were no sleeping cars or meals served in diners in those days. Mother (about thirty years old) had all sorts of problems, but pluck and fortitude brought her safely through. She managed a sick man, two babies, baskets of food, and clothes-hampers or satchels, (no suitcases in those days) and she was ten or eleven days on the train. On the steamship, Daddy was more comfortable and got about the deck with a little help.

In Liverpool poor, cheerful, optimistic, mother was nearly crushed and defeated, for the doctors there said so many months had passed since the accident they could do little to help him, but they bound his body tightly in bandages and put on a form of corset which was very un-comfortable at first, and he found it difficult to take a deep breath. However, he endured it, and as the weeks went by it got more comfortable. (I think mother said daddy had to wear the corset day and night.)

In Liverpool unfortunately Carrie (under two years) fell and broke or dislocated her arm. So poor dear mother, had her hands more than full. How she managed caring for daddy, and baby Carrie with an arm in a sling, I don't know. Will, at four years couldn't have been much help to her.

Later when grown up, we would ask, "how did you manage?" She would say, "I hardly know, but certainly the Lord was with me all the way." Daddy complained very seldom. He was so eager to get to the Island (The Isle of Man) believing the Manx air would do much toward curing him. I think they stayed seven or eight months that trip. Seeing his people, old friends, and acquaintances did help him but that lung was left to heal as best it could. Great believers in nature, and rest in those days, doctors were not expert, or experienced in treatment of broken bones.

—Annabel

Will was to recall this trip many years later. He could remember little, except for crossing the Atlantic Ocean. Silas owned a team of horses in Jordan Valley, that he had named Prince and Charley, and Will remembers standing on the deck of the ship and telling his father, "I'll bet Prince and Charley could wade across this water." Even then, at four years old, horses appeared destined to forever be a part of Will's life.

As a result of his trip to Liverpool, Silas had regained at least some of his health. While continuing the operation of Trout Creek Station and the toll road, as well as his interests in the mining industry, Silas continued to accumulate a large herd of grade horses that carried the Standardbred blood.

By the mid-1860s in the eastern sections of the country, and to some degree the southwest, steam power had started to come into use, but it was not until 1889 that railroads finally reached into the Northwest.

SS

8

Bannock Indian Wars—1878

The dark clouds of war once again appeared on the horizon in 1878. Indians, led by the Bannock tribe from Idaho, began recruiting other disturbed tribes to make what they surely must have known would be a futile effort to drive the settlers from lands they believed had been taken from them.

In 1868, the Indians had been returned to their reservations, but the conditions they were forced to live under were intolerable. They continued to suffer tremendously from starvation, disease, and dishonest Indian agents. What little money the government allocated for the Indians often went into Indian agents' pockets. Indians were hired for pennies to raise food for their use, but corrupt agents in turn sold that food to settlers and pocketed the money. The Indians consequently ended up with neither food nor money.

Uprising

With no resources to feed their families, and disease rampant, the Indians began to realize their death was imminent from starvation and disease during the coming winter. They became resigned to the sad fact that they had as well meet their fate gloriously in battle against the settlers rather than to see their families slowly starve and freeze to death during the winter months.

Under the leadership of Chief Buffalo Horn, the Bannocks came off their reservations and aligned with a number of other tribes in the Northwest to form a force large enough to take the battle to the settlers and the army.

Sarah Winnemucca wrote in her book, *Life Among The Piutes* that the Bannocks made many attempts to recruit the Paiute Tribe, and did entice a few to take up arms against the whites. The majority of the Paiute Tribe, however, was not warlike, and made every attempt to remain neutral.

During this same period, the Skinners continued to operate their stage station and provide for travelers. Later that same year they traded the station for property on Jordan Creek. Following is a quotation from the writings of my mother, Johanna Skinner. The information was told to her by Will Skinner, who was a child of about seven when the following events took place.

1878 was the summer of the last Indian outbreak. When we first got word at Trout Creek that Indians were really on the warpath, it was about six one evening. My mother and a niece of my father, Miss Lilly Callister, four of us children (I was the oldest at seven years), one hired man, and the stage company stock tender, whose name was "Bud" Dryden from Reynolds Creek, were home. A friendly Indian employed by the Skinners, whose name was Paiute Tom, apprised settlers in the Jordan Valley area of this. He said to Annie Skinner, "I will go up on the hill (near Trout Creek) and see what the Indian fires say tonight." When he returned he said to her, "Fires say Bannocks are coming by way of South Mountain, maybe tonight."

My father and G. W. Clinton, a brother of E. H. Clinton, were out at what is known as Parsnip (peak) with a bunch of horses and one of his prize Standardbred stallions named Alcona. The report was that Indians were sighted southeast of South Mountain headed toward this Jordan Valley section. My mother's first thought was getting word to my father. Neither of the men who were at the station, had been to Parsnip. My mother had been there twice, and me also. I wanted to go, but she would not hear to that, so she saddled up a workhorse we had that was gentle to ride, and in the dark of night started for Parsnip Peak.

At that time, there were not many fences in the way and no roads where she wanted to go. She found her way okay. The horses were in the corral, the stallion tied up, the saddle horses picketed out nearby. My dad and Clinton saddled up and moved the horses to Trout Creek that night. During the excitement, we lost no horses, but the bedding and supplies left at Parsnip disappeared.

Our mother wrote in her journals:

For some time prior to 1878, the Bannocks, not without some cause, had been raiding the settlements, stealing horses, wantonly slaughtering cattle, and even murdering the settlers. In June of this year (1878), they became actively hostile, and urging the Paiutes to join them in one last concerted effort to regain their territory, they made their plans to go on the warpath.

The cause for the Indians' anger can be traced to the treatment they received from the settlers and Indian agents. As prisoners on the reservations, they were denied adequate food and shelter. Many thousands died of starvation and disease. Their food-gathering areas and fishing and hunting grounds were off-limits to them, claimed by the settlers. In hindsight, it is difficult to understand how the Indians could be blamed.

The settlers hurriedly organized the Volunteers, numbering about 100 men, with O. H. Purdy, who had been a schoolteacher, as captain and leader. They were armed with all the available rifles. The only firearms that were left at the Trout Creek Station were three shotguns and a few side arms. Had the Indians made a raid on the station, they would have met little resistance. Mounted on horses, the Volunteers went up South Mountain Creek to intercept the Indians.

They met the Indians, but quickly realized they were numerically overwhelmed. They estimated there were four hundred fifty Bannocks, so the settlers decided to retreat. Captain Purdy and another man named Steuden attempted to cover the volunteers retreat, facing the enemy to the last, but were killed and scalped. With war whoops and yells, the Indians led by Buffalo Horn followed the volunteers to a nearby creek where an experienced old scout named Nick Maher had hidden in the high brush with a young, unarmed sixteen-year-old lad named John Connor.

Maher, taking aim over the shoulder of John Connor, surprised the Bannocks by shooting the palomino horse Buffalo Horn was riding, and mortally wounded the Chief. The Indians suddenly without a leader, and seeing dust rising in the distance, thinking soldiers had joined the volunteers, turned in retreat toward the Owyhee River. It was later determined that the dust the Indians observed was from the volunteers retreating and not from added army forces. Had the Indians not made this error, this story would most likely have ended much differently.

Settlers Seek Safety

Captain Purdy had been mounted on a horse that belonged to young Will Skinner. After the battle, word came back to the stage station that

The Stateline House as it is today. Half the house is in Idaho and the other in Oregon. This is where the settlers came for safety.

Captain Purdy had been killed, as well as the horse he was riding. Will was in bed when he overheard this news. Ever the horse-lover, he set up a howl proclaiming he "didn't care about Purdy but sure hated losing his horse." At this point seven-year-old Will got a good spanking from his mother, on an unclothed rear end, because of his remark. Will remarked many years later, "It was a lesson hard learned and long remembered." Happily, several days later Will's horse wandered back to the station quite alive. He had indeed been wounded in the battle, but not seriously, and was soon nursed back to good health.

With the Indians on a rampage, it was deemed prudent to move all the women and children to a safer place until hostilities cooled down. They were first taken to the "Stateline House," the only building from that era that still stands and continues to be lived in today. It is divided by the Idaho-Oregon state line. The home was so crowded they had to move some people to the Farnaman home, another safe stone house on the Gusman ranch further up Jordan Creek. This home was well-protected but very overcrowded.

The next move to safety took Anne Jane and her children to Silver City in a buggy during the night, with guards riding in front, alongside, and behind the buggy for protection. They stayed at the home of a family named Bigelow who were storeowners in Silver City. Their home provided decidedly more protection from an attack by Indians than the stage station would have.

After several days in Silver City, Anne Jane, ignoring the possibility of another attack by Indians, felt compelled to return to the Trout Creek Station to keep it up and running. The children were being cared for in Silver City during their stay at the Bigelows' home by Silas Skinner's niece, Lilly Callister. Lilly was the daughter of Silas's deceased sister, and had accompanied Silas and Anne Jane back to Idaho when they returned from a trip to the Isle of Man.

In sharing his recollections with Johanna Skinner, his daughter-in-law and our mother, Will Skinner remembered that during this period of excitement, horses were kept saddled night and day for every person remaining at the station, in readiness for a hasty evacuation should the Indians have attacked.

The Death of an Indian Chief

There are at least two versions of the demise of Bannock Chief Buffalo Horn. In her book *Life Among the Piutes*, Sarah Winnemucca tells us that the slayer of Buffalo Horn was an Indian named Piute Joe. The battle setting she described is much the same as Will Skinner's version, told to him by John Connor, the young man over whose shoulder Nick Maher took aim. Connor asked Will Skinner not to relate the story until Nick Maher was dead, in order to insure the safety of both men. Will Skinner obliged Connor's request, keeping his confidence until both Nick Maher and John Connor were dead.

We will probably never know which version is correct or who was responsible for the death of Buffalo Horn, which brought an eventual end of the Indian Wars. At any rate, with the loss of Buffalo Horn, the Indians lacked strong leadership, and except for intermittent raids against settlers, they straggled back to the reservations, essentially ending the Indian Wars.

Depressing Conditions

It did not, however, end the deprivation and sadness the Indians continued to suffer for many years at the hands of corrupt Indian agents and a national government that made many promises for food, clothing, and shelter, but provided little or none, essentially ignoring Sarah Winnemucca's pleas on behalf of the Indians.

Sarah Winnemucca was bright—a striking personality and an attractive representative of her tribe. She was a bit flamboyant, an excellent rider, and possibly clairvoyant. Very early she realized that it was impossible for her people to compete with the whites, so she set out to educate them in the ways of the white man. Sarah Winnemucca, granddaughter of Chief Truckee, and daughter of Chief Winnemucca of the Paiute Indian Tribe, dedicated her life to the betterment of her tribe. Sadly, Sarah was largely ignored by those in the U.S. government who were capable of giving aid. Even more sadly, she was seen by many of her tribe as somewhat of a traitor for what they considered her sellout to the whites.

More than anything else, under the leadership of this family the Paiute Tribe wanted to accept the white settlers and to be accepted by them. Sarah, like her father and her grandfather before her, lived that philosophy to the highest degree. Sadly, it was not to be. The settlers had little or no use for the Indians.

The Paiute hunting grounds, the lakes where they caught their fish, and the highly productive lands where they collected seeds for their winter food supply all were taken over by the settlers. Still this tribe wanted nothing more than peace with the whites, and to be left alone to their ancient activities.

They did fight back on occasion, only to fall prey to the white man's laws, often cruelly applied and just as often unjustified. *Life Among the Piutes* is a litany of brutality and dishonesty that they and other Indian tribes received from the white man, and government agents.

An Indian's Advocate

In the uprising of 1878, Sarah Winnemucca had previously agreed to drive a man and his young daughter in her buggy from Central Oregon to Silver City, Idaho. She heard on the way that the Bannocks had gone on the warpath. It was late at night when they arrived at the Stateline House on Silas Skinner's Toll Road. She was immediately suspected of carrying arms and ammunition for the Indians and was put under guard by the suspicious soldiers. An inspection of her wagon the next morning proved differently, and Sarah actually received apologies. Volunteering her services to the army, she borrowed a horse and sped to the Sheep Ranch to offer her services to Captain Bernard, the officer in charge of the army contingent there.

Always the Indians' advocate, she also worked closely with General O. H. Howard in Boise. At Captain Bernard's request, Sarah and two of her brothers volunteered to ride horseback from the Sheep Ranch to Steens Mountain, a distance of well over a hundred miles, to scout out the location of the hostile Bannocks for the army. She was to report to General Howard on the location of the warring Bannocks who had essentially kidnapped the Paiutes in an effort to force them into helping make war.

Sarah found the encampment of the captive Paiutes, and as the darkness of evening fell, she had the women of the tribe steal away from the camp one or two at a time with their children on the premise that they were gathering wood for the night. She had them reassemble far away from the Bannocks. Sarah also convinced her father, Chief Winnemucca, and other men of the tribe to follow in the darkness. The group rendezvoused at Summit Springs. When they realized their captives were gone, the Bannocks pursued them. When the Paiutes' children slowed them, Sarah had them bury the youngsters in the ground, leaving only breathing space, cautioning the little ones to make no sound lest the Bannocks find them.

The Paiutes avoided capture and returned under the cover of darkness to retrieve their terrified children, and took them to their new camp. With her people safe, Sara returned to the Sheep Ranch to report to General Howard and Captain Bernard. This trip of more than two hundred miles on horseback over extremely rough country was completed in about two days and nights. Her brothers and her sister-in-law, whom she had saved, accompanied her back to the Sheep Ranch.

In later years Sarah made many trips to San Francisco and Washington D.C. in an effort to bring government aid to the Indians on the reservations. She became an accomplished public speaker and had no fear of high-powered politicians, including a president of the United States. Political leaders made many promises for assistance but did not fulfill them. Thousands of these people from many tribes on reservations across the nation were to starve to death and die of disease while she tried mightily to save them.

Despite all, her efforts to bring relief to the Indian tribes did not cease. After General Howard successfully put down the Indian rebellion, she worked tirelessly and often at her own expense to set up schools in order to educate and work with Indian children, attempting to bring them into the white man's world by teaching them to read and learn the white man's ways.

SS

9

Silas's Dream— His Own Ranch

Silas had not forgotten his dream of owning land. He and E. H. Clinton—businessmen and visionaries—traded all their road equipment, work stock, and the Trout Creek Station to C. D. Bachelor for one hundred and twenty acres of land on Jordan Creek about thirteen miles west of the town of Jordan Valley. One hundred and thirty years later, the land for which they traded is now a small part of the present-day Skinner Ranch west of the Jordan Valley community.

Both Skinner and Clinton had invested in livestock by this time, but which they ran separately. Silas Skinner, in addition to his growing herd of registered Standardbred trotting horses, owned both cattle and grade horses, branded with the now famous SS iron, known then and today as the "double ess." Clinton's stock was branded with a $\overline{C}$ (bar C). In partnership, they also bought three hundred and fifty cattle from a man named Mike Hyde, a rancher in the Reynolds Creek area, and branded them with "OO" (double O). They bought a bunch of horses from him as well.

In 1879 Silas Skinner sold his interest in the Jordan Creek property to E. H. Clinton. Silas then bought a small ranch from Jack Strickland, located about five miles to the east up Jordan Creek, and moved his family there. Skinner and Clinton's livestock partnership continued, however. Clinton retired and moved to California, where he died in 1884. In his absence he had hired Will Skinner to manage the property. Following E. H. Clinton's death, his brother, G. W. Clinton, inherited the property, after which G. W. also died. Will was then hired by the brothers' heirs to manage the property. During this time, Will began to formulate his dream of ownership and expansion of the property.

The ranch property that Silas bought from Jack Strickland was to become known in the Skinner family as the "Old Skinner Place." Skinners continued ownership of this property until about 1917, in conjunction with The E. H. Clinton property, which W. S. (Will) Skinner bought in the early 1900s from the Clinton heirs and which then became the home place.

Children on the Ranch

Two more children were born to Silas and Anne Jane after their move. Horatio (Ray) was born in 1879 on the "Old Skinner Place"—the Jordan Creek ranchland Silas had traded for. Ray died in 1918 in the flu epidemic, and he is buried in the Jordan Valley Cemetery. Sarah Ellen, born in 1881, died in 1883 at about age two. She, too, is buried in the Jordan Valley Cemetery.

Mona May, the youngest, was born in April 1883 after Silas had moved his family to the "Old Skinner Place" on Jordan Creek.

With the range continuing to produce adequate feed, Skinners continued to run their cattle and horses on the range year round. It was about this time that nine-year-old Will Skinner, Silas and Annie's oldest son, started to take responsibility for herding the horses owned by his father. Due to predations from the Indians, the horses were kept close to home during the night and turned out during the day. It was young Will's job to keep the horses together and on good feed, and to see them home safely at night.

Butter-Making Operation

When Silas and Anne Jane moved their family up Jordan Creek to the "Old Skinner Place," they brought with them a herd of milk cows. It is doubtful these cows were from dairy stock, more likely from Skinner's herd of range cattle. Jim Fell, a neighbor, also bought a bunch of milk cows. The Skinners and Fell formed a partnership on the milk cows and went into a butter-making business. Jim Fell eventually married Lilly Callister, Silas Skinner's niece. Anne Jane and Fell's hired man did the milking. Automatic milking machines and cream separators had yet to be invented, so Fell skimmed the cream and Annie Skinner took charge of the butter-making process.

The skimmed milk was fed to a bunch of pigs, which doubtless were destined to become ham and bacon on the dining tables of the mining people in Silver City and the surrounding community. There were a number of Chinese nationals working in the Silver City mines. Quite often one would buy a pig, tie a rope to its front leg, and drive it from the Skinner place near Jordan Valley to Silver City, a distance of some twenty-five miles.

The butter was salted, packed in barrels, and later molded and sold to merchants in Silver City and Jordan Valley. During the hot summer months, the partnership suspended the butter-making and went into the cheese-making business. Will Skinner, still a child at the time, reminisced in later years about watching as Mr. Fell operated the large cheese presses. Like their butter, the cheeses produced were marketed to local merchants and to stores in Silver City and the mining area.

The partnership marketed the butter under the name of "Fells Butter." It became famous in the area, demanded by merchants and their customers. Soon all butter being made and sold in Jordan Valley and Silver City was called "Fells Butter," regardless of who produced it. To protect his reputation, Jim Fell had a special set of molds made up that imprinted his name in the butter to stop impostors from using his brand on their inferior product.

Young Will also had a hand in the butter-making operation. It was his job to watch over and take care of the milk cows' calves, which, as the calves grew rapidly, was not an easy task. His experience with the calves turned out to be a valuable lesson in the business of cattle ranching in later years.

SS

—Four-mule team and a cook wagon out on the range. Circa 1900.

10

Will's Education

Silas and Anne Jane saw to it that Will also attended school for about two months each summer. He rode his horse to and from the school, a distance of about nine miles each way. After two months the school closed, and he was kept busy herding horses over the land that would one day develop into his childhood dream, the Skinner Ranch.

The teacher got married about two years later, and the tiny school located two miles east of Jordan Valley closed. For the present at least, Will's education had come to an end.

The Desert Bloomed

From the time he arrived in America and went into the ranching business, Will's father, Silas, had never observed a season when the rangeland didn't provide an abundance of livestock feed. Because of that, and very possibly because of his failing health, Silas was much less of a visionary than was his young son Will. Silas did not believe there would ever be a need to produce more feed for animals. He believed that what little supplemental feed might be needed could be produced easily on land next to Jordan Creek, which was watered by flooding during the spring runoff.

But there may have been another reason for Silas's line of thinking. He had started to develop other interests, and with the abundant feed being produced naturally, growing more animal feed was not something he felt was important. His mind was more attuned to his Standardbred trotting horses, which by now were producing outstanding colts that were showing signs of racing greatness.

In 1881 Silas leased a ranch about two and a half miles west of the town of Jordan Valley, and built a racetrack in a field on the north side of his once-owned toll road. He hired an experienced trainer whose

The remains of the willow fence built by Silas Skinner for his stallions.

name was Goldsmith, to train his trotting horses. He needed an exercise area for his stallions, so he built a large corral out of willows for that purpose. To this day, the willow fence continues to stand beside Highway 95, one hundred and twenty-six years later. The willows next to the ground have now rotted away, but there is still about two and a half or three feet of willow fence still existing. Through the years the "Goodrich Ranch" has been owned by a number of families and several years ago was purchased and is now part of Skinner Ranch's Incorporated.

Silas's best trotting horses were taken to California to compete on the tracks, where several made significant marks in racing circles. A number of the stallions he owned became famous as sires. Among them were Altamont, Alcona, Alcona Jr., Alcona Clay, Clay Duke, and Split Rock. Split Rock was named for a topographical landmark near Skinner's Trout Creek Stage Station. A mare that Skinner named Flora Belle became an internationally famous trotter, winning wide acclaim on the tracks. Will, who was just a youngster at the time, remembered rubbing and massaging her legs the nights before she raced.

Continuing Education

In 1881, Silas and Anne Jane became increasingly concerned about continuing an education program for their two oldest children. At this time, Frank Callow, a cousin of Anne Jane, came west and worked with Silas and Anne Jane for a summer. He had previously made marriage plans and would be returning to Ohio to get married.

After some discussion and planning, Silas and Anne Jane decided to send Will, age ten, and his sister Carrie, eight, back to Ohio with Callow for a more formal education. Arrangements were made for the children to live with Mr. and Mrs. Will Fitch, relatives of Anne Jane, who lived in Kingville, Ohio. In due time Callow and the two children boarded a buckboard driven by Tom McCain, a longtime friend of the family, and they started the six day trip to Winnemucca, Nevada, to catch the train to Ohio.

Little Carrie became very, very homesick along the way, and when they stopped for lunch she decided to hide in the sagebrush. She believed if they were unable to find her, they would go on without her; she would then catch the next stagecoach back home. She knew all the stagecoach drivers on the road, and believed she would have no problem getting a ride. Callow and McCain, however, found her hiding place and the trip continued.

At the same time, Carrie's mother was also having strong misgivings about sending her little girl so far away, and for so long. She sent word to McCain by stagecoach to bring Carrie back home. By the time McCain got the message, Will and Carrie were on board the train and well on their way to Ohio.

A story Will gleefully told in later years about their trip to Ohio must be related here. While the train made its way across the country, several gentlemen had started a card game. According to Will, it was the custom for vendors to go through the train from car to car, selling pastries and pies to the passengers.

Another passenger, an elderly lady, had a talking parrot in a cage, taking it with her to her destination. She was being very careful that the parrot did not overhear any off-color language. Alas, a vendor came through the train selling pies, and a gentleman playing cards, no doubt suffering from some bad luck, loudly informed the vendor, "No, no, no, go to hell with your damn pies."

The next time the pie vendor came through the car, informing the passengers he had "pies for sale," the parrot informed the vendor, as well as everyone else in the car, "No, no, no, go to hell with your damn pies." Will recalled there was a roar of laughter from the other passengers following the parrot's emphatic refusal, and a very angry parrot owner.

After two years of schooling in Ohio, Will and Carrie's parents decided it was time for them to come back to Oregon. Will was quite ready to do so. His heart had always been in the western country, with the horses. Carrie, on the other hand, had made many friends among her classmates, and she was not one bit anxious to come home.

In honor of their departure, the school they attended let out for the day. The boys were singing, and the girls were all in tears as Will, Carrie, and their luggage were loaded onto a wagon to be taken to the train. Their parents' wishes had prevailed over Carrie's sadness in leaving her friends, and the two children were soon aboard a train bound for Idaho.

In 1884, the railroad had been completed only as far as Pocatello, Idaho. Beyond Pocatello to the west, the tracks were being used only by work trains. So it was that young Will and Carrie boarded a work train and became the first paying passengers on the tracks from Pocatello to Caldwell, Idaho. Being a work train, the children rode in the caboose with the conductor. Will and Carrie both remarked many years later that they had been treated like royalty by the train crew; their slightest wish was a command.

When the train arrived in Caldwell, Will and Carrie were informed there had been a big storm in Jordan Valley, and that their parents would be unable to meet them at the train station. The children remained under the wing of a trusted hotel proprietor in Caldwell who cared for them until Tom McCain, the man who had taken them to Winnemucca two years previously, arrived a few days later with a team and buckboard. A short time later the two children were back in the arms of their parents.

SS

11

SS

A Hopeful Move to a Warmer Climate

The accident Silas previously suffered when his horse fell with him and broke his ribs, eventually ended his life. He had not fully recovered from the injury, and his health had gone into a lengthy decline. His physician had suggested that a milder climate might be conducive to healing. Additionally, Silas and Anne Jane had often discussed the importance of providing an education for their now six children. Educational facilities in Jordan Valley were substandard at best, with classes conducted for only three months and then only in the summer and if a teacher was available.

With the physician's suggestion in mind, and the abiding need to educate their children, the couple left their children in the care of Lilly Tapp, Silas's niece, and took the stagecoach to Winnemucca where they boarded the train for the Napa Valley in Central California. There, on Big Ranch Road in Napa, they found the ideal ranch property to accommodate their family and their horses. In 1884 they bought the property and moved their family and the trotting horse operation there.

In the back of Silas's mind, the Standardbred trotters were a third reason for the move, and the close proximity of the California racetracks was enticing. The desire to get his trotting horses onto those tracks was a major factor in their decision to move.

Once relocated to Napa, he began a training program to which the horses responded very well. Several quickly became prominent trotters who were also well-known as sires of outstanding Standardbred horses throughout California and the West Coast.

Meanwhile, Silas's herd of horses in Jordan Valley continued to increase in number and in quality because Silas had introduced the Standardbred blood into his less valuable mares.

Skinner's horses fit very well with the increased use of Standardbreds on ranches and in livery stables. Livery stables of that era would be compared to automotive garages of today; they provided a service for travelers, allowing them to stable their horses for a fee while traveling. Livery stables also provided rental horses, other horse equipment, and conveyances such as buggies and wagons for a fee.

Silas the Entrepreneur

Never one to overlook an opportunity to make money with his horses, Silas promoted another use for them when he arrived in California. He contracted with the city of San Francisco to provide them with one hundred and fifty horses annually, to be delivered for use by the city—to pull ambulances, streetcars, fire engines, and garbage wagons, as well as for other drayage purposes.

That contract, however, posed other obstacles for Skinner, whose health continued to deteriorate. His horses were in eastern Oregon, approximately four hundred miles from Napa Valley. If he were to drive them to Winnemucca, Nevada, and load them into railway livestock cars for shipment to Napa, his costs would be prohibitive. There was only one alternative available to him. That alternative was to gather the horses and make preparations to drive them overland to Napa.

Silas returned to Jordan Valley with Will, age thirteen, and Will's younger brother, Tom, only a few months over seven years old. Will, Tom McCain, and a man named Jim Allen gathered up one hundred and fifty-eight horses, and plans were made to drive them overland from Jordan Valley to Napa Valley. Tom was still too young to be of much help to Silas on horseback.

Following is Will's written account of the drive.

Leaving here from the "Old Skinner Place" in Jordan Valley on August 7, 1884, we arrived at Napa, California, October 7, 1884, with one hundred fifty-six horses, and a wagon to carry the camp supplies, driven by my father, with Tom on the seat beside him and pulled by a four horse team. Driving the horse herd were myself at about thirteen years of age, Tom McCain, and Jim Allen.

The fourth night out from the home ranch in Jordan Valley, camp was made at the head of Crooked Creek. Two horses were missing the next morning and Jim Allen and I were sent back to follow them as their tracks were headed towards home. We tracked them to the Owyhee River Crossing and the man there, a Mr. Fletcher, told us the horses were two hours ahead of us.

Since there was no chance of catching them we turned back to go to the head of Crooked Creek. We got to the creek and got off our horses to get a drink at a cold spring and upon drinking the cold water Allen stiffened out with something like an epileptic attack and was unconscious for several hours. It was late at night and no help near. I covered him with saddle blankets and kept a fire near him as he seemed to be chilling. Some time toward morning he regained consciousness and with my help was able to get on his horse and we started for camp.

We had gone but a few miles when we met Tom McCain who my dad had sent back to find us. That was some experience for a thirteen-year-old boy. McCain sent me on to our camp at the head of Crooked Creek which was about twenty-two miles. He came at a slower pace with Allen. As we had been nearly thirty-six hours without food, my father was careful that I ate very sparingly for several hours.

We proceeded following the Honey Lake Road to Cedarville and on to Pittville, where we stayed in hotels. We camped out all the other nights. When going through the white pine forest we found it hard going. The timber was so thick and the road so narrow, when we met a team, we had to get the horses off the road. The horses were scared in the timber and it was hard to keep them in a bunch and get them all back on the road. Neither McCain or I, or the horses we were riding liked the timber any better than the horses we were driving.

While staying at either Cedarville or Pittville, my father began dealing with a man who offered $115.00 per head for the horses but my father wanted $125.00 so we continued on our way. While camped at night the saddle horses were always hobbled. On the whole trip we only had to buy pasture for horses four nights, three at Cedarville and one at Madeline Plains.

On leaving Madeline Plains we drove about twenty-five miles to watering troughs where sheep had been watering. The horses were not used to sheep and would not drink. During the night all the horses, except the hobbled saddle horses and workhorses, left this camp ground and returned to the camp of the night before. Tom McCain and I followed them and caught them at the former camp location, corralled them, and took them the next day to the camp they had strayed from.

The rest of the trip was quite uneventful and routine, and the drive reached Napa on the seventh day of October, exactly two months from the day we left the Skinner Ranch in Jordan Valley. When the horses were sold from the Napa ranch one week after their arrival, we received $125.00 per head. In that era the price difference of $10.00 more per head that he (Silas) received, made a very significant difference and a significantly improved bank account.

Delivering the Product

Silas and his crew made two drives the next year taking horses to California. Thereafter the drives became an annual event for the next several years. Skinner's horses became more popular in California as their name spread. The team and wagon that carried the supplies for the trips, returned to Winnemucca by train then went to Paradise Valley where the wagon was loaded with flour for delivery to Silver City, thus making the trip home pay and avoiding returning to Jordan Valley with an empty wagon.

Death of a Pioneer

In the meantime, Anne Jane put the younger children in school in Napa, and the family had been introduced into the social affairs of the Napa community. Silas's health did not improve as they had hoped, and instead, continued to worsen. The physicians there diagnosed his illness as consumption. He eventually became bedridden, which must have been difficult for such an active and vital man. On April 10, 1886, apparently realizing death was near, Silas deeded the ranch property in Napa to Anne Jane.

Silas died on June 12, 1886, at the age of fifty-two. With his last words, he would remember his old and dear friend Michael Jordan from their toll road and gold mining days, and whom he had buried on the banks of Jordan Creek following Michael and his brother James's massacre by the Indians.

In a letter to family, Silas's daughter Annabel wrote that Silas, with his wife Anne Jane at his bedside on the day he died, said to her, "It's alright Annie, Mike is beckoning over there for me. Can't you see him? He's waving for me to come on over." Silas is buried in the Tulocay Cemetery in Napa, California.

A Look at His Life

It is interesting to look back on the accomplishments of Silas Skinner over the short fifty-two years of his life. He had been a successful sailor, who at twenty-eight felt he wanted something more, something different. He took a huge step when he left the sea for a new life. Over the next twenty-six years, Silas appears to have been successful at everything he tried.

(I'm sharing this with you, which expresses how I feel
about a Certain Man in these late years of our lives together)

How dear and good he is -
My living friend of so many years!
My heart is saddened when I see
how very thin he's grown.
How bravely he tries
to stand straight -
There was a time he stood tall,
with no effort.
Thru memory's eyes I see him
strong and erect astride his horse,
as he reined up beside the old rail fence.
It is now as tho his body had been sabotaged
one starless night, by some unseen enemy.
I know, too, he feels that way -
Yet when I look at him each day,
I feel a tenderness toward him
I had not known those years ago
when he was strong,
and seemingly invulnerable
O my dear beloved one -
Time-ravaged, with health frail,
camouflaged by courage & pride -

Anne Jane's note to her husband Silas in his last years.

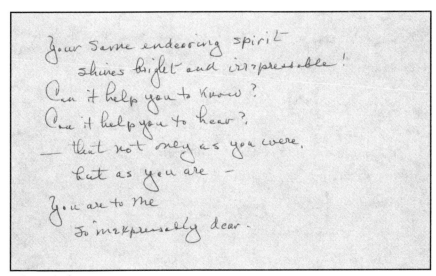

The end of Anne Jane's note.

His successes were not limited to the sea and sailing, but also in the mining industry, and as a construction engineer, road builder, frontiersman, businessman, livestock rancher, and last but not least, the owner of fine racehorses. He accomplished all of this in a relatively short period of twenty-six years. He also proved he had the ability to keep a cool head in stressful, potentially life-threatening situations as when he and David Shirk were attacked by Indians, a time when lesser men would have crumbled.

Silas and Anne Jane had a strong marriage. Together they raised and educated six children to adulthood. They lost only one child to diphtheria, very early in her life, in an age and in an area where medical care was primitive at best. These two also worked well together in their business ventures, relying heavily on their previous experiences in life to guide them. Silas was once quoted saying, "I have no problem making the money; Annie is the one who knows how to save it."

In the stacks of letters, papers, documents, and history we waded through in pulling materials together for this book, we found this note (see picture) she wrote to Silas during his last days. It gives us an insight into her tenderness and the respect she had for him.

SS

—*The Skinner family. Standing (left to right): Tom, Carrie, Will, and Annabel. Seated (left to right): Annie, Mona, Ray, and cousin Lilly Tapp. A picture of Silas Skinner is on the wall in back.*

12

Anne Jane and Young Will Take Over

With the death of Silas, the reins of management of the Skinner holdings in Napa Valley and Jordan Valley were passed into Anne Jane's capable hands. Will, the eldest son, who was then barely fifteen years of age, felt a strong responsibility to his family and to his father's memory. He made plans to return to Jordan Valley soon after his father's death to work, with Tom McCain's assistance, in the management of the family's ranch and livestock interests in eastern Oregon.

There were loose ends hanging in California, however, that the family felt should be tied up before any big decisions could be reached. Will was deeply involved in the Oregon property and wanted to make that his home. Caring for a young family while managing the Napa Valley ranch and Silas's racehorses had placed an onerous burden on Anne Jane.

Additionally, the mortgage on the Napa Valley ranch was only about half-paid when Silas died. Anne Jane called a meeting of her family at which some hard decisions were made. She came to the realization she did not have the time, the desire, nor the knowledge to continue working with the Standardbred trotters. With Will returning to Jordan Valley and the rest of the children too young to be of significant help, it was agreed they would sell the Standardbred trotting horses and pay down the mortgage on the Napa Valley ranch.

Plans were made to hold a dispersal sale of the trotters. Advertisements were placed in strategic locations in California cities. The Southern Pacific Railway ran a special train from San Francisco and Sacramento to the Skinners' Napa Valley property. Buggies, hacks, and horse-drawn buses were provided free of charge. The family served a huge free lunch to the buyers to put them into a bidding mood before the auction started.

When the sale ended about three hours later, and the proceeds had been tallied up, it turned out that the return was much better than the family could have anticipated. Prices paid had averaged over a thousand dollars per horse with several horses going for five thousand dollars each. The family was able to pay down the Napa Valley Ranch property, leaving it nearly clear of debt for Anne Jane and her family. With the annual sale of the range horses in Oregon, a large portion of the debt on the Oregon property was also paid, with a small operating fund remaining.

An interesting side note to the above sale occurred in the 1940s, some sixty years after the date of the sale. The building that housed the harness shop and schoolroom in which Will and Ella's children attended school on the Skinner Ranch in Jordan Valley was being renovated to make it more available for current use. As the siding on the building was being removed, we discovered many sale brochures advertising the above dispersal sale.

These sale brochures had somehow found their way to Jordan Valley and had been nailed to the inner walls of the old building to provide insulation against the wind and cold weather. In light of this current endeavor to document the history of the Skinner family, it would have been interesting to add a picture of one of Silas's prize horses. Sadly, the sale brochures no longer exist. My brother, Bob, thinks our mother burned these because of the threat of some disease going around during the period of the sale.

Will

Taking a man's place and a man's responsibility on his young shoulders, fifteen-year-old Will Skinner returned to Jordan Valley after his father's death. He traveled by train from Napa, California, to Winnemucca, Nevada, then by horseback across the Owyhee desert to Jordan Valley. It was a lonely trip for Will. He missed his father and was lonesome for his mother and his family. He remarked later that he had "many a good cry on that trip across the Owyhee desert."

Along with family friend Tom McCain, Will managed his family's livestock and was also hired by Silas's business partner G. W. Clinton, brother of E. H. Clinton, now deceased, to work on and manage the Clinton property on Jordan Creek.

The following year, again with the helpful guidance of Tom McCain, Will successfully organized and made two drives of about one hundred and fifty horses, overland to Napa to fulfill the contract with San Francisco. In the years following his father's death and until 1891, Will continued to make one drive annually to deliver horses to Napa. His ability and his reliance on the experience of Tom McCain to help plan and organize an undertaking of such magnitude was quite a feat for a teenage boy.

Who Was This Man, Tom McCain?

We should make special mention of Tom McCain, having referred to him a number of times. We have reason to believe Silas may have employed him, but we cannot prove it. The name Tom McCain has a prominent role in almost every story, and every historical event that Will Skinner discussed over the years.

Tom McCain was obviously one of Silas and Anne Jane's most trusted friends. Few parents would entrust their young son and daughter to an unrelated person, yet it was McCain who drove Will and his sister Carrie in a buggy to Winnemucca, over two hundred miles over a period of six days, to board the train for schooling in Ohio. It was McCain who picked them up in Caldwell, Idaho, when they came home.

Following Silas's untimely death, it was Tom McCain who took young Will under his wing and gave him guidance as Will managed Skinner family interests in Jordan Valley and took on management of the Clinton properties in their absence.

Tom McCain imparted his vast knowledge of livestock management, and served equally well as a surrogate father to the teenager. We suspect that while Will received most of the credit for his activities and knowledge in later years, Tom McCain was standing in the shadows in those early years, directing the traffic, and he deserves much of the credit for many of Will Skinner's successes.

When Tom McCain died, he was buried in the Jordan Valley Cemetery. We are not aware of any of his family, or if he even had one. We suspect Silas and Anne Jane and their family may have been among those closest to him.

Changing Times

In August 2007, approximately eighty members of the Skinner family from across the nation gathered in Napa, California, for a family reunion at Silas and Anne Jane's old ranch, now a vineyard. Carole and I drove from Salem, Oregon, to Napa in a little less than eight hours. After reading Will's own account of his trips requiring two months to drive a herd of horses to Napa from eastern Oregon, and another he made alone on horseback in the dead of winter to Winnemucca, I marvel at his ability, durability, and organizational aptitude. Not many teenaged boys in today's society could handle, nor would they have the ambition for, such an undertaking.

As many in this extended family do, I take pride in the fact that I am a direct descendant—the great-grandson of Silas Skinner, the grandson of Will Skinner, and the son of Kirtland. But I am not alone in my pride. The members of this now large and relatively close-knit family meet every two years to stay connected, and we obviously take pride in the accomplishments of our pioneering forebears. They provided us with strong genes.

I am also amazed at how the advanced methods of travel have reduced the time required to cover the distance between two points in the relatively short period of about one hundred years. Those trips that took Will Skinner up to two months, took my wife and me a short eight hours. I have to wonder: are we moving a bit too rapidly for our own good? Will we, in the next one hundred years only have to think about where we want to be, and we will be there? It's scary!

In his later years, Will Skinner wrote of an experience he endured during the winter of 1888–1889. He was seventeen years old, living on his own at the time in Jordan Valley. He had become lonesome to see his mother and the rest of his family. Because of the extreme cold and deep snow, the stagecoaches had stopped running. He decided to make the trip from Jordan Valley to Winnemucca, Nevada, on horseback—two hundred and twenty miles—and then take the train from Winnemucca to Napa, California.

Will seldom used punctuation or paragraphing of any kind, although his sentences were usually complete. The following is written just as he wrote it, though commas and periods have been added for clarity. In his words:

To give an idea what the winter was like, I left here January 10, 1889, to ride to Winnemucca on horseback to go to California. There was about two feet of snow here in the valley. It was forty-two below zero the night before I started. There was neither stage nor travel on the road between here and Summit Springs. The snow across the Owyhee Desert was two to three feet. I saw little bunches of cattle bunched up around high brush across the desert pulling the sagebrush back to eat. Some places I counted them. When I came back in May, the carcasses were there. The first days ride from the river (Owyhee), going down, took me to the Bowden Ranch. Mr. Bowden there had a few cows and few horses he was trying to feed. Hay was gone. He had a shed, which had been covered with rye grass of two or three years before which he was tearing off to try to save that stock but winter lasted too long. He lost all of them. The next day I went over to Battle Creek, which had been a Stage Station at foot of Summit Hills. There was a sheepman there with a band of sheep which were corralled by the snow and been there for twelve days and were already dying. They were owned by the man with them and a captain at Fort McDermitt. It was eight miles from there to Summit Springs. The man with the sheep told me no one had been over the summit for eight days and said "you are a foolish boy to try it." But I had a good horse and was anxious to get home to Napa, California. So against his advice I started and was seven hours making eight miles. I walked through snow three to six feet deep but made it and was about froze. A family by the name of Packard lived at Summit Station and took fine care of me. They thawed the frost out of my feet and hands with snow. So all the ill effects were blistered feet and hands. The roads from there to Winnemucca broke so I made better time. It took six and a half days riding to reach Winnemucca. Snow through Quinn River Valley was two and a half to three feet. Two bands of sheep there were being fed in a snow corral. Cattle on feed could not move around much. Winter lasted too long for their hay so there was big stock loss there also. Mr. Wm. Baxter had eleven hundred and fifty ewes on desert and lost every one. When the captain at the Fort heard his sheep were dying, he got some teams on bob sleighs loaded with some grain at the Fort and got through with it. Saved seven or eight hundred out of eleven hundred fifty so my getting through with word to the captain probably saved some of their sheep for them, But after I got through, I realized it was a foolish trip for me to tackle at that time. But looked to me like all our horses here were sure to die. A lot of them were around home here. We could do nothing for them except keep water open. I had a man here with me. [Will was most likely referring to Tom McCain here.] I knew he could do that and I did not want to see these horses die. I was homesick and wanted to go home so I took the risk. There came a thaw here about Feb. twenty. It let the snow down to a foot or so, and horses could then get some feed. Our loss was plenty but we did not lose all. The snow from Winnemucca to Reno was two to four feet, then to Truckee, four to six feet, and from Truckee on over the summit you rarely could see any telegraph wires. I got down to Auburn and everything was green and some flowers were blooming. It was a very lovely sight after being in snow for weeks. Anyway, I never have forgotten that trip. Now we can leave Jordan Valley at one p.m. by bus and be in San Francisco the next morning at seven thirty.

Will's Dreams of the Future

Will Skinner's experience during that severe winter gave him pause. He later spoke of how he couldn't help thinking of the livestock that could have been saved had adequate feed been available. He recalled how as he rode over the land, he had thought, *What if the land had been cleared and irrigated?* With the land that was so available, his only thought was of what could have been. *Maybe if the rudimentary dam Clinton and his neighbor Ike Sharpe had put in Jordan Creek could be beefed up to hold back more water, and to supply that water to land cleared of sagebrush and planted to meadow grass....* C. D. Bachelor, who had owned this land and later traded it to Silas Skinner and E. H. Clinton, and Bachelor's neighbor, a man named Tracy, had together put a rudimentary dam in Jordan Creek, which was later added to by E. H. Clinton and his neighbor, Ike Sharpe.

At the time, Will figured if that dam could be beefed up to hold back more water, and then to supply that water to land cleared of sagebrush and planted to meadow grass, large numbers of livestock lost because of the lack of feed during that very severe winter could have been saved

As he herded his family's horses over the range the next few years, Will's vision of how this land could be more productive became clearer. Still, his father's comments rang in his head. "Why worry about raising hay, when the range produces more than needed for livestock?" But Will could not get the visions of starving animals out of his head. Those animals could have been saved if they had only had feed available.

Will Skinner was a teenager, but he was also a visionary. It would be necessary for him to put his plan and his dreams on hold, since he did not own that land and had no money to buy it. Above all, he was determined. Somehow, someday—he would find a way to realize his dream.

—Anne Jane Callow Skinner

Anne Jane, Widow

After Silas died, Anne Jane went about raising her family and continued managing her business interests in Napa and ranching interests in Jordan Valley. During the years following Silas's death, she made a number of trips to visit her family and friends on the Isle of Man. When Silas died, he left Anne Jane in reasonably good financial condition. The sale of the Standardbred horses and the sale of some of the Napa property also kept her financially solvent.

She remained in Napa for a number of years and was quite highly placed in the community's social structure, and according to her obituary, she was "a lady of forceful character, always active in every good community enterprise." She made sure her family was educated up to the standards of the day, as well as in the social graces. Correspondence often made mention of card parties, dances, and picnics held among the neighbors on Big Ranch Road.

Ray Melville, who married Nancy Skinner, daughter of Bob and Sara Skinner, made a recent examination of the handwritten records of the sales of the ranch in Napa. The language in the records is quite interesting. The following hand-written document is quoted in part, from an official record of transfer for Napa County when Anne Jane sold some of the ranch property: "To Wit: Commencing at a post, set in a mound and glass standing on the east line of the road surveyed through said ranch and distant 60 chains from the most southerly line thereof at a point from which a white oak tree 30 inches in diameter, bears 70 degrees E. 1.83 chains…to another post set in mound and glass…" The questions that come to mind are how permanent those types of landmarks were, or what happened in the event the tree died or grew to forty inches, and how long it was before an accurate survey was completed. But this method obviously worked to the satisfaction of all parties to the sale.

Following the final sale of the ranch property in Napa, Anne Jane moved her family to Berkeley, California, in 1898 to be near her daughter Mona. Few members of the family living today remember Anne Jane, but her history, her life story and the pictures in our files, indicate she had a very determined jawline and a strong personality. Anne Jane died in 1928 and is buried next to Silas in the Tulocay Cemetery in Napa, California.

SS

*—Wedding picture of William Silas Skinner
and Ella Sackett. November 11, 1891.*

13

Will and Ella

Will Skinner continued to look after his family's interests in eastern Oregon and made annual trips delivering horses to fulfill the contract with the city of San Francisco. In doing so, he became acquainted with a number of families in the Napa Valley. His mother and his brothers and sisters, who were in school, became known and were socially active in community affairs. His mother and his siblings made sure that Will was made aware of the gentler side of life during his visits. Will's brothers, Tom and Horatio (Ray), had developed into quite handsome young men who were prominent among the social set and sought after as worthy companions for many of the young ladies in the community.

Will was not one to hang back or be a wallflower. During one of the social occasions, he met and fell in love with an attractive, young socialite who was a member of a prominent ranching family in Napa. The young lady's name was Ella, the daughter of Kirtland Sackett and his wife Nancy (Henery) Sackett.

Ella, born June 21, 1868, was an attractive and talented young lady, and she soon caught Will's eye. She played the piano and sang beautifully, which attracted him. Will was a good dancer, and a better-than-average mixer at social events. It was at a community event that Will and Ella were properly introduced, and a big smile would appear on Will's face when he would later make the comment, "Another fellow brought Ella to the dance, but I took her home."

Will was twenty and Ella was twenty-three when they married. He was required to have his mother's permission before their wedding could take place. With Ella's father and Will's mother as their attendants, Will Skinner and Ella Sackett were married on November 11, 1891. After a honeymoon of several days in San Francisco, they re-

The Sackett family. Standing (left to right): Margaret, Charley, Hattie, George, and Ella. Seated (left to right) Nancy, Kirtland, and Sam.

turned to Napa. Soon after, the couple boarded a train to Winnemucca, Nevada, and then traveled by buggy to the old Skinner Ranch in Jordan Valley.

The Sackett Family History

Ella Skinner's ancestors had arrived in America 232 years before Silas Skinner left his ship in California in 1862. The Sackett family has traced their heritage back to Thomas Sackett, born in 1531 on the Isle of Thanet, in England. He was the great-grandfather of Simon Sackett, born in 1595 on the Isle of Thanet, and a native of the Isle of Ely, Cambridge, England, and the first in the Sackett family to migrate to America.

Along with his wife and baby, Simon Sackett boarded the sailing ship *Lyon* in England during the fall of 1630, and set sail for the new world. After a very rough and lengthy crossing, the *Lyon* arrived at Nantasket Roads off Boston Town on the fifth day of February 1631. The ship's arrival was greeted with great happiness, since the colony had run dangerously low on provisions, with famine imminent.

Deputy Governor Winthrop Dudley, because of the colony's precarious supply of provisions, had previously ordered a day of prayer and fasting. When the *Lyon's* sails were sighted, he immediately proclaimed a day of feasting and thanksgiving. It has been said that due to this fact, we are indebted to the late Governor Dudley for our traditional American Thanksgiving Day.

In 1631, Governor Dudley and several other prominent men, including Simon Sackett, erected housing on land granted to them by Governor Dudley, naming the settlement Newtown, laying the foundation for what is now known as the city of Cambridge, Massachusetts.

The Sackett family has had a colorful history since migrating to America. They have prospered and grown immensely in numbers. There are few communities of any size in the United States today in which the Sackett name is not a part.

Reverend Don Emmel, along with his wife, Esther Skinner, granddaughter of Will and Ella (Sackett) Skinner, conducted a lengthy investigation of the early history of the Sackett family in America and located the following information from *Westfield and Its Historic Influences 1669–1919* by John Hoyt Lockwood:

In 1675, a descendant of Simon Sackett, built the first home constructed in Westfield, Massachusetts. The Indians attacked and burned this home down, and also kidnapped the family's youngest daughter Elizabeth who was about six years old. The Indians took the child to northern New York, and raised her as an Indian, and she eventually married a member of the tribe.

Around 1810, Elizabeth visited her family with her Indian husband, and their son and daughter. The family was unaccustomed to living in a house and so, put up a tepee in the yard to live in while they visited. After they left, Elizabeth never returned for a visit with her family. Her son grew up to become an Indian Chief well-known for the raids he conducted on the colonists. Known as Chief Sackett he, with a superior force attacked a much smaller, but very well trained British military contingent of forty men. Trained in the finer points of protecting themselves in battle, the British took cover, and firing well aimed shots, soundly defeated Chief Sackett. He made several charges, attempting to dislodge the military, but in doing so, lost so many of his braves he soon retreated to safety.

The Skinner family happily reports today that others of Chief Sackett's mother's descendants were much less warlike, and in later years made many visits to their maternal family's home.

Kirtland Sackett, Ella's father, a direct descendant of Simon Sackett, had a curiosity and pioneering spirit similar to that of Silas Skinner. Kirtland Sackett, however, took a different route than the sea to arrive in California. He was a captain, or master, of wagon trains traveling west across the country. He eventually settled in the Bay Area of California, where he joined with the wagon wrights in Sutter's Fort. Kirtland married Nancy Henery on November 5, 1861.

Nancy Henery, Ella's mother, came to California by train from the East with her aunt, Mrs. Goodrich, and her two daughters. They settled in Napa, California, where Nancy acted as a third daughter to her aunt and took the name "Nancy Goodrich" until her marriage to Kirtland Sackett. This was a common occurrence at that time since train fare for families was more reasonable than for singles. Many otherwise lone travelers were temporarily adopted by friends or relatives.

The following narration was written in the early 1900s by Agnes Sackett, daughter of one of Ella (Sackett) Skinner's brothers. It was given to Verna (Skinner) Van Matre, daughter of Will and Ella, who handed it down to her daughter-in-law Julie Van Matre, wife of Ernest Van Matre.

Kirtland Sackett became a very close friend of General Mariano Vallejo's youngest brother. General Vallejo owned a home in the town of Sonoma, California. [General Vallejo was a Mexican Army Officer who helped guide his beloved California from a Mexican district to an annexed American state. He founded and is the namesake of the California city of Vallejo, once intended to be the state's capitol.]

It was there while I was on a visit, I met and talked to General Vallejo's youngest daughter. At the time, I mentioned my Grandfather Sackett's friendship with her youngest uncle. She recalled the name Sackett, then described him and Nancy, and recalled that her uncle asked his father if he (Kirtland) could get married in the General's home. She then described the wedding and how she (at a very young age) had watched the ceremony in their parlor.

The Skinner family recognizes that the foregoing information written by Agnes Sackett differs form other accounts. The Vallejo family and the Sackett family were definitely well acquainted, however. Whether the wedding took place in General Vallejo's home is questionable. Apparently, there are also existing records that indicate the marriage took place in the family church in Napa.

The Story of Ella Sackett Skinner

The Sackett and Skinner families were neighbors in Napa and grew to be close friends. Kirtland and Nancy Henery Sackett became the parents of eight children. Their sixth child, a girl, was born on June 21, 1868. She was named Ella and would one day become the bride of William Silas Skinner.

There has been a bit of family speculation at times as to what Will's new bride must have thought of this country her husband was taking

The "Old Skinner Place"—where Will brought Ella as a bride.

her to. Their trip by buggy took them through the Owyhee Desert on their way to the family's ranch in Jordan Valley. Ella, daughter of a prominent family, born and raised in the lap of luxury in the lush Napa Valley, was taken to the arid, as yet undeveloped and unpopulated remote country of eastern Oregon. She must have wondered what she had agreed to. She may have decided it could only get better. Will remarked in later years, that he "must have had a lot of nerve to bring his bride into such primitive surroundings." He was also quick to say that his new bride readily stepped into the role of ranch wife, and efficiently turned the house in which they lived into a home. They set up housekeeping at the old Skinner Ranch on Jordan Creek while Will continued looking after his family's livestock and land holdings. Following the death of G. W. Clinton, Will took over management of the property (which would later become the home of the Skinner Ranch) for the Clinton heirs who were living in California, and continued to look after his family's property and livestock interests as well.

Will continued to see far more potential than just grazing livestock on this raw land. It was flat, it had ample water in Jordan Creek available for irrigation, and he knew it could be quite easily managed once the sagebrush was removed. His dream would not go away. By necessity, however, that dream would have to remain on hold for a while longer.

The Birth of Silas Kirtland Skinner

On November 27, 1892, in the little home on the "Old Skinner Place," another Skinner entered the world. Will and Ella became parents to the firstborn of their nine children. This child, a boy, was named Silas Kirtland in honor of his two grandfathers, and who many years later would become my father, though five others would precede me and one more would follow.

Our dad, who became known as "Kirt," was followed on March 6, 1894, by a brother whom Will and Ella named Thomas Harold. Two days after Harold's birth, a spring thaw in the Owyhee Mountains caused an ice breakup in Jordan Creek, and as the ice began to pile up near their home, the water began to rise around them. Will became concerned for his wife, newborn Harold, and less than two-year-old Kirt as the creek water was suddenly lapping at the home's foundation.

Will tied a boat to the doorknob of the house, bundled his wife and babies into warm clothes, and evacuated them by boat, which he towed on horseback to higher ground. There he put the family on a horse-drawn wagon and transported them about two miles east, up Jordan Creek to the Company Stage Station which was being operated at that time by the Henry Scott family. The elevation there was high enough to avoid the flooding.

Following a stay of about a week, and a drop in the water, the family returned to their own home. The flooded creek had reached the floorboards of their home before receding but the home sustained no damage.

By 1896, Will had moved his family to Caldwell, Idaho, and was working in a livery stable. This move may have come about to insure that better medical care would be available for the expected birth of another child. Will and Ella also may have made their decision in light of the spring flooding two years earlier. On March 1, 1896, a daughter named Ruby Aileen was born to the couple.

It would not be long before Will and Ella moved back to Napa, California. Their oldest children were approaching school age, and according to family history, the couple felt it was important to provide their children with a good start on their education. Will went to work at a job in the Aetna mines near Napa to support his growing family. On September 25, 1897, daughter Verna Claire was born in Napa. Another daughter was born while they lived at the Aetna mines. She was named Nancy Irma, born on October 26, 1898.

The "Old Skinner Place." Kirt and Harold were born here. This picture was taken in the 1960s by Cliff Carlsen.

Will and Ella's first seven children in front of the old Clinton Home. Back (left to right): Ruby, Harold, and Kirt. Front (left to right): Ella, Bill, Irma, and Verna.

At the Rockville Station. Tom Skinner is the driver, and Annie and Annabel Skinner are in the back seat. 1910.

By 1901, Will had moved his family back to Jordan Valley. The Skinners continued to own property, and their livestock in Oregon needed looking after. On August 5, 1901, their sixth child was born and christened William Callow Skinner. Ella Marjorie was born in Jordan Valley on January 12, 1903, as were Anna Beatrice, born March 26, 1907, and Hugh Sackett, born January 12, 1909. It is remarkable that in a day and age when medical knowledge was still primitive, and in an area far removed from any medical facility, Will and Ella Skinner raised all nine of their children to adulthood and beyond. Isolation from the outside world slowed the spread of disease and may have been a factor in the family's health.

No available information definitively explains Will and Ella Skinner's relocations during the first ten years of their marriage. Education for the older children may have been a factor, as we have noted, or the reason may have been economic. Perhaps it was the inability to cope with loneliness, or the hesitance to sever close family ties in California. Perhaps it was a combination of all those things.

SS

*—Harold and Dad (Kirt) in the willow corral
with Uncle Tom (Will's brother—in the middle).*

14

Will's Dream

Afriendship may have been what pulled Will back to Jordan Valley. During the time that Will Skinner worked at the Aetna mines in California, he made the acquaintance of Willis G. Thompson (Tompy). Theirs was a friendship that continued for life. Thompson was not married and was a frugal man. He had worked hard through the years and had saved his money.

It is unknown if Thompson was acquainted with ranching life, but in his friendship with Will, he may have recognized a man with a dream, a man who partially owned a small ranch, and who also had his mind set on developing some prime property in Jordan Valley. More importantly, he had a reasonable plan on how to get it done. We are not sure whether Will talked Thompson into coming to Jordan Valley with him, or if Thompson decided to tie his future to Will's dream. Information on their early association is sparse.

A Dream Come True

Will Skinner's dream began to materialize June 17, 1891. It was just a glimmer on the horizon, but the glimmer was significant. On that day, his mother, Anne Jane, sold Will and Ella one-half interest in the "Old Skinner Place." Earlier that same year a local man named Hicks had been running his horses with the Skinners' horses. Hicks sold all his horses to a horse buyer for nine hundred and fifty dollars. Less than a month later, the buyer sold all those same horses to Anne Jane Skinner for five hundred dollars.

The good business sense Anne Jane had developed in Ohio proved fruitful in this horse deal. On June 20, 1891, she sold her herd of horses—including one two-year-old stallion named "Norton" and one

Will and Ella raised four capable young men. Standing: Bill. Seated, left to right: Harold, Hugh, and Kirt. Circa 1915.

three-year-old Standardbred stallion named "Alcona Clay"—and all her cattle to Will and Ella.

Two years later, Anne Jane sold the other half of the "Old Skinner Place" to Will and Ella. The sale included four hundred and five horses and all of the cattle branded "SS" (double ess) or "Y" (wine cup) for two thousand dollars, at two percent interest. At long last, Will was beginning to see his dream come true. As he continued to manage the Clinton heirs' property, he made his plans to expand. It would not be long before the Clinton property would also come under the owner-ship of Will and Ella Skinner.

Dad hunting ducks near the bridge across Cow Creek on the Skinner Toll Road.

Will had been unable to get the pesky idea out of his head that there was a wonderful opportunity in Jordan Valley, if only he could swing it financially. After some bickering among the Clinton heirs, Will was able to close the deal and buy the property. This property on Jordan Creek was the land Silas Skinner and his partner E. H. Clinton had originally traded for in 1878 with C. D. Bachelor. The acquisition of additional Bachelor property north of Jordan Creek would come later.

Expansion

Will had gained a foothold now and began accumulating more property. Among these land acquisitions were several sections of the sagebrush land that Will had coveted for so many years. Judging from the size of the sagebrush growing there, it was clear to Will that this land had good fertile soil.

His friend Willis Thompson bought a small ranch on the Owyhee River and took up Homestead rights on property adjacent to the land Will had acquired. No known documentation indicates that the two men formed a partnership, but they obviously worked closely together in developing their properties.

Dad (Kirt Skinner) looking over the dam on Jordan Creek.

The Forces That Built This Valley

In prehistory, spring thaws caused creeks and waterways to slice their way across the land making new channels and filling old ones with gravel and silt. With the water, came the beavers. Beavers dammed off these sloughs and smaller waterways, and through countless centuries, gravel and silt washed down Jordan Creek and settled in the beaver ponds. This combination of water, erosion, and beavers built up level floodplains composed of highly fertile soil along the waterways. Underlying the rich topsoil was a heavier gravel layer that provided excellent drainage.

It was this land that Will Skinner had watched and pined for as he herded his father's horses. It was nearly flat, with the natural fall that would make it easily irrigated. This was indeed land that could become highly productive with the addition of water. A channel, or slough, branched off to the north from Jordan Creek and then divided again leaving three main waterways running east to west through the property. During the spring runoff there was ample water in the creek to run water into these sloughs. When the flow dwindled after the main runoff, the water returned to the main channel of Jordan Creek.

The first settler on the property, C. D. Bachelor, had placed a primitive diversion dam in the main channel of the creek in order to force water into these sloughs to irrigate his property along Jordan Creek.

Bachelor then traded his property to Silas Skinner and E. H. Clinton for the Trout Creek Station and Clinton's mining property. Several years later Silas sold his share of the property to Clinton and bought the "Old Skinner Place." Clinton developed some additional property further north and improved the dam; this land later came under ownership of Will and Ella Skinner.

In conjunction with the development of an irrigation system, Will and his colleague Willis Thompson began clearing the newly acquired land of sagebrush to make way for planting crops.

Contracts to clear the land of sagebrush were offered to the Paiute Indian Tribe from McDermitt, Nevada. Each Indian family contracted and was responsible for clearing a set area of the land. The men removed the brush, and their wives cut the wood into firewood lengths. Will recalled they had a pile of grubbed sagebrush firewood that lasted for several years.

The Indian families brought their tents and teepees to live in, and Will and Ella Skinner provided a store of sorts, from which the Indians could purchase staples such as flour, sugar, and meat. Will and Ella Skinner's children played with the Indian children while their parents were busy clearing brush. They became familiar, though not fluent, with each other's languages. For many years, a number of these Indian families would return to the Skinner Ranch to hunt or just to visit, and in later years their offspring would do the same. Among the Indian families the Skinners counted as friends were descendants of Chief Winnemucca, the old leader of the Paiute Tribe, who was prominent in the area's early history.

During the time they were grubbing brush, the Winnemucca family constructed an elaborate camp. They dug a hole in the ground several feet deep, cutting out bench-like seating around the perimeter, with a fire pit in the center. They placed their tent over the excavation, which made for cozy living. During that winter, however, one of their children became ill and died.

The Winnemucca family immediately burned down the entire structure and its contents, believing that this type of housing was the cause of the child's death. It also may have been an ancient tribal tradition used to stop disease from spreading to other Indian families.

Sagebrush, The Be-all, End-all Fuel

Sagebrush was the fuel of choice for cooking and warmth during the early days of the ground-clearing operation. It was in fact, the only

Will and his daughter Ella Skinner stand in front of a sagebrush wood pile. Kirt is in the background by the saw. The old lava rock building is in the back (before the roof was put on it).

fuel available; the nearest trees were in the mountains, many miles distant. After the railroads arrived in Boise Valley, coal from distant mines was freighted into Jordan Valley. However, sagebrush continued to be an important fuel for cooking and for heating until the Idaho Power Company brought electricity into the area in 1947.

While the land was being cleared of sagebrush, work continued on the irrigation system. Early water rights were established by the first landowners along with Sherman Castle and Ike Sharpe, who owned property irrigated from the dam on Jordan Creek. This land would later come under ownership and development by Will Skinner. Water rights established by early settlers who first diverted the water from Jordan Creek would become an important asset to the Skinner Ranch in later years, as more and more demand was made on the available water.

Skinner and Thompson improved the dam by hauling in wagonload after wagonload of good-sized lava rocks that they placed across the main channel to build up the spillway and divert water into the slough. At the same time, they constructed a series of headgates in the sloughs, to control the flow of water and force it into the irrigation ditches. This served quite well, until the ice breakup in the spring. Ice and high water carried the rocks down the channel.

In the following years, after the runoff slowed, it was necessary for the crew to wade into the maelstrom and roll or carry the rocks twenty or thirty yards back up the creek to the spillway. During the spring, the water was still cold and the current strong. Even on a warm sunny spring day, only the young and the strong could withstand the torrent.

Several years ago, the Skinners significantly improved the dam with a reconstruction project using reinforced concrete walls, a concrete floor in the spillway with steel pillars or uprights to hold boards to divert the flow when irrigation water is needed. They are easily removable when irrigation water is no longer needed. In anticipation of spring runoff, the boards' removal allowed for the free flow of water down the main channel.

To complete the project, concrete headgates have been placed at intervals in the sloughs to raise water levels high enough to put it on the land. As a result, the irrigation system on the Skinner Ranch has been developed into a sophisticated, highly efficient, environmentally friendly project.

Land Preparation

Clearing the land of sagebrush continued, and it was prepared for planting. Leveling took place with equipment known as the "fresno." The fresno was a horse-drawn implement used to move dirt from high to low areas. Once leveled, the land was planted and irrigated. After the crop was removed, the leveling process was continued to correct areas where the ground had settled. Where the natural lay of the land was nearly level, ditches were dug following elevations to provide adequate fall.

During this time, Will divided the house Clinton had built on Jordan Creek into two sections and moved it from that location to a more central location that he planned to make the ranch headquarters. At about the same time, another building was moved to the headquarters area. It is well over a century old and is currently still in use. It ranks as the oldest building on the ranch. At one time, it housed the Skinner school and the harness shop and was used for storage and as a granary. Its usage has changed often through the years.

The family now included nine children, and Will and Ella had found it necessary to add several bedrooms onto the home. Will's two oldest sons had grown into hard-working, capable assistants under Will's management. Their brothers, Bill and Hugh, were a bit too young yet to accept much responsibility, but they would soon take their place in the operation.

SS

—A tired "crew" after a long hard day's work.
Photo taken from the top of the windmill.

15

Ranch Life

While living and working in Jordan Valley during those early years of his marriage, Will contracted with the Mexican government to buy horses for the Mexican Army. In this capacity, he traveled by horseback and buggy through eastern and south-central Oregon and into northern California, buying horses from ranchers in the area. His travels took him to Harney, Lake, and Baker counties in Oregon, and Modoc County in northern California. (At this time Baker County encompassed all of eastern Oregon, including what later became Malheur County.)

During these buying trips, Will established friendships with ranching colleagues in southeastern and south-central Oregon and northern California. He was a personal friend of Pete French, a prominent pioneering rancher in south-central Oregon. French had put together the biggest cattle and horse ranching operation in the Northwest, and the largest ranch acreage ever to exist in the state of Oregon. Ultimately, a jealous neighbor got into an argument over access to land and shot and killed Pete French. The neighbor was tried for the murder, but was not convicted.

Another acquaintance Will often spoke of was John Devine. Devine was owner of the Alvord Ranch east of Steens Mountain near the Alvord Desert, and he also owned the Whitehorse Ranch, southeast of Steens Mountain in Harney County. Devine was a horse lover. In addition to his ranching operations, he owned a number of fine racehorses that he raced on many California racetracks.

Will often talked with family members about his travels buying horses, but no one can recall that he ever discussed how or where these horses were to be delivered to the Mexican government. We suspect he may have had them driven to Winnemucca, Nevada, where they

were put on a train to southern California. We also believe the horses
he bought for the Mexican government were required to be broken to
lead but never ridden. They were trained by Mexican vaqueros to the
Mexican Army's standards.

Will also sold and delivered one of his Standardbred stallions to
John Devine. The stallion was an offspring of the Standardbred trot-
ting horses Silas had brought to Jordan Valley from Kentucky. We
have reason to believe the horse he sold to Devine was one that Will
Skinner often spoke of named "King Orry," named after an ancient
Manx king.

Home Life

The older girls in Will and Ella's family were committed to assisting
their mother with household chores. With a growing family, one of
those chores Will talked about was laundry. The motor-driven washing
machine had not been invented yet. On washday, water was pumped
from the nearby well and carried by bucket to the house to be heated
on the kitchen stove. After being scrubbed on a washboard in hot water, and then rinsed, the girls hung clothes on the line outside to dry.
With the size of their family, there were always large piles of laundry
to be done each week. A clean house, clean clothes, and clean sheets
for the beds were considered a must. Company could be counted on
and most often arrived unannounced.

The area was remote, and it was many miles between neighbors. A
state education system had not yet been established. Most families who
settled in the area hired a teacher for their children and held school in
their homes, or sent their children to a neighbor's home for schooling.
Such was the case with Will and Ella Skinner. The matter of schooling for the family's younger children was placed high on the family
agenda.

In 1908, Will leased the Ruby Ranch from the William Beers family
and moved his family there. The house was larger and better equipped to
meet the family's needs, and, importantly, the house had a schoolroom.
The better accommodations allowed Ella to get back to entertaining
guests and family, which she thoroughly enjoyed doing. A piano was ordered and freighted into Jordan Valley by wagon from Boise, Idaho, and
became the centerpiece of entertainment. The piano, with its well-worn
ivory keys, has a place of honor in our living room today.

ty

Ella was an accomplished musician who had grown up with parties, dancing, and community social events in Napa, California. She saw to it that there would be ample time to host social events in the Skinners' home. There were five attractive young ladies and four young men in the home, adding to its intrigue. Ella made positive her children were well-versed in social graces, regardless of the remote area in which they lived. Social events were attended by neighbors from many miles distant. These occasions were presided over by Will and Ella. She played the piano and sang, aided by other musicians among the guests.

With little daily interaction in the community, these events served to keep the family current with their neighbors. Such events were essentially the radio and newspapers of the day, as well as a way to introduce new people to the community. Ella also took charge of the menu prepared by the Chinese cook, to be served to the guests and family.

In later years, these events were held in other homes as new neighbors arrived in the community. Each family brought potluck for the midnight feast. Every conceivable dish appeared, including sandwiches of all description, salads, desserts, cakes of all kinds, and gallons of coffee. After the meal and cleanup were finished, the music continued, often going on until sunup.

One memorable event took place when a party (actually it was a "chivaree" to celebrate the wedding of a local couple) was scheduled to be held at a neighbor's home in late winter or early spring around 1935. It was cold and the roads were so muddy that cars could not negotiate them. Not to be denied a good time, our family went to the event on a hay wagon pulled by a team of horses. The distance was not great, maybe less than two miles, but after an evening of dancing, the return home was very late. Today, with warm cars and good roads, would we venture to such an affair with elderly people and very small children on a horse-drawn wagon? Maybe.

Eventually, several leaders in the community— Dad, neighbors Hol Parks from the Ruby Ranch, and Dale Sinclair—formed a committee and along with others bought a building that had once housed the offices of a local irrigation district. They remodeled the building into a community gathering center with space for dancing and a room for kids to sleep while their parents continued dancing. Over the years, this building became a community gathering place used as a Grange

Mona Skinner, Will's youngest sister, and Dr. Jones in front of the drug store.

Hall, a church when the circuit rider came around, a place for school programs, and as the dance hall.

Children's Education

The couple were determined their children would be well schooled, and prior to their move to the Ruby Ranch they provided a school very near their home for their younger children, and neighboring children in the community. The schoolroom was very small, located in a room in the back of a harness and leather repair shop. The students varied in numbers but consisted mainly of the youngest four or five Skinner children. One of the first teachers of the Skinner children was Will's youngest sister Mona, a graduate of the University of California in Berkeley.

SS

16

Johanna and War Years

In 1913, Will and Ella advertised for a teacher to come to Jordan Valley to teach their younger children in the private school that was held in their home. The young lady who submitted her application for the teaching job was named Johanna Murray. Ella was impressed with the applicant's qualifications, and she was hired. It is not a unique story, or maybe it is, because this young woman happened to be of foreign birth, well-educated by the standards of the day, and adventuresome. She was a remarkable young lady who deserves to have her story told. She would also become the mother of seven children, of which I, John Skinner, am the sixth.

This is her story.

Homeland

In the far north of Scotland in the Shire (county) of Sutherland, hard by the banks of the River Shin, lies the little village of Lairg. It was here, on the family farm home known locally as Drumnahaving (home by the water), that a daughter was born to John and Christina (MacKenzie) Murray, on November 14, 1889. The young lady was given the name "Johanna." She joined a sister, Ella, and a brother, Robert. She soon became known to her Scottish family, friends, and acquaintances as "Hanna."

Her father was a farmer by profession, and a religious man. Early in life, Hanna learned from her parents the wonder and beauty of God's creations. Her father's eyesight was failing, and he often asked Hanna to read aloud from what he called "The Book" (the Bible) for him during family times.

Hanna was bright, a thinker, and above all she was very inquisitive. In time she would develop her own set of beliefs and values which carried her through life, and which were to become the principles of

How Drumnahaving looked when Johanna Murray lived there from her birth in 1889 until she sailed to America in 1909. It had been occupied by the Murray Clan from 1520, when it was built, until Jessie Murray (Johanna's sister) died in 1970. It is located in Lairg, Scotland. Circa 1970.

her existence. She did not preach, nor did she wear her religion on her sleeve, but her early knowledge of God's work continued to be her guiding light until the day of her death.

The Murray family eventually grew in numbers to seven siblings—five girls and two boys. A sister and brother, Ella and Robert, preceded Hanna's birth. A brother, Alexander, followed Hanna into the family; then a sister, Christina, died very early in life; another sister, Diana, was born but then died at about ten years old. Finally came sister Jessie, who lived in the family home of Drumnahaving until she died in 1970. The Murray family ancestors had occupied Drumnahaving for well over five hundred years and the Clans Murray and her mother's family, MacKenzie, were both prominent and well-known in Sutherlandshire, and in the north of Scotland.

Ancestors

Hanna's father's ancestors were cattlemen who grazed their cattle on the moors and drove them to the markets, riding their horses bareback. Hanna's

Johanna's parents, John Murray and Christina McKenzie Murray, with Johanna's two sisters, Christina (left) and Ella. Mom is wearing her wedding frock.

mother, Christine, was born into the MacKenzie family, many of whom were adventurous sailors and explorers. Her grandfather, John MacKenzie, was a master carpenter who built one of the prominent churches in Lairg.

Hanna counted among her ancestors such luminaries as MacKenzie King, one time Prime Minister of Canada. Another of Hanna's ancestors was Alexander MacKenzie, the brother of her great-grandfather. Alexander migrated to Canada, and as a teenager went to work in the fur trading business. He later became famous as an avid explorer in the Canadian North, and in 1789, preceding the Lewis and Clark Expedition by over a decade, became the first white man to conduct an expedition across the North American continent, north of Mexico, while in search of the Northwest Passage. He reached the Pacific

Johanna Murray Skinner, in later years, visits Fort Clatsop and reads about her great-great grandfather's brother, Alexander McKenzie. His picture is on the wall. 1971.

Ocean in 1793 but did not find the hoped-for waterway that would link the Atlantic and Pacific Oceans.

The scenic MacKenzie River in western Canada is named in his honor. MacKenzie's expedition across the Canadian North America was the impetus for President Thomas Jefferson's appointment of the Lewis and Clark Expedition to explore Western America ten years later.

Another ancestor of Johanna Murray, Donald MacKenzie, was a cousin of Alexander and a partner in The Northwest Fur Company of Canada. He led a large fur trapping expedition into the Oregon Territory in the early 1800s. Among the members of this group were a number of French Canadians, Iroquois Indians from the New York area, and several Hawaiians, or "Owyhees," which was the Hawaiian to English translation at that time.

The main group of MacKenzie's trappers decided to remain in the Boise Valley over the winter, but the Owyhees elected to explore the country in southeastern Oregon and southwest Idaho for possible fur trapping. When the group reassembled the next spring, the Owyhees were not among them. It was assumed that the Indians had killed them. Since that time, southwestern Idaho and southeastern Oregon have been known as "Owyhee Country," with the main waterway in the

Before Johanna came to America, she wrote of her class from Tain Royal Academy, with teacher Miss McGill, going on a picnic in Scotland. They had climbed to the top of a mountain and found a rainstorm. They hurried down and were welcomed into a farmhouse to dry off and have lunch. Johanna remarked that it was a "highland welcome." Johanna is second from the right. 1908.

area being the Owyhee River, which drains northern Nevada, southern Idaho, and eastern Oregon.

Donald MacKenzie also had a hand in the construction of Fort Boise in 1819, and was instrumental in opening up the rich Snake River country to the fur trade. MacKenzie's group continued their explorations throughout the Oregon Territory, and into the Willamette Valley. The popular and beautiful McKenzie River in western Oregon is named in his honor.

Several of Hanna's uncles, her father's brothers, had previously migrated to Central Oregon and settled in the area of John Day and Prairie City, where they established several ranches and ran cattle and several large bands of sheep. One of these uncles, Alexander, returned to Scotland for a visit with his family in 1909.

Johanna comes to America

Hanna, who had inherited the adventurous spirit of her MacKenzie ancestors, joined her uncle Alex for the return trip to America. She fully intended to return to her family and her native Scotland after several years, but that was not to be. In 1914, the ominous clouds of World War I rolled across Europe, and it soon became too dangerous for her to attempt to return to her home.

Hanna was twenty years of age when she arrived in America. She had attended primary schooling in Lairg, with her more advanced education at the Tain Royal Academy in the north of Scotland, where she received training roughly equivalent to that of an American senior high school.

Following her arrival in America, she and her uncle journeyed across the country by train to Ontario, Oregon. Several days later they went by buggy to Baker City, Oregon, where they boarded what we believe was the inaugural trip of the Sumpter Valley Railroad to Austin, Oregon. She taught in several small schools in Central Oregon, and in 1913 was hired by Will and Ella Skinner to teach their younger children.

Hanna began her trip from Vale, Oregon, to Jordan Valley on the uncomfortable seat of a primitive freight wagon driven by Preston Wroten. When she at long last arrived in Jordan Valley, she took a room in the Jordan Valley Hotel. Her introduction to the little town was punctuated that night by a shooting outside her hotel room. The town marshal thought the poor fellow was reaching for a gun, but he was only attempting to retrieve a bottle of whiskey from his pocket. That episode was one of many in her introduction to the frontier West.

Hanna was gathered up the next day by the refined and genteel Ella Skinner who arrived at the hotel by horse and buggy, with several of her younger children in tow. Following the shooting of the night before, Hanna surely must have been relieved to see that more refined citizens also inhabited the little frontier town. They placed her trunk in the buggy and started for Ruby Ranch, the Skinner Ranch headquarters, some eighteen miles to the west. At this time, she probably hadn't the faintest hint that this valley, tucked away in a remote part of the state of Oregon, would eventually be her home for the rest of her life.

Mom Meets Dad

As they neared their destination, they passed through one of the hayfields, where Hanna noticed a man apparently sleeping in a shock of hay. It crossed her mind that this fellow should wake up and get to work or else he would be soundly chastised or possibly fired by his boss. Little did

Hanna know, this napping young fellow would in time become one of the most important persons in her life. She was to find out later that he was Silas Kirtland, eldest son of Will and Ella Skinner. He had taken ill that day, and in seeking some relief, had lain down in the shock of hay to rest a bit, thereby missing the buggy that passed by carrying his future wife.

The arrival of a new teacher in the community never failed to create a stir among the young men, and such was the case upon the arrival of Miss Murray. Her arrival did not stir Dad's curiosity to any great degree that day, but with the passage of time he took more serious notice of Miss Murray, who became known to the Skinner family by a shorter version of her given name—"Jo." The name "Hanna" fell into disuse among the Skinner family, though not among her Murray relatives.

Schoolmarm

Miss Murray taught school that year, then returned to Drewsey, Oregon, where she lived with cousin Christina Altnow and her husband Harry, also ranchers in that area.

Will and Ella Skinner were impressed with Johanna Murray's teaching ability and the way her young students were responding to her methods. They decided to rehire her for the following year. Will wrote her a letter offering her the job, and handed it to a neighbor, G. B. Glover, who was on the Malheur Board of Commissioners, and was on his way to Vale, the county seat. Will asked him to put the letter to Miss Murray in the mail for him.

It would be several months later that Mr. Glover would find the forgotten letter in his coat pocket, but at long last he mailed it to Miss Murray. She, believing the Skinners had made other plans for a teacher, had already accepted a teaching position at Riverside, Oregon. She informed the Skinners, however, that she would like the teaching position the following year. In the fall of 1915, she returned to the Skinner Ranch and taught there for the autumn and winter of 1915 and 1916.

World War I

In the meantime, in 1914, World War I had begun in Europe. Germany was flexing its muscles and declared war on France. Soon thereafter the British Isles became involved, and in 1916, the United States. Eventually the conflict infected almost the entire

Johanna Murray riding to school for a day of teaching in Riverside.

world. Young men from all walks of life were being called up for duty in the army.

Dad and his brother Harold were called up for their physical exams for army duty. A hired man once remarked that Dad was so skinny "he had to stand up twice against the sun to make a shadow." He was so underweight for his height that he failed to pass his physical exam for service in the army.

His brother Harold, however, was drafted into the army and was trained and prepared for overseas duty. He was about to board a troop carrier headed for Europe when the armistice was signed, and his orders were changed. To the relief of his family, Harold was soon discharged.

The Murray family in Scotland did not fare so well. Our mother's youngest brother, Alex, served in the British Army was sent to France. He was trained in the British signal corps and was on the front lines where he was exposed to poisonous mustard gas spread by the German Army. Mustard gas, heavier than air, settled into

The building behind the auto was covered when the Warm Spring Reservoir went in. In auto from left to right: Mrs. Hoglun, Johanna Murray, and George Jordan, foreman of the ranch. Circa early 1900s.

the protective trenches and low-lying areas. The deadly gas seared his and many other soldiers' lungs and caused his death within just a few very painful weeks. He was not alone. Many of his comrades from both sides of the ocean would suffer death from poison gas, and for those who survived the gas, there were many years of suffering ahead.

Many Allied soldiers were to lose their lives in Germany and France before the German Army was vanquished and the Armistice signed in 1917. Our mother's brother, Robert, also served in the British Army in France and luckily survived the war without injury. He later became a farmer in the north of Scotland and died in 1934.

As with the end of all wars, there was great happiness in the nation and across the world when "Johnny came marching home." Unfortunately, the "War to End All Wars" didn't.

SS

—*Wedding picture of Silas Kirtland Skinner (Dad)*
and Johanna Murray (Mom). October 16, 1917.

17

Education and Romance

In September of 1914, with Johanna Murray unavailable to teach the Skinner children, Will and Ella had to replace her. The county school superintendent recommended a young lady who lived in Lynn, Indiana. Her name was Edith Jones, and she had been recommended by friends from Indiana who were presently teaching in Oregon. The superintendent sent Miss Jones a telegram offering her the teaching position for the Skinners and she accepted. She boarded the train in Chicago and arrived in Caldwell, Idaho, three days later at four in the morning.

At six o'clock that same morning, she boarded the stage and was on her way to Jordan Valley, seventy-five miles away. The "stage" was actually a heavily loaded freight wagon drawn by four horses, with only one seat for herself and the driver.

Riding on a road that was little more than a trail up and down the hills between Homedale, Idaho, and Jordan Valley, hanging on for dear life to the high spring seat of a freight wagon, proved to be a long, rough, uncomfortable trip. She didn't know exactly where she was, and she was more than a little concerned to be alone with the driver, who was a scruffy looking fellow. After one stop to have lunch and change teams, they finally arrived in Jordan Valley at eleven o'clock that night. She stayed in a hotel that was on the second floor of a saloon that served as the stage station.

The next day Miss Jones, with her bag in hand, walked several miles out of town to visit a friend who was also teaching in Jordan Valley. A day later, Ella Skinner and her son Bill picked her up, and after having dinner in the fine new Jordan Valley Hotel, they started for the Ruby Ranch. On the way, they stopped at the Skinner Ranch where Ella Skinner introduced Miss Jones to her son, a wild looking, long-haired and whiskery young fellow who was busy feeding a bunch of hogs. Miss Jones found nothing attractive and was rather put off by this twenty- plus-year-old man whose name was Harold.

When they arrived at the Ruby Ranch, however, Miss Jones was impressed with Will and Ella's five daughters. As in all small communities, when a new schoolteacher arrived, the young men also gathered around in the evenings to meet her. With Ella at the piano, the family sang popular songs of the day. Someone asked Miss Jones if she played the piano, and although she was an accomplished pianist, she declined, not yet comfortable with the people in the community. She was impressed with the Skinner young folks, though, and it was not long before the Skinner men had taught her to dance.

Miss Jones taught the younger Skinner children and several neighboring children that year in the upstairs schoolroom of the Ruby Ranch house. The following summer she returned to Indiana to visit her family following a trip to the San Francisco World's Fair. She returned to Oregon and attended a teacher's school in Salem. That fall she took a teaching job in Drewsey, Oregon, a position she did not enjoy. It was a cold winter with heavy snow, and she was required to ride a horse three miles to school and back each day.

That Christmas, Ruby, the Skinners' oldest daughter, invited Miss Jones to return to Jordan Valley to spend the holidays with the Skinner family. She accepted the invitation and Harold, second son of Will and Ella, and the young fellow who had previously sported the long hair and whiskers, offered to meet the stage in Jordan Valley to fetch Miss Jones back to the Ruby Ranch.

The story is not clear about just what sort of conveyance Harold used to make the trip. It may have been a horse and buggy or a horse-drawn sleigh, or possibly an automobile. It was night, and a very romantic one at that, by all accounts. Lots of snow on the ground, the stars twinkling brightly in the sky. Many years after she and Harold had married, she would tell her family quite wistfully, "All was a dream that night."

When asked by a granddaughter if that was the night romance had bloomed, she answered in her charming midwestern drawl, "I think probably. I had a little bit of an idea. I think he did, too."

The wedding of Edith and Harold in June 1919 was the first of many weddings to occur in the living room of the new Skinner home. Following their wedding, the couple were at home in Will and Ella's big house. The *Jordan Valley Express*, the local newspaper, noted in a quite lengthy column that "the wedding party descended the stairway of the luxurious Skinner home into the living room, and the groom's mother played and sang the song 'I Love You Truly'."

Later Harold and Edith managed the ranch on the Owyhee River for several years and then returned to the Ruby Ranch. Their first two children, Eleanor and Ernest, were born in Will and Ella's home. Later they moved into Jordan Valley where Esther was born. In the mid-1930s they moved to Caldwell, Idaho, where they lived the rest of their lives.

Romance in the Sagebrush

During the second year in which Johanna Murray taught the Skinner children, and maybe even a bit earlier, Kirt started to take special notice of the young Scottish schoolteacher, and she of him. Those long eastern Oregon evenings in the fall and spring provided a wonderful time to take a walk or a buggy ride. Not too different from today, really, except that cars were not yet common.

What was common were the hijinks were often played on young lovers. Dad and his younger brother Harold were very close to mirror images of each other, and it was common for even close friends to be confused about which one of the two they were talking to.

One evening Kirt and Jo made secret plans to take a long walk in the moonlight. He would be waiting for her in the dining room at dusk. The time for the tryst arrived; in the dusk she saw her beau waiting for her, a shawl wrapped high around his neck against the cold, and off they went for that long walk. She did not realize her companion was Harold, the brother of her beau, until their return. The real beau had been hidden away by his other siblings, tied up out of sight while the walk took place. She always said she knew it wasn't Dad who walked with her that evening, but we still wonder.

From the many stories told when the family gathered over the years, it is evident the young folks worked long hard hours but also had a lot of fun with family members and the other young people in the community. There were lively times at the Skinner home with ice-skating parties in the winter, picnics on summer Sundays, and dancing. Many people in the small community enjoyed the Skinners' hospitality, and these activities were a magnet for the young folks.

It must also be said that these were some very lonesome times for our mother. She was homesick for her family and her native land. To add to her sadness her younger brother, Alexander, had died from mustard gas poisoning in the war going on in Europe.

Her parents were aging and heartbroken by the death of their son and by Hanna's absence from the home hearth, but it was far too dangerous for her to travel on the seas. German U-boats prowled the oceans, and no Allied ship was safe from attack. Johanna Murray was a most stalwart young lady, but there were many tears shed on her pillow on those long nights away from her family, and it would be far too many years before she could make the voyage back to her home in the north of Scotland.

Still, there was a bright side. She had found a man and a family who loved and cherished her, but she must have had misgivings along the way. When she had journeyed from Scotland to America, it had been her intention to return to Scotland. She realized she was now committing herself to a life in America with little chance of returning to her native Scotland in the near future.

Above all, Johanna was pragmatic. She realized she would have to make the best of the situation that faced her. This war would not go on forever. Peace would eventually prevail. She would recall to us how she so often thought, *Then I will make that trip to visit my homeland and my family.*

But that was not to be. During the school year, the romance between Kirt and Jo began to warm up, and it was not long before plans were being made for their wedding. With his mother Ella and his sisters Ruby and Verna as witnesses, the couple was married in The Westminster Presbyterian Church in Portland, Oregon, on October 16, 1917. After a short honeymoon in Seaside, they returned to the ranch and moved into Will and Ella's new home.

SS

18

Will and Ella Build Their Dream Home

In 1916, a year before our parents' (Kirt and Johanna's) wedding, Will and Ella finally realized their dream of building a house on their ranch and began construction. Only the finest lumber—seasoned to avoid warping—was freighted to the Skinners by eight-horse teams pulling wagons from Caldwell, Idaho, to Jordan Valley. The couple hired an expert carpenter to build their home; every board that went into the framing of the home was sawed to exact dimensions before he ever hammered a nail, and the finish work was expertly accomplished.

The home would be built to accommodate not only their family, but also the many guests who came to visit. This would be a *big* home, one with all the modern conveniences available at the time. There would be a pressure water system, primitive by today's standards, but in that era, state of the art. A gas engine powered a belt-operated pumpjack that pumped water from the well into the pressure tank. The engine had to be started several times a day, and on occasion it would be necessary to pump air into the storage tank with a hand operated tire pump to maintain adequate air pressure in the tank to force water into the pipes running into the house.

Water was piped through the kitchen cooking range to be heated, and stored in an uninsulated hot water tank for use in the kitchen and bathroom. Facilities in the bathroom on the ground floor consisted of a basin and a bathtub. Because of the number of family, hired men, and guests to be fed, there was a fire in the kitchen range from early morning until late evening. Constant water usage made water pressure and hot water temperature difficult to maintain. The uninsulated hot water tank stood in an alcove next to the cooking range. A four-legged stool next to the hot water tank was a favorite place to warm a back on cold winter days.

Will and Ella's dream home. Circa 1917.

Because of the area's remoteness, electricity was not yet available. A carbide gas plant was installed that generated and piped gas into every room in the house for lighting. It was necessary to recharge the gas plant with carbide almost monthly.

There was a large kitchen on the ground floor, and an icebox on the entry porch for keeping food cold. An insulated cabinet above the icebox was made to hold blocks of ice harvested from Jordan Creek in winter. The ice was stored in a bin in the granary, and covered with insulating layers of straw to keep it from melting. The ice usually lasted until mid to late summer.

Next to the kitchen was a dining room that would accommodate, if necessary, thirty to thirty-five people or more at two long tables. The living room was at least twice the size of the dining room, and by opening its wide double doors, the living room could be pressed into use for additional dining or dancing space. A screened porch on the north side of the house was used for family gatherings, dancing, or entertaining guests on pleasant spring or summer evenings.

Finally, two large connected bedrooms and the bathroom were on the ground floor. A hallway ran nearly the full length of the house from the front door on the north that provided access to the two bedrooms,

Old ranch house. Left to right: Verna, Grandma Ella, Ruby, baby Ella, Irma, Grandpa Will, Dad (Kirt) on first horse, Harold and Bill on second horse. 1905.

the living room, and dining room and to the stairway to the second and third floors.

Four bedrooms and a ballroom occupied the second floor, along with two screened sleeping porches, one on the north that would accommodate up to four or five double beds, and a smaller one on the east that was adequate for two double beds. Every bedroom in the home would easily accommodate two double beds, and more if required. The schoolroom, and a storage attic were located on the third floor. It was indeed, a big home.

Some Inconveniences

Soon after the home was built, Will and Ella decided the ballroom should be converted into two more bedrooms. There was fear exuberant dancing might crack the ceiling plaster and cause it to drop into the rooms below.

By today's standards, there were some inconveniences. For heating, there was only one big potbellied wood and coal stove in the living room, and the cooking range in the kitchen. Both were totally inade-

North porch of the main house. Left to right: Verna, Irma, Edith Jones, Ruby, Ella, and Beata.

quate to heat such a large home. The distance between the living room seating and the stove was a barometer of the outside temperature. In deep winter, the old potbellied stove was often red hot all day. Anyone who opened doors into the hall in an attempt to warm the upstairs area a bit before bedtime was met with strong derision from Will.

There were accommodations for three stoves in the upstairs area, but for fear of fire, these were rarely used. Sagebrush was good firewood, but the bark was a bit messy. Carrying it through the house and up the stairs left an unsightly trail and an irritated person who had to clean it up. In later years, an oil stove was added in one of the downstairs bedrooms, but it had little warming effect on the upper stories.

There was another inconvenience, and that was the lengthy path leading to the outhouse with its outdated Sears Roebuck and Montgomery Ward catalogs, both common necessities in that era. Nights could be very, very dark, and in the winter very, very cold, but everybody seemed to make the best of the situation. There were no alternatives at that time, and because we really didn't know differently, we all thought we had it pretty good. Nevertheless, when the temperature on a winter night would settle to thirty or more degrees below zero, one could find good

In the living room of the Skinner Home—looking south into the dining room. Will, Ray, and Ella are seated. 1917.

reason to wish for warmer alternatives to that long path to the outhouse in the dark.

Outbuildings

In due time several outbuildings were added for convenience. The first, we believe, was a building constructed entirely of lava rock, except for the roof. This building continues to stand today, in testimony to the ability of Sarafin Aburasturi and Antonio Lavin, the Basque masons who built it more than a century ago, and is an icon of another era on the Skinner Ranch. It is divided into three rooms that have been used for various purposes through the years. One room was historically the meat house where meat was kept. The middle room was where the milk separator stood, and where the milk was processed. The third room had various purposes. It was where the well was located and was used as the laundry room. A gas motor operated the Maytag washing machine, and water for the wash was heated in a 200-plus gallon vat that stood nearby. This sometime storage room also housed the gas motor that pumped water from the well and supplied it to the house.

That huge vat that heated water was also used to render fat into lard for cooking purposes. After fat was cut into small pieces, a fire under the vat melted the fat into lard that was stored in five-gallon tins to be used later in the kitchen. One of the byproducts of that process was a tasty morsel we called "cracklin's," a product which can be found in stores today, and has become more commonly known as "pork rinds."

The Yard

Ella's flower garden was another structure on the property. It was enclosed in wire netting to keep the birds away and provided a wide array of colorful flowers. There was also a chicken house and an exercise area for the chickens. Rarely was it necessary to buy eggs. Each year hens were "set," a process required to produce baby chicks. They grew to replace laying hens, and the roosters provided the much-anticipated fried chicken dinner on July 4th and on an occasional Sunday.

Moving In

In 1917, with their new home finished at last, Will and Ella moved their family from the Ruby Ranch back to their home ranch. The old E. H. Clinton house they had previously lived in had long ago been out grown and converted into the bunkhouse for hired men.

In this sparsely populated area of Oregon, people who lived many miles distant were considered neighbors. There were no telephones but communication between neighbors was highly important. It was an era when people in remote areas interacted by visiting each other, and in doing so often made their own entertainment or there would have been none.

Winter evenings were occupied with reading or playing cards. The Skinner family had a passion for playing a card game called "Five Hundred," an uncomplicated but thought-provoking game that family members play to this day. Cribbage was another popular game often played in the evening. One or the other of these games was played almost nightly for entertainment among the family.

Some additional excitement took place one summer evening during the 1940s. The family was gathered around the piano singing, accompanied by the piano player and several harmonica players. Some of the hired men heard the music and came from the bunkhouse to add their voices to the songsters', and some came just to listen and enjoy themselves.

The west view of the big house in later years with trees grown around it.

One other guest was quite uninvited. A rather large bull snake had worked its way up the outside steps, across the front porch, through an open door, and when noticed was having some trouble moving on the linoleum floor. Somehow, it had made it into the center of activities before anyone noticed it. Amid loud exclamations and a few screams, George McCauley, one of the hired men, calmly picked up the snake and turned him loose outside. The snake, of course, was not a rattler, and of the much less dangerous variety. What attracted the snake into the festivities, we will never know. We do know it didn't know the words to the songs nor how to keep time with the music.

SS

—*All of Will and Ella's children. Back (left to right): Kirt, Harold, Hugh, and Bill. Front (left to right): Ruby, Ella, Verna, Irma, and Beata.*

19

SS

Family and Home

With the end of the war in 1918, there was another reason for celebration: Will and Ella's first grandchild was born. Our parents' first son, William Murray Skinner, was born on October 25, 1918, just days before the armistice was signed. There was great joy in the hope that there would never again be armed conflict among nations, in which young people would have to serve.

Following Armistice Day and a thankful end to the war, America embarked on a period of significant growth and expansion of industry, historically known as the Roaring Twenties. An upbeat mood pervaded the country.

Ella began to convert her new house into a home. One of her first endeavors was to plant a flower garden. A border about six to eight feet wide encircled the house from the east entry to the front door on the north, and from the front door around the house to the west entry. Many trees and ornamental bushes were planted around the yard, for shade and beauty. Many of those are still living today. A nearby garden provided vegetables and many kinds of berries and fruit.

Another wedding was to take place in the Skinner Family in 1919. Ruby Aileen Skinner, the third child born to Will and Ella, and their first daughter, married Evan Gheen, a native of Pennsylvania. In his family's tradition, Evan had trained to be a lawyer. Following the completion of law school, about 1910, wanderlust brought him and his brother Ed to Weiser, Idaho, where they worked in a lumber mill for a time. Ultimately Evan decided he wanted to farm rather than practice law. Having heard about a new irrigation project near the Owyhee River, he moved there and began farming. He and Ruby met after he was injured in a farm accident. Ella Skinner, accompanied by her daughter Ruby, drove to his farm to check on him. Evan become

Will and Ella's first grandchild, Bill, held by our mother Johanna. The others, left to right, are Dad (Kirt), Ella, Will, and great-grandmother Annie. 1918.

enamored of the attractive Ruby Skinner, and they were married in Berkeley, California, at the home of her grandmother, Anne Jane, on December 19, 1919.

New Home, Old Traditions

Certain strong traditions continued to be observed after the Skinner family settled in their new home, some of which are still observed today. One such tradition centered on patriotism, but began with a circus. During World War I, a circus had come to Jordan Valley, where it went bankrupt and sold its equipment to the local citizens. Will Skinner had not yet had time to build a granary, so he bought the circus tent as a place to store harvested grain. After a granary was built, the center pole of the circus tent was placed at the front gate and became the flagpole. Ella saw to it that the American flag flew from the top of the pole on every national holiday from the time their son Harold entered the armed service during World War I. Early on, she taught each of her children and grandchildren to sing "Columbia, The Gem of the Ocean." After the flag raising, everyone gathered and sang that song, honoring America.

The flag pole, made from a circus tent mast, still stands on the Skinner Ranch compound. Two of the four houses on the ranch are shown here—the big house to the left and Bob and Sara's house to the right. Bob and Sara's house was the old homestead that was moved here in 1953.

In later years following Ella's declining health, the custom continued on every national holiday. Everybody—including the hired crew—gathered on the front lawn on the Fourth of July to recite the Pledge of Allegiance when the flag was raised.

The American flag continues to fly from that same flagpole every Fourth of July and on other special days. It has been moved from the front gate of the old house to a pasture in the center of the headquarters complex, so to be visible to every home. The pole is getting shorter due to rot, and every few years it must be reset. It is now propped up by three fence posts.

On those special summer holidays, all hands gathered to crank the ice-cream maker after retrieving a block of ice harvested from Jordan Creek during the winter and stored under sawdust or straw in the granary. If none was on hand, a block of ice was brought down from Dr. Jones's ice plant. Making ice cream was a major operation from the time our mother stirred up the mixture to the time it was finally dished up to be eaten. The ice-cream maker was a metal can set in a wooden barrel filled with crushed ice and rock salt. A churn with paddles turned the mixture and the "work" began. Two, sometimes three hours of churning was required to freeze the cream. Every adult male took a turn on the churn. The longer it took, the harder it got to turn. (Also, the better it tasted.)

The ladies doing the cooking went above their normal good work on those special days, and put a spread on the table that included potatoes and thick milk gravy, fried chicken or steak, boiled potatoes, a vegetable or two, potato salad, jello, and fruit salads—topped off with ice cream or watermelon, and homemade pies and cakes for dessert.

The family also traditionally observed Thanksgiving and Christmas. On those days, the crew did only those tasks that were required, such as caring for the livestock or milking the cows. On Thanksgiving and Christmas, the table groaned with turkey and all the trimmings.

There were no grocery stores nearby to run and pick up needed items. In early days, going to the grocery store was an all-day trip into Jordan Valley by horse and buggy, and in later years by vintage automobiles, over roads sometimes nearly impassable because of mud. Some items such as flour, and sugar, were purchased once or twice annually and brought from Boise Valley in wagons pulled by four-horse teams.

The Family's First Automobile

The early 1920s Overland Blue Bird automobile, the dilapidated body of which is still lying out in the sagebrush, was well received, especially by the younger members of the family. It attracted several young men from town who may also have been attracted to Will and Ella's daughters. Everyone knew how to harness and drive a buggy horse, but hardly anyone knew how to drive a car.

One pleasant Sunday afternoon, several fellows from Jordan Valley arrived to visit, naturally expecting to get a ride in the Overland. Off they went with one of Will and Ella's daughters at the wheel, and her sisters and the young men as passengers. By this time, fences had been built and gates constructed where fences crossed the roads. As the story goes, the driver, possibly Verna Skinner, pulled up to the gate, stopped for but an instant, then proceeded to drive the car through and tore up the gate, to which one of the young men remarked, "If you had only waited for just a minute, I would have been happy to open the gate."

Behind the old rock house, a load of Skinner girls, with one or two added, and an unidentified man.

There is a moral to that story: cars did not then, nor do they now, respond to the word, whoa!

Financially, the country appeared to be in pretty good shape in the postwar 1920s. Henry Ford had earlier developed the prototype of the production line, and built huge numbers of Model T Fords. The Model T was followed by the even more famous Model A. It was not long before the automobile became an absolute necessity.

A necessary requirement on-board all cars in that era was a tire repair kit to repair the flat tires that occurred every few miles, and an air pump to pump up the repaired tire. If a car left home without those items, a long walk home was guaranteed. Another necessity—the service station. The automobile had sparked a new industry in the form of oil and gasoline refineries, and the ever-present service station could be found on every other corner of towns across the country.

Every family soon sported one of these smelly, sometimes dangerous, automotive creations. In those days, a crank was required to start a car. If the "spark" wasn't set just right or if the engine backfired, causing the motor to suddenly jerk the crank out of the starter's hand, the starter's hand could be severely bruised or fractured.

Bill and Bob Skinner. Circa 1922.

Horses continued to hold their own against the gas motor in agricultural communities and wherever livestock was produced, providing the power required for many chores in towns and cities. Tractors, though costly, were being produced by this time but they were not yet as useful, versatile, or inexpensive to operate as a horse.

A few years prior to his death in 1960, Will Skinner remarked—and he firmly believed—that one day horses would make a comeback against gas-powered equipment. We smiled at his remark then, but he may have been right. With world supplies of oil dwindling, and with inefficient solar, wind, and ocean tide electric power production, we may once again look to some sort of alternative power sources. But we seriously doubt it will be the horse.

On the wagon in front of the Homestead House, are (left to right) Bob and Bill. Kirt Sr. is holding Kirt Jr. on the horse. Circa 1922.

The Big Home Shrinks

The big home Will and Ella had built seemed to shrink as the family grew. Whether they had planned to house their entire family remains a question. They may have assumed that their daughters would marry and move away. With their firstborn, William, our parents lived in the home, alongside Harold and Edith and their families. In addition to Will and Ella, Bill and Hugh, both unmarried, and several unmarried sisters also occupied the home.

Living with Dad's parents and his eight siblings presented a problem. The new infant in the family was adored by all. Little Billy had everything going his way; according to our mother, he was a spoiled brat. She said that if he asked for a clean spoon for each bite of food, his five aunts would vie for the chance to wait on him, or his grandmother would be the one to rise to his beck and call. A second son, Robert Harold, was born to the couple on June 26, 1920, and then Bill, the "big brother," had to start learning to share.

Will and Ella Skinner's family would eventually present them with thirty-one grandchildren. The first was born in 1918, and the last was

Left to right: Bob, Bill, and Kirt Jr. wearing drop seat drawers. Circa 1925.

Standing (left to right): Bob and Kirt Jr. Seated (left to right) Bill holding John, Dan, and Christine. 1929.

born in 1940. Of those thirty-one grandchildren, thirteen were born in the Skinner home. Five list their birthplace as Jordan Valley. The birthplaces of the younger additions to this growing family are scattered.

A Temporary Move

During this period Will Skinner and Willis Thompson had, for unknown reasons, dissolved their relationship. From Thompson, Will bought a small ranch on the Owyhee River, adding considerable debt. Will also bought land adjacent to the Skinner Ranch property, land that Thompson had homesteaded. Thompson had started to build a small home on the property, and then abandoned the project when he

Left to right: Dan, Chris, Bob, Kirt Jr., and Bill. The dog is protector Lindy. Circa 1929.

Left photo: Dan by the rock house. Circa 1930. Right photo: Joanne and John. Circa 1935.

sold the land. The basement and foundation had been completed by the time the two parted company.

Our dad and mother hired a carpenter to have a home built on the foundation. Their "Homestead House" was finished in 1922 and they moved in shortly before the birth of their third son, Silas Kirtland Jr., on July 3, 1925, and Daniel Herbert followed on August 12, 1927. I (John Sackett) was born on April 10, 1929. Jessie Johanna, our youngest sister, was born on November 22, 1932, a year after our dad and mother had leased the ranch and moved back to the big home.

SS

—*A visit to the grain fields in the old ranch buggy
(left). This buggy is still on the ranch today.*

20

Losing the Ranch

While they had still lived at the Homestead house, Will asked Dad to manage the operation of the ranch from the new large house while Will and Ella visited relatives in California. Will's mother, Anne Jane, was living in Berkeley at that time, and many of Ella's family lived in Napa. On Will and Ella's return from visits to California, Dad would move his family back to the Homestead house. Prior to this, however, it was becoming apparent that Will's financial problems might have reached an insurmountable level.

Historically, Will had financed his ranch operation through the Jordan Valley Bank and several of its subsidiaries managed by a man named Fred Palmer. Palmer was a wealthy man who owned ranching property and, with his sons, was involved in raising cattle and sheep. In a 1925 preview of the country's economic future, Palmer's bank and several associated banks went bankrupt.

At that point Will turned to Lumbermen's Trust Bank in Portland and borrowed operating money to help pay off the debts he had incurred. He was never able to successfully and consistently meet his financial obligations after that.

It could have been Will's pioneering spirit or possibly an obsession to expand his operations beyond the home ranch, or he may have been considering setting up his sons in the ranching business. Whatever his motive, Will's rush to expansion added to his financial undoing.

An enticing opportunity arose when an acquaintance and neighboring rancher named Dave Summerville, owner of two ranching operations in the area, approached Will about buying both of his ranches and livestock. Summerville's main operation was located approximately fifty miles distant on Juniper Mountain in Idaho. The other, a smaller ranch, was located near Grassy Mountain about fifteen miles south of the Skinner Ranch.

Will went to Lumbermen's Trust Bank, to which he was already indebted, to borrow the additional money. The bank agreed that these two ranches were attractive opportunities, but they discouraged him from taking on extra debt until he was in better financial condition. In the bank officer's opinion, land was not an attractive place to put money in that particular financial climate.

The bank agreed to loan Will Skinner an additional $125,000 to buy all of Summerville's cattle, horses, and equipment. Will placed options to buy the two Summerville properties, and at the same time placed an option to buy the Ruby Ranch from the Beers family.

Will and Ella had raised four capable young men who were hard workers, very handy and knowledgeable about the ranching operation. Our dad had responsibility for the home ranch management. His brother Harold took over management of the livestock operation and moved his family to the Juniper Mountain ranch. Will and Ella's other two sons, Bill and Hugh, at this time unmarried, worked primarily on the home ranch. Bill, however, soon married a lady named Edna Matheson and left to manage a ranching operation in Prineville, Oregon. Hugh soon took over management of a band of sheep owned by Will.

Disaster Strikes

Following the rapid expansion, dark days lay ahead. Will's bank in Portland was hesitant to leave itself unprotected, and elected to back the loan to Will with the sale of interest-bearing bonds to a group of investors. Prices of cattle and grain crops were not always adequate to meet the payments on the debt, and the ranch operation began to fall behind financially. As the economy became softer, prices received for ranch products declined, and the debt became increasingly more difficult to service.

During the mid-to-late 1920s, Will Skinner's financial world began to fall apart. Will and Dad made trip after trip to Portland to meet with the bondholders and their attorneys. The Skinners' attempts to pacify the bondholders and educate them on the vagaries of weather and cattle prices largely fell on deaf ears.

The bondholders had in good faith backed the banks loan by buying the bonds. Quite naturally, they expected and had the right to receive regular payments on the interest and principal. As the Skinner ranching operation fell deeper and deeper into debt, each meeting between the bondholders and the Skinners brought added disappointment to both parties.

Payments were being made on the debt, but the amounts were not sufficient to retire the debt or satisfy the bondholders. When cattle, hay, or grain sold, some of the proceeds went to pay the bondholders—though more often than not, inadequate—and the rest went to ranch operation. On several occasions, the bondholders required the basic herd of cattle be sold in order to make payment on the loan. In doing so, the bondholders limited themselves from receiving payments in subsequent years. Had they allowed the Skinners to maintain a sufficiently large herd of cattle, it still would have been difficult for the family to pay the debt in full, but it might have been easier for the bondholders to tolerate the delinquency.

To add to the deepening financial problems, another disaster befell the family. During the late 1920s, Ella began having a series of small strokes. Each one took its toll on her condition, and soon a part-time nurse was required to provide for her care. Ultimately, Will felt Ella would benefit if removed from the trauma of their financial problems, so he took her to California to live with their daughter Ruby and her husband, Evan Gheen.

Financial problems continued to mount. Family files include letters written to Will from his mother during the late 1920s, indicating that Will's financial problems went beyond ranch liabilities. His mother, Anne Jane, living in California, and by this time quite elderly, had sold her ranch holdings in Jordan Valley to Will and Ella, and was now pleading with him to make at least a partial payment to help cover her living expenses.

The 1929 Stock Market Crash

Then, in the autumn of 1929, an even deeper financial pit befell Will Skinner and his family, along with millions of others across the nation. The sudden and complete financial disaster brought the entire country to its knees. On October 29, 1929, the stock market crashed. The nation's economy failed in the most disastrous and rapid period of deflation the country and the entire industrial world had ever experienced.

Those who lived through the Great Depression will forever remember the pain and the frustration caused by losing everything they owned.

Throughout the country, banks failed and filed for bankruptcy. People who had money on deposit lined up at the doors to withdraw their money, only to find that they would receive just a few cents on the dollar. Some would receive nothing. A few banks hoping to gain confidence with their depositors, decided to pay out in full as long as they had funds to do so. Some of those depositors felt comfortable enough to redeposit their money, only to find out a few hours later that their banks had closed their doors and the depositors were left with nothing.

Properties that previously had value were suddenly devalued and in many cases became worthless. Hundreds of thousands of businesses went broke; no one had money to buy their products. Highly placed business executives suddenly became paupers, searching alongside their former employees for any type of work that would provide food, clothing, and shelter for their families. In desperation, many of these people would commit suicide.

Families were left with no place to go, and no money to go anyway. People lost their homes, businesses, ranches, and farms—any property that was not clear of debt. There are no words to describe the deprivation and devastating hardships endured by hundreds of thousands of honest, hardworking people during those years. My mother remarked that during this time in history, she believed that on any given day, the entire community in which we lived would have been extremely hard pressed to put together even five dollars in cash.

When the Depression hit the country, Will was even more deeply affected. The bondholders assigned a Resident Manager to work with Will. This person had the grand idea to build a big cattle feeding operation near Homedale, Marsing, and Wilder in Idaho. The feed yard was near the rail lines for easy shipment, but it also meant that cattle from Skinner Ranch being put on feed had to be trailed from the ranch to the feed yard, a distance of about seventy miles.

Lumbermen's Trust Bank had also financed a ranching operation in Prineville, Oregon. Feed cattle from that ranch were brought to the feed yard by train. Huge problems arose—expenses for labor, housing for employees, and feed costs for the cattle more than ate up any profit. This experiment added even more to the Skinner debt and was abandoned.

Skinner Home built in 1917 by Will and Ella Skinner. It has also been the home of Kirt and Johanna, Dan and Cathy, and Bob and Karen Skinner. Painted by Sara Skinner.

Skinner Ranch fields and Cottonwood trees planted over 100 years ago. Juniper Ridge and Parsnip Peak in the background.

From the ranch looking west to Steens Mountain.

Buckaroos, working cattle, enjoy lunch on the range with South Mountain looming in the background. Photo by Marty Owens.

A mother cow watching over her baby calf while keeping an eye on the camera.

A cowboy works on the range near the Antelope Reservoir.

Working cattle out on the range. Photo by Marty Owens

In Spring, Wild Pinks explode from the earth between twigs, lava rock and hard soil. Photo by Marty Owens.

Silas shoeing a horse. Photo by Marty Owens.

The oilhouse/ grainery is the oldest building on the Skinner Ranch. The center section was pulled by teams of horses to this location. The ends came from another structure that was also pulled in, split in half, and added to each side. Both structures were probably built before 1878. Both have been in this location more than 125 years. Its many uses have included a grainery, schoolroom, bunkhouse, shop, oil room, harness shop, and machine storage.

Rock house on the ranch containing a meathouse, milkhouse, and wash- house. A well was dug under the washhouse. Rock kept the rooms cooler.

Sheep Ranch Station, located on the Skinner Toll Road.

Kirt and Johanna's 50th wedding anniversary in their new home. October 1967.

Kirt and Johanna's 50th wedding anniversary, 1967. Standing: Duane and Joanne Owens, Dan Skinner, Chris and Bill Moore, John and Carole Skinner, and Bob and Sara Skinner. Kirt Jr. and Naida Skinner are shown in the wedding photograph on the table in front. Seated are Mom and Dad.

Johanna's sister Jessie visits from Scotland (left in picture). Circa 1969.

Kirt and Johanna standing by the first historical marker at Charbonneau's grave. They were instrumental in the identification. Rocks in the foreground originally marked the graves. 1971.

Mom's Apple Blossom box on her sewing machine. See page 282.

Balla Callum, home of the Callow family on the Isle of Man. Circa 1900.

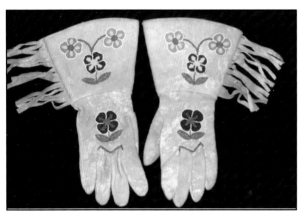

Hand-smoked and beaded gloves given to the Skinner family by Bannocks. Photo by Sherry Green.

This fourth generation of Skinners were raised on the ranch (Kirt Sr. and Johanna's children). Back (left to right): Kirt Jr., Chris, Joanne, and Bob. Front (left to right): John and Dan. These are the people who have made this book.

It took a significant amount of time for the bondholders to come to grips with the fact that the real value of the property had decreased, and they would not be able to recoup their full investment in the foreseeable future. Nevertheless, they continued to try. With no improvement in the financial conditions by the fall of 1930, talk of eviction was in the air.

On March 30, 1931, the bank wrote a letter demanding payment and enforcement of the agreement Will and Ella Skinner had signed. Eviction was imminent.

The letter was written by the Secretary and Trust Officer of the Trust Company. It illustrates the hopelessness of Will's financial situation and brought the sad future of the Skinner Ranch into focus.

March 9, 1931
Wm. S. Skinner and Ella Skinner
Husband and Wife
Jordan Valley, Oregon

Dear Sir and Madam:
You are hereby notified that default has been made in the provisions of the Trust Deed, executed by you under date of March 1, 1922, running to Lumbermen's Trust Company, now known as Equitable Trust Company, as trustee, in that $15,000.00 par value of bonds of W. S. Skinner secured thereby and maturing on March 1, 1931, have not been paid, and further in that interest falling due on March 1, 1931, upon $75,000.00 par value of the bonds secured thereby has not been paid. Formal demand is hereby made upon you for the payment of the said bonds and interest maturing March 1, 1931. Failure to make payment will subject you to the enforcement of the provisions of said Trust Deed.

Will was unable to make any positive response to this formal demand for payment and was quite naturally overwhelmed by the negative forces life was piling on him. He wrote Ella, still living with her daughter Ruby Gheen and her family in California, and advised her of the actions being taken by the bank. She desperately wanted to be home in Jordan Valley. She was becoming increasingly paralyzed as strokes continued to devastate her body. Now her world was crashing in on her and she was losing her beloved home. Though her body was failing her, her mind remained sharp.

Following is a typed version of her five-page handwritten letter to her family, but sent to and directed almost entirely to our mother, telling her what she wanted done to preserve the many treasures she had collected in the family home, and also how deeply she wanted to go back to Jordan Valley just one more time. She had developed a deep love for the eastern Oregon country and the ranch home that held so many warm memories.

September 13, 1931
My Dear Folks:

I suppose you are all busy packing up and moving. How I wish I were there to tell you what I want done with my few treasured belongings. I have scarcely been able to stand these last two weeks. I know it would have been a thousand times easier for me to be there and see things in their accustomed places and bid them a final farewell. Be sure and empty every bureau and chiffonier drawer and put all the things in boxes for me. I want every thing saved. Then my pictures that hang on the wall, I want every one packed carefully. In the living room table drawer, Ella [her nurse, Ella Sweep] left my father's and mother's pictures. I told her to be sure and bring it but she didn't do it. Then there is a box of photos in my big closet in the front bedroom and a box on those book shelves. In the attic there is a big box with photos in it and a lot of my loose music. My trunk I had when I was married is there and there is a trunk with a loose lid that has some things in it that I want. There are so many things I want to see about and it has been so long since I have been through the house I scarcely know where any thing is. My quilting frames were in the schoolroom and that big frame with the hair wreath I made years ago. Oh! Daddy please let me go up and see things once more. I am so depressed and homesick. I just can't stand it. Put what jewelry of mine that is there, in my trunk.

Jo, [Johanna] if you come across a trunk key tied with a red ribbon please put it where I can get at it easily as it belongs to my big trunk in the attic. Jo did you ever find my wedding ring? I need my silk and wool union suits and my woolen stockings so keep track of them. Jo is it asking too much of you to do all these things without help and I want to be there to help. The picture Bobbie [grandson Robert] made for me I want carefully put in my steamer trunk. I love it and the 23 Psalm picture in the back bedroom where I slept before leaving the ranche [sic]. There are a few of the pictures that almost seem a part of me and I want them carefully packed. Daddy dear, please let me go home once more. Don't deny me this after all these years I have helped that home. Don't you or any of the folks appreciate what I have done.

Carrie [Will's sister] was here yesterday and told us that Dr. Coleman who was up at the ranche [sic] with George

Imrie [her brother–in-law] died a week or two ago. He has had sinus trouble and there was a tumor developed on a gland leading from the nose under his eye and brain. They operated and for 14 days he was unconscious and out of his head by spells. Then he passed away. The Napa people regret his death greatly. Lew [Carrie's husband] said he never saw a larger funeral in Napa. He left a wife and three children about the ages of Ruby's three. He seemed so well and strong when he was up in Jordan. One never knows what is ahead of them.

Carrie is down for a week with Ruth and Don.

It sprinkled a little last night but very little. [Ruth and Don were Carrie and Lew Norton's children.]

We got the Statesmans and Caldwell paper yesterday. Thanks a lot.

I bet Beatsie [granddaughter] is pleased to start school.

What is to be done in the school at home. I have asked so many times and you forget to answer me. Give all the kids my love and tell them to write to me. Tell Johnnie Macca still loves him ten dollars and wants to go up to see him and give him a big kiss. I hope he is still Macca's boy. I miss his dear little curly head coming to me and begging for some of my breakfast.

I have a lot of the pictures put up in the living room and I love them all. I told Ella [her nurse] to put Irma's children's pictures in my suit case but she didn't and I want them.

Please pack all my music and hymn books and all my books in the book cases and on the chiffonier or any place else you find them. I wanted Ella to bring two hymn books but she didn't so I haven't a thing to play. That is why I want to be home. Everyone forgets and think they know more about what I want than I do.

It would be nice if we could rent the house for the fall and winter till the different ones found something definite to do so we would have some place to go and have a definite plan ahead. It will be so expensive to move and try to locate without something in view. You see I am simply a blank as to what your plans are. It makes everything so hard on me. While you are good about writing there are so many things you forget to mention in your letters. Do write every thing and often. Is there any man there from Portland? Mr. Oakes or Mr. Cecil.

It is cloudy today but the bay is pretty as there is no fog on it.

Jo please have John Wright [a hired man] send me those pictures and the enlarged one of the house. The Virginia Creeper vines down here are all turning red. I wonder if mine at home is? I forget that I shouldn't say home and also that it isn't my vine. I wonder if Dad would walk me out to see it. I have seen lots of those vines here but none such a beautiful shape as that one was, when I left.

I want to see little Suzanne so much [daughter of her son Hugh and his wife Merle]. Carrie was so wonderfully pleased with Merle's letter. She spoke of it two or three times. Well I must stop for this time.

Jo there are 3 or 4 silver cake stands in the top part of the kitchen cupboard over the coffee pot place. Be sure and get them and all the other silver pieces there. Some of those pieces were my mother's. There is an old fashion syrup pitcher too. Be sure and get them all. Oh! I want to be there and see every thing. Don't forget one of the pictures or books or music. And all my pillows & bedding and my coats. The fur one too and my hats. There are a lot of my underclothes and things and my vases for flowers. Please let me go and see my things there. Get all my fancy work that I have there. So many pieces have been given to me. Don't lose them. I want them all.

Jo—You can take care of the family Bible till I am through with it then you and Kirt can have it. I don't think you will have long to wait for it as my heart feels like it was broken. Take good care of it for Mother loved it so and so have I.

Hope all are well.

Lots of love and kisses to you all.

Lovingly, Mother

Foreclosure, Receivership, and Sheriff's Sale

With the huge and growing debt against the property and the Depression's debilitating effect on property values, the bondholders inevitably foreclosed on the Skinner Ranch in October 1931. A receiver was appointed by the court and ordered to take possession, and to hold safe the home, the land, and personal property until an auction could be arranged.

The ranch livestock were sold by private treaty in two different lots, prior to the sale of the equipment. One lot was sold to a rancher in Cascade, Idaho, and trailed there. The other lot was sold to a cattle buyer from the area named Ben Hunt. Hunt hired a crew that included Dad and his brothers Harold and Hugh and several others to feed the cattle with hay he bought from the bondholders. The hay had been put up during the previous season on the ranch.

89 Bonnie Lane
Berkeley,
Cal.
Sept 15 - 31.

My dear Folks:

I suppose you are all busy packing up and moving. How I wish I was there to tell you what I want done with my few treasured belongings. I have scarcely been able to stand these last two weeks. I know it would have been a thousand times easier for me to be there and see things in their accustomed places and bid them a final farewell. Be sure and empty every bureau and chiffonier drawer and put all the things in boxes for me. I want every thing saved. Then my pictures that hang on the wall, I want every one packed carefully. In the living room table drawer, Ella left my

Page one of Ella's hand-written letter to Johanna. Note that the "Ella" referred to in her letter was Ella Sweep, who was Ella Skinner's nurse at the time this letter was written.

Some of those pieces were my mother's. There is an old-fashioned syrup pitcher too. Be sure and get them all. Oh! I want to be there and see every thing. Don't forget one of the pictures or books or music. And all my pillows & bedding and coats. the fur one too. and my happy There are a lot of my underclothes and things and my vases for flowers. Please let me go and see my things there. Get all my fancy work I have there. So many that have been given to me pieces lose them. I want them Don't so you can take care of all. family bible till I of the through with it same and Kip can have it if you don't think you will have long to wait for it as my heart feels like it was broken. Take good care of for Mother loved it so it is so have I. Hope all are well and Lots of love and kisses to you all
Lovingly Mother.

The last page, page nine, of Ella Skinner's letter.

The only exception to the sale of livestock was a herd of Jersey dairy cattle being fed for their owner, and a small bunch of pigs that belonged to Dad. The Jersey cattle were later awarded to Dad by the court for nonpayment of the feed bill and labor costs.

All equipment required to operate the ranch was sold at auction. The only piece of machinery remaining on the ranch was a grain grinder that Jack Swisher, a neighboring rancher, bought and asked Dad to keep on the ranch and use it to grind the grain he bought.

After the sheriff's sale was held, the real estate went on the block. No bids were received, so it remained under the ownership of the bondholders and in the hands of the court-appointed receiver. Will Skinner was devastated that his beloved ranch was now owned by the bondholders. Until the day he died, he could not bring himself to admit out loud that the ranch was lost.

In retrospect, the bondholders committee did not do themselves any favors in forcing the foreclosure. They recouped some revenue from the sale of the cattle, hay, and equipment, but with no bidders on the property, they were now owners of a cattle ranch devoid of any hope of producing any revenue. Animal feed could be produced, but with all the livestock sold off, the only way to dispose of the feed was to sell it. But remember, the bondholders had also sold the equipment. With no equipment to operate, there could be no preparation of the ground for planting, and no harvesting of crops.

Will and Ella were not the only losers in their attempts to keep possession of the ranch. In a desperate effort to stave off foreclosure, several of Will and Ella's family had rallied around them, some contributing their life savings or labor or both, to no avail. The contributions, the years of hopes and dreams and hard work were all gone, now in the possession of the bondholders committee and the court-appointed receiver.

Will Skinner's financial credibility had evaporated. He would never again be given credit or be able to borrow money.

As we look back, it is difficult to determine or understand Will and Ella Skinner's long-term plan for the home they built. The home was known far and wide for the hospitality it provided. It was built with a large family and entertaining in mind. Extravagant parties and the home's size and amenities contributed to the expense that in later years helped to bring about its downfall and the near eviction of the family. We believe if Will could have been satisfied with his accomplishments, been patient and waited for the economy to recover, he could have successfully realized his dream of what seems today to have been the building of a family ranching dynasty.

Following the foreclosure, Will and his sons—Dad, Harold, and Hugh—and Will and Ella's daughter Verna, being knowledgeable about the property, were hired by the president of the bondholders committee. A man whose name was M. E. Gunderson asked the Skinners to continue living in the house and work on the ranch until the ranch sold. They received modest salaries for their continued labor, salaries that reflected the country's poor economic conditions.

Gunderson appointed a resident manager for the ranch property, an arrangement that did not work well for the bondholders. The manager proved ineffective in running the operation to the committee's satisfaction.

The Skinner Ranch was not Alone in Foreclosure

The Beers family who owned the Ruby Ranch had previously sold it to Fred Palmer and his sons. Caught in the vise of the desperate economy, it was necessary for the Palmers to turn the Ruby Ranch back to the Beers family. With only a small debt owed on the property, the Beers family still owned the property and came through the horror of the depression reasonably unscathed. The Palmer family took the deep loss.

The neighboring Azcuenaga ranch was lost to its owners during the same period, due to debt problems. Their family was not able to recover that property.

SS

21

The Depression

The ranch remained on the market following the foreclosure. At some time thereafter, the attorney for the bondholders committee, the court-appointed receiver, and an unknown third party placed a bid on the property for thirty-five thousand dollars. The bid did not include the payment of back taxes or court costs. The Skinners' attorney questioned the ethics and eligibility of the receiver to be a party to this offer.

Soon after, Will and our dad and mother made a counter offer of thirty-eight thousand dollars to buy the ranch back. Their offer did include payment of back taxes and court costs. The bondholders considered both but did not accept either bid, instead hoping for higher offers.

While working on the ranch and seeing possible but slim opportunity to regain ownership of it, our dad and mother met with M. E. Gunderson, chairman of the bondholders committee, and offered to lease the property. Gunderson was a fair and honest man who had been given authority by the bondholders committee to deal exclusively on the property. The committee had received no additional bids beyond the two previously received, and Gunderson liked and was comfortable with the Skinners. He reasoned that to even partially satisfy the bondholders, he needed a hard worker who knew the ranching business as well as the property.

A Lease is Negotiated

After weighing the available options, Gunderson put his faith in the couple he knew had the necessary ability and were intimately familiar with the property—and who had a strong and passionate desire to stay

Left to right: Dan, Joanne, and John on Bally. Circa 1934.

connected with this land. He knew the Skinners to be hardworking, trustworthy, and honest. As chairman of the bondholders committee, Gunderson decided to grant them a lease on the ranch as the most qualified persons available to him.

Because of his financial history, Will was not included in the lease Gunderson negotiated. The lease was to be renewed annually, with the bondholders retaining ownership while hoping for higher bids on the property, but beyond that, the lease terms are largely unknown. A search through the volumes of family files, letters, and documents found no such written lease. However, we did find a letter to our dad and mother from their attorney, advising them that the lease was valid and binding, and that as long as they were in possession of the property, that was adequate proof of the lease's existence.

Darkness still loomed on the horizon for our parents, and it would get even darker, but with a lease in effect there was a tiny glimmer of light, and with that light came hope of recovery.

The lease was entered into in 1932. Whatever the terms of the lease during this period following the Depression, it is evident that the Skinners had a very hard time meeting them. The lease Gunderson negotiated with our dad and mother did not ease the financial problems

Left picture (from left to right): Mom (Johanna) holding Joanne, and Ruby holding Eddie—taken in Berkley in 1933. Right picture: Mom (Johanna) with Joanne. Circa 1934.

that existed, and the bondholders continued to be difficult to deal with. In looking back and examining all the letters and records from those years, we see that investors from the Willamette Valley were unfamiliar with the climate and vagaries of agriculture on the eastern Oregon Desert, and certainly none were familiar with cattle ranching.

The Skinner Ranch is located at an elevation that provides for a short growing season, and therefore is not conducive to raising row crops that produce cash on an annual basis. This climate is best suited for cattle ranching. This was not to the liking of the bondholders. Before the foreclosure and even after the lease with the Skinners went into effect, the bondholders forced the sale of part of the cattle herd to get a return, even if only a partial one. There were tough years ahead for the couple, but they worked long hard hours, applied good management practices, rolled with the punches, and with a whole world of faith in themselves, eventually began to put the ranch back on the road to success. As we look back and begin to understand the trauma and heartache, the worry and frustration of those years, we wonder how our parents came through this period without crumbling or giving up all hope.

From left to right: Dan, Dad (Kirt), Joanne, Mom (Johanna), Chris, and John. The dog in front is Lindy. Circa 1936.

During the six years they leased the ranch, our parents maintained their standing offer to buy the property from the bondholders for thirty-eight thousand dollars. No other bids were submitted that exceeded their offer. Even after the lease had been negotiated, periods of hope would be followed by long periods of deep dejection. Dad would be required to make trip after trip to Portland to meet with the owners and their attorneys.

Parental Protection of Family

During those troublesome years, our parents did not burden their family with their worries. As children, we were not aware of the forces that guided them; we were well protected from their worry and despair. The older siblings were more aware, comprehending the discussions more fully than the younger ones. We heard the whispers, and we saw the frustrations. We heard the quiet discussions late into the night.

As children, our connection to The Great Depression was insignificant. To be sure, we wore patched and hand-me-down clothes, darned socks, and very often we put cardboard cutouts in our shoes because the soles were worn through. But our psyches were not overly bruised by this; we were no different than any of the other children in the com-

Back row (left to right): Grandpa (Will), Dad (Kirt Sr.), Bob, Kirt Jr., and Bill. Front row (left to right): John, Dan, Mom (Johanna), Joanne (in front of Mom), and Chris. Circa 1937.

munity. What could we have done had we been more fully informed? At our ages, very little.

We never went hungry at any time during those years. We raised our own meat to serve the crew and family. We planted a big garden that provided potatoes, squash, carrots, turnips, corn, and other small vegetables in season. We had eggs from our chickens, and we had milk from our cows. Our mother made homemade cottage cheese, churned butter, and made homemade bread. A dessert of some sort was served at every dinner and supper.

Because of the short season, some of the less hardy garden plants would freeze, but the ones that didn't freeze made it to the table. A nearby dirt cellar, dug into the side of Skinner's Ridge, was filled each year with potatoes, carrots, turnips, and any other vegetables that could be stored.

The growing season was too short for fruit to ripen, but fruit growers from the Boise Valley traveled through the country selling their produce to ranchers out of trailers and pickups, and took orders for

Bill Skinner with his car and guitar at Uncle Harold and Aunt Edith's home in Caldwell.

The car in front is Bill's 1938 Ford Coupe. It is towing his Model T Ford that he'd just bought for $10. Bill got it running.

Dan and his horse, Cricket, in the willow corral.

their next trip through. Hundreds of two-quart jars were filled annually with peaches, apricots, cherries, plums, and jams and jellies of all kinds. After canning, these were stored in the cool basement of the house for the coming year.

A Rocky Road and Stumbling Blocks

After the lease had been negotiated, no equipment remained to operate the ranch. There was the small herd of Jersey cows, and Dad had a small bunch of pigs, but it wasn't until a year or so later that he was able to buy a small herd of cattle. Beyond those few assets, there was a huge desire on the part of our parents to be successful.

By leasing equipment or borrowing it from neighbors, Dad was able to get the crops in. The small herd of cattle, as well as sales of grain and hay, kept the Skinners' operation afloat but did not ease the financial problems. Oftentimes prices for even those products failed to make ends meet. Eviction was still a constant cloud over their heads.

During the time our parents were leasing the ranch, a series of long and disappointing meetings were held in Portland with the bondholders, with little or no progress being made. To add to our parents' frustration, the bondholders were divided on any solutions to the problems that existed. Despite confusion, anguish, sleepless nights, and many

Chris on Bounder.

Playing "500," a popular family card game. Will is sitting with his back to the camera. Dan is seated to his left. John is standing. Kirt Jr. is seated at the table and Kirt Sr. is in the rocking chair to the right. Notice the piano in the background and the pictures on it.

Left to right: Chris, Joanne, John, and Dan. Circa 1938.

tears shed in frustration, the Skinners' desire to regain title to the ranch remained strong, even in the face of their dwindling chances.

On a cold and windy March day about a year after the Skinners' lease on the property had become effective, the bondholders' attorney appeared on the Skinners' doorstep with potential buyers for the property. In the party with the attorney were his wife and the potential buyer and his wife. Through this attorney, the buyer, who was interested in buying distressed property, had joined with the court-appointed receiver, a possible breach of ethics by the receiver. The buyer appeared to be an innocent party to this deal, unaware of the problems involved.

The attorney had previously represented the Skinners on several ranch issues. Now it appeared he wanted to see the Skinners evicted, which would allow him to feast on the remains as a possible co-owner or at least a vendor of a ranch.

Our mother met the two men at the door. The attorney advised her who he represented and demanded that she allow them access to the house for their examination. With a lease in effect, which was in good standing at that time, our mother felt she and Dad were legally in possession of the property, and the demand did not sit well with her. With broom in hand and fire in her eye, the wee Scottish lady with the heart of a lion pulled herself up to her full four-foot-eight-inch height and

Kirt Jr. on the back porch of the ranch house. Note the canvas water bag hanging on the door behind him.

denied them access. She informed them they were not welcome and demanded they get off the property immediately, that there had been no notice of eviction, and that they had no right to be on the property and even less right to make such a demand.

The attorney, still pushing, asked for Dad. She informed him that Dad was out in the field and would be in soon. The attorney, being familiar with the ranch, informed our mother that he would take his party up to the Skinners' dam on Jordan Creek to eat their lunch. They wanted to inspect the ranch irrigation system. He advised her they would be back later to discuss the issue with Dad. They didn't get a chance to do that. When Dad came in for lunch, Mom made him get back on his horse, go find the intruders, and tell them in no uncertain terms to vacate the place—now! Which he did. And, which they did, hastily!

Records indicate the attorney made no further attempts to get his fingers on the Skinner Ranch. In later years, we have questioned our mother's actions. The property was indeed for sale, and we wonder if she might have overstepped her rights on this occasion. Whatever the effect of her outrage on the visitors that day, it worked, and when Dad "evicted" them, they left.

The Holiday from Hell

The disagreeable and hostile attitude of the bondholders committee became even more evident in an occurrence that took place on a Thanksgiving Day soon after the lease had gone into effect on the property. The bondholders had placed a representative on the ranch to look out for their interests. The first year he mainly stayed in the bunkhouse and did little except for a small plowing job in one field. During the first year, his employers paid for his meals and he ate at the Skinners' table along with the hired men. He was a polite and pleasant gentleman who seemed to get along quite well with Dad.

The second year he was there, his employers required that he cook his own meals in the bunkhouse. On Thanksgiving Day, this man called Dad aside and informed him he had received orders from his employers, the bondholders, to immediately evict the Skinner family.

We will never know when the eviction order was received, but it would seem unfortunate, irresponsible, and untimely to inform a family they were being evicted on a day of Thanksgiving. When had this man been notified to evict the family? There was no mail, due to the holiday, and telephones did not exist yet in Jordan Valley. The only answer to those questions is that he was told well beforehand to inform the Skinners they were being evicted at the most inopportune, inconvenient, and hurtful time possible.

Before the sun had gone down that day Dad was again on his way to Portland to meet with the bondholders. The outcome of that particular trip remains uncertain. What we do know is that our parents did not give up possession, and continued with their lease. The Skinners, it can be said, were not dealing with nice people on that occasion.

SS

—*What is left of Jessie Anderson's General Store. He was one of the people who helped provide for many others in the community during the Great Depression. Photo taken 2006.*

—*Danner Hall, where many community events took place.*

22

Community

In the years following the Depression, with banks everywhere failing daily, local merchants and business owners in Jordan Valley came through with great support for the community. Two of these merchants— General Store owners William Helm and Domingo Yturri —stepped up to the plate and served essentially as bankers for the Skinners and most likely for many other ranch people in the area.

Their supply of merchandise necessary to the ranching community was without equal. They carried almost every item in their store that would be required by an isolated ranching community. Their stock of supplies included groceries, hardware, harnesses, some farming and ranching equipment, and replacement parts and repairs for the equipment, clothing, shoes, and boots, and for children there was always a small paper sack of candy handed over the counter at no charge.

These merchants cashed employees' payroll checks and "deposited" the amount to their store account as groceries and other merchandise were written down on account. When folks such as the Skinners sold their cattle, grain, or hay, they paid off Helm and Yturri.

Others in Jordan Valley provided services willingly during those bleak years. Sam Scott and later Hugh and Dorothy Scott of the local IGA grocery market; Pete Laca's service station supplied ranchers with gas and oil; and Dr. W. W. Jones, the local physician. There was never a person more dedicated to the health of the community he lived in than Dr. Jones. Did he get reimbursed for all the wounds he repaired, or the babies he brought into the world, or the drunks he sewed up after a fight? The answer is, of course, he didn't. But he took care of them anyway. There were yet others.

In the small community of Danner, a settlement about eighteen miles west of Jordan Valley, Jessie Anderson, a Danish immigrant, built

Dr. W. W. Jones, beloved physician who rode horse-back, and later in a car, to deliver babies and tend to the sick and injured for many miles around Jordan Valley.

a small general store and post office that provided basic services to the community. He too, kept many families in food and clothing during the depth of the Depression, and on occasion took on the role of the banker. It is very doubtful he received payment on many of the grocery bills of itinerant farm and ranch laborers owed him when they left the community. Jessie's store building still stands today, a bedraggled icon of history.

Never to be forgotten during this period was the cooperation be-tween community members; work, equipment, and labor were will-

The hired hands on this crew were kept on for feeding cattle in the winter. Standing (left to right): Bruno Gluch, Hank Reed, Bill Spiegel, Kirt Skinner Jr., and Bob Skinner. Kneeling (left to right): Bill Skinner, Willard Fretwell, George McCauley, and Ira Bowdich. In Front: Ed Fredwell. The car is Dad's old Chrysler. Circa 1936–1938

ingly exchanged. Through those years, there were many occasions when the goodness of people brought heart-warming if only temporary relief and brightened that glimmer of hope. There were people who admired and had respect for the Skinners. An example of that respect involved their hired men.

In the early 1930s, Dad had negotiated a loan from an apparently solvent bank in Boise to cover payment on the lease from the bond-holders, and operating expenses for the year. Additional men had been hired for the haying season. With no warning that trouble was brewing in this bank, he was notified that it had gone bankrupt and closed its doors.

Dad had a big crew working, and all were happy with their jobs. He was aware that it was entirely possible he would not be able to pay the men for their labor then or even after the hay was put up. Following a sleepless night and worrying all the next day, he made up his mind about what to do. For him, the only option was to take the high road, to be honest and level with the men.

That evening, the men had eaten their supper and were resting after a busy day, just visiting, sitting around and on a wagon used to carry supplies to the field. Dad called the men together and informed them of the bank's failure. He closed by telling them they had two options, and they were free to make their own decisions as to what they wanted to do. If they wished to leave and seek work elsewhere, he would understand. The other option he offered was if they continued on through the completion of haying, he would do his best to somehow work out a deal in which they would all receive payment in full for their summer's work. Some asked a few questions. Silence followed.

Then one of the older men spoke up. "Here's how I see things. Right now we're getting three good meals a day and a place to sleep. If we go someplace else we can't be sure of getting anything better, maybe not even as good. My suggestion is we stay and help Kirt get his hay in the stack and see if he can't figure out some way to pay us when haying's finished."

The man's short speech resulted in every man on the crew agreeing to stay and finish the job. When haying was done that summer, Dad was able to pay every man his full wages for the summer's work.

The man who made that statement was Jesse Bryant. On that evening, he became a hero to our dad and mother and continued to be a cherished friend of the family until his death many years later.

Ella's Homecoming

In 1933 Will and Ella's daughter Ruby and her husband Evan Gheen brought Ella back to the ranch by car from their home in Berkeley, California. While in California she had become totally paralyzed, unable to communicate. She had completely lost the ability to move, but she remained mentally alert. Though she could not handle them, she was now happily back among her treasured possessions in the home she and Will had built.

With deep respect for his parents, our dad and mother informed our grandfather that he and Ella would have a home on the ranch and would be supported as long as they both lived. They assumed the cost for Ella's care and the constant nursing help required to attend to her needs. Her ability to move was limited to her eyes, which remained very expressive, and she could only issue a plaintive cry. But she was at last at home under the attentive and loving care of Will, her family, and her nurses.

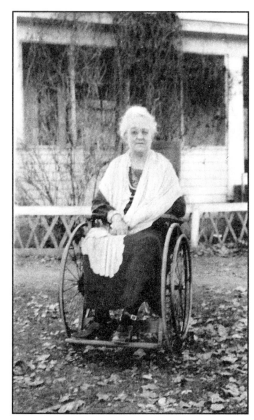

Grandma Ella Skinner.

Will and Ella Skinner continued to make their home on the ranch for the remainder of their lives. Both died in their beloved big house, Ella in 1941, and Will in 1960. Both are buried in the Canyon Hill Cemetery in Caldwell, Idaho.

The Tragedy of the Dust Bowl

Another tragic phenomenon—the Dust Bowl—arose concurrently with the extremely depressed economy, adding even more stress to the nation's sad conditions. While the western states were not directly affected by the Dust Bowl, this weather-related tragedy had a big effect on other parts of the nation in the early to mid-1930s. Hundreds of thousands of acres of prairie grassland had been plowed up and converted to dryland farming in the midwest, known as the breadbasket of the world. With the onset of severe drought conditions and the arrival of high winds, the breadbasket became a dust bowl.

An enormous area of land was involved, ranging from central Texas throughout the midsection of the United States and north into Canada. Huge dust storms developed that turned day into night and eventually affected distant areas such as Chicago, New York, and the whole eastern seaboard of the United States and eastern Canada. Millions of farming families who had been able to weather the Depression were now forced into bankruptcy.

The incessant wind-driven dust inundated homes, farm buildings, and equipment, all of which had to be abandoned. Livestock developed pneumonia from breathing the fine dust and many thousands died before they could be moved. The rich, fertile prairie soil literally blew away, leaving nothing but desolation. In many cases even families were abandoned, with their breadwinners away searching for employment that would let them send money home, or possibly move their families to a more favorable area.

The Depression and the concurrent Dust Bowl were a double whammy that just about did the country in. Thousands of refugees from these disasters flooded into the western states and other sections of the country where as many as possible were absorbed into the workforce. Thousands of people changed professions in order to find any kind of work that would provide for their basic needs. The years between 1928 and 1938 were a sad and disastrous period in American history.

The Hired Help

During the Depression and the Dust Bowl, many of the hired men who worked on the ranch were fugitives from one or both of these tragedies. Many, in fact most, had at one time owned their own farms. They knew how the work had to be done, and most did their jobs well. Some were hired on for the full year, and many came back to work year after year during haying season and at harvesttime. The going wages at the time amounted to about one dollar per day, three meals a day served in the dining room of the house, and a place to sleep. Each man provided his own bedroll, did his own laundry, and was housed in the old Skinner home that had been converted into the bunkhouse.

Our Work Day

During those years, summer working hours did not start and end with sunup and sundown. Our parents readily accepted the responsibility placed on their shoulders. In spring and summer months, depending on our ages, we were up well before the sun to start the day. After breakfast our dad, Kirt, managed the farming and planting, haying, and harvesting crews. After his supper in the evening, he did necessary bookwork or went back out to the field to do the irrigating, or both. During the winter he worked right along with the hired employees to insure the livestock were properly fed and cared for. Dad's work habits were learned early and continued throughout his life.

The Kitchen and House

The operation of the kitchen and the household, so much different than today, fell under the direction of our mother, Johanna. Monday washday was an all-day affair and not an easy task, especially in winter. An old photograph of a washday clothesline reveals over one hundred pairs of socks, washed and hanging on the line to dry. Piles of bedsheets and dirty clothes were collected and sorted. Mother carried water by bucket from the well to a large vat where it was heated using sagebrush wood.

It took several hours and loads of sagebrush wood to heat the water, after which it was delivered by the bucketful to the gasoline motor-driven Maytag washing machine. Instead of today's more modern laundry soap, our mother shaved slices off bars of Crystal White soap.

Ten to fifteen pairs of sheets would be washed on a typical laundry day. When the sheets had been washed and rinsed, mother carefully put the hems together before putting the sheets through the wringer. In this way they could be hung on the line for easy folding and handling later. Other laundry was sorted by color and then by degrees of dirt, with the most soiled going into the washing machine last.

Six clotheslines were filled entirely, each near seventy feet long. Rain was a problem, as was snow and freezing weather in the winter. On those days, the laundry was hung in the house to dry.

When they were old enough, Johanna's two daughters, Chris and Joanne, were great help to their mother. They made the beds and helped in the kitchen and with cleaning. There were no carpets in the home, and both levels of the house—including two flights of stairs and two long hallways—were dust-mopped every other day without fail, as heavy traffic brought both dust and tracks. The wooden floors and stairs were varnished annually. The daughters' daily jobs included the

Wash day—148 pairs of socks, plus sheets, towels, and personal items for everyone went out on the lines. Each pair of socks was washed, turned inside-out, and washed again—then paired up and hung on the line.

aforementioned laundry as well as feeding and caring for the chickens and collecting the eggs.

At a time not too long ago, it was a rare occasion to see a lady on horseback, working cattle with her husband and her kids, or with a group of neighbors in a corral roping calves during branding. Today it is not unusual to find women doing all these things, as well as operating heavy equipment in the fields.

The Skinner ladies all take an active part in the total ranch operation and are as aware of the requirements for success as are their husbands. They have essentially replaced hired men. And yes, should anyone ask the question, these ladies are equally as adept in their homes and in their kitchens, and are capable of putting on a delicious meal at a moment's notice, and still maintain very nice homes for their families.

No Idle Time

While my sisters helped my mother with the house chores, we boys would make it a point to be "involved" in the outside chores because if

Chris with her chickens. The chicken house, pens, and roost are in the background.

we were found idle, our mother would be sure to hand us a dust mop, or put us to work washing or drying dishes.

In the winter there were fewer hired men and less company, but we kids were in school so were of little help, putting an even heavier burden on our parents. On rare occasions, Dad was available and stepped in to help Mother if he had time.

During the school year, the older boys in the family had little time beyond milking the cows by hand, morning and evening, and processing the milk. During winter we also made sure the woodboxes were filled, usually twice a day. Coal scuttles were filled at least twice a day, more often on really cold days.

Electric power didn't reach the Jordan Valley area until 1947. Until then sagebrush wood and coal provided fuel with which to cook, to heat water for washing clothes and dishes, and to heat the house. There was no such equipment as the automatic dishwasher, automatic washing machine, or automatic dryer in that era. After meals had been served, youngsters very often became dish washers and dryers.

Team and wagon. On board are Joanne, Uncle Harold, and Dan.

On some cold winter days, we didn't make it to school on time because of our chores. We had a lady teacher who had been a missionary in Korea for many years. She was accustomed to being waited on hand and foot by her servants in Korea, and since she had room and board in our house, she expected like services from the Skinners. To her sorrow, she had to learn to take care of herself. She didn't like it that our chores occasionally kept us from getting to school on time, but because of her attitude, we didn't much care that she didn't like it. She complained to our parents that we were tardy. Dad informed her rather quickly that since she was riding to school with the Skinner kids, she was also late for school. Had our parents been able to afford another hired man to do the chores, it would have helped, but dollars were still very hard to come by, and there was a World War going on. Everybody did what had to be done—except her. She complained. We certainly weren't injured by learning to work and to share the load, and what school we missed was negligible.

Ranch Kids and Their Pets

Ranch kids are often pressed into service quite early in life and given jobs that are safe and easy to handle. One such kid's job was irrigating

*School House
District #69
Cow Creek.*

*Cow Creek School class.
Back (left to right): Miss
Fleming, May Lees, Chris
Skinner, LaVonne Carson,
Dan Skinner, and Grant
Carson. Front (left to right):
John Skinner, David Lees,
Allen Lees, Jimmy Carson,
and Joanne Skinner. 1936.*

the yard. It was important that the yard be watered to keep up the garden and the lawn. Water was pumped from a nearby irrigation ditch and the kids were responsible for making sure the water went where it was supposed to go, as best we could, usually with help from an adult. It was a learning process that was used a great deal later when irrigating the fields.

Irrigating involves the use of a shovel, which at that early age was too heavy to carry over my shoulder like the big guys did, so I dragged it along behind me by the handle. While doing that I found out some chickens are smarter than we give them credit for. A little white hen, of which there were quite a number, began following me around. She realized that when I dug, there would likely be a worm or some other tidbit to eat. Then she got even smarter. When I dragged the shovel, she hopped on and rode. We became great friends that summer.

The morning came, however, when Mom commissioned Dad to provide two or three old stewing hens for supper that night. Around the corner of a building came my little hen on a dead run and right behind her came Dad. When my pet saw me, she flew straight into my arms and tucked her head under my elbow, safely hidden from danger. Dad came to a dead stop, his mouth and eyes wide open, speechless. I don't remember whether we had stewed chicken for dinner that night. If we did, I do know it was not my little white feathered friend.

Animal nature can be hard to fathom. For whatever reason, sometimes a cow will be unable to take care of her calf, or occasionally a cow will take sick and die leaving a small calf to be cared for. When that happens, it usually falls to the kids in the family to make sure the calf is fed and cared for. This is excellent training for a child and of course, the calves become great pets. Caring for them teaches responsibility and invariably a love for animals, which is a strong requirement for anyone interested in the livestock business.

In many cases during my youth, these pets were also the beginning of a future herd of cattle. The orphaned calves were fed their milk for several days from a bottle, and then were taught to drink from a bucket. That process was the spark for the following poem that appeared in the *Western Livestock Journal* many years ago. Any person who has taught a calf to drink out of a bucket will appreciate this little poem.

Picture of John taking care of favorite pet, LuLu. 1941.

The hardest thing on a ranch I think,
Is trying to teach a calf to drink.
You pull and haul, get his head in a pail;
He'll stand there and twist and wiggle his tail,
Then the very first thing, kerplunk goes his nose,
And most of the milk goes all over your clothes,
Hang on to your patience, your teeth you can grit;
If you can't hold your temper, you might as well quit.
For Old Mother Nature, whose methods don't fail,
Never meant for a calf to drink out of a pail.
Just back him in a corner and straddle his neck;
He won't damage you much, you're already a wreck.
In his mouth, put your finger, and maybe with luck,
That little old calf will start in to suck.
Now pick up your bucket and push his head down,
And away you go again, around and around.
Just do this a week with your back in a kink,
And maybe by then, you'll teach him to drink.

—Author unknown

Bob carrying milk cans.

During early years on the ranch, youngsters of ten or eleven were expected to contribute, consistent with their age. Before and after school
my sisters were expected to help clean, make beds, and learn to cook
and sew. The boys were first given the chore of hauling chopped wood
to fill all the woodboxes in the house. At that age we were not yet
allowed to chop the wood, but to carry it, certainly. There was a big
woodbox in the entry porch off the kitchen. Because sagebrush was
used for cooking for a big crew, the box was filled at least once daily, if
not added to again. Another box was on the west porch near the living
room. Will Skinner watched carefully to make sure we filled it for the
heating stove in the living room. Both these stoves also burned coal,
and that was another of the chores we had. Coal scuttles were to be
filled morning and night, and on extra-cold days, even more often.

The older we got, the more responsibilities we were assigned. By the
time the boys reached their early teens, we had learned to milk the
cows and process the milk. During the school year that meant very
early hours and very late hours. My older brothers first had that chore,

and later my brother Dan and I milked twelve to fourteen cows, morning and evening. That doesn't sound like many by today's dairy standards, but remember, there were no milking machines in those days; we did it by hand.

In the winter, milking was started by lantern light well before sunup, and finished at night by lantern light once again. We didn't complain because every other kid we knew was doing the same thing. It wasn't work all the time; we always seemed to have some time for play.

A ranch is a wonderful place to raise a family. Very early we observed nature at its kindest and at its most raw. We learned to accept gracefully that which we could not alter. We learned to accept responsibility almost from the time we started walking. We had the whole outdoors as a playground and we used it.

We learned to make mistakes and then how to avoid them. We learned the value of human relationships as well as how to deal with and respect our animals. We were probably considered rubes when we went to town, but we learned how to accept and be accepted there as well. As children, we had excellent opportunities to learn the business of life and liberty, the love of family, and the love of this wonderful country we call America.

The Loss of a Great Woman

In October 1941 we lost our beloved grandmother. The following editorial from the Malheur Enterprise was written by Arthur Bone, editor, on October 30, 1941. It accurately captures the essence of Ella Skinner, a fun-loving and accomplished pianist, vocalist, and otherwise very talented and devoted pioneer ranch wife, mother of nine, and grandmother to thirty-one. Ella had lived in a sad state of paralysis from her strokes until her death.

> THE DEATH OF ELLA SKINNER
> The death of Mrs. William S. Skinner of Jordan Valley marks the end of an epoch in Malheur County. She was the pioneer mother in the grand manner who was able to combine the amenities of gracious living with the ruder requirements of pioneer life and extract the best from both.

Coming to Jordan Valley early in life from California, she soon made the Skinner Ranch famed far and wide for its hospitality and the warmth of its welcome. Eventually, the ranch embraced within its vast precincts a civilization all its own. In those early days, with so much to be done, there was a natural tendency on the part of some pioneers to neglect the cultural opportunities that life in older communities offers.

Not so with Mrs. Skinner. She showed that gracious living could be a part of pioneer life by making her own household an example. The Skinner Ranch became the center of social life for a vast territory. Her interest in community and religious activities never waned until invalidism over took her.

Good roads and automobiles have ended the isolation that made necessary the development of such ranches as the Skinner Ranch. But they illuminate a picturesque period in our pioneer history. The county was fortunate to have had as its mistress one of the greatest, one so charming and gracious a lady as Mrs. Skinner.

The Long Summer Day

During these years our late Grandmother Ella's legacy of hospitality continued. Neighbors, friends, and travelers always knew there would be a meal or a bed or both available at the Skinners'. But that big house had to be kept up and kept clean, with bedsheets sometimes changed daily because of departing and arriving visitors. It was apparent that the big house was becoming a problem, but it would wait until the 1960s to be corrected.

Chris and Joanne on the steps of the west porch. The dinner bell, to the right, was made of an old disk. This bell was used three times a day to let the hired men know when breakfast, dinner and supper were served.

In the summer, with the full haying crew, family, and frequent visitors, there would be between twenty-five and thirty-five meals or more served at a sitting, with three meals served daily for an estimated average of ninety meals per day. (We guess many restaurants would vie for that much business today.)

Our mother always tried to keep kitchen help to relieve her of cooking duties. These ladies were much like the men who worked in the fields. Some were excellent cooks, some good, some mediocre. And some had absolutely no ambition, skill, or even the ability to function. Those sorts didn't last long as employees. At that point, the job again fell on the shoulders of our mother and our sisters until help could be recruited. Of those hired ladies who proved to be competent and had the ability and the ambition to learn, most would remain loyal and many were considered by the Skinners to be almost family. The cook had her own room in the house and was expected to be on the job by five o'clock in the morning and to have breakfast prepared by six.

For the teamsters, a typical day in the summer months would also start at five. After the wrangler gathered and corralled the horses, the teamsters caught, groomed, and harnessed their teams, and fed them hay and

A family picnic. Seated from the left: Tompy is first, Chris is third, Will is fourth, and John is sixth. Standing from left: Johanna is third, and Kirt is fourth. Dan is seated far right, and Joanne is on the ground far left.

oats. The crew then got ready for breakfast and waited for the cook to ring the breakfast bell. Visitors often vied at the noon and evening meals for the privilege of ringing the bell (a disk blade hung on a post).

Each person had his or her place at the long table and seldom gave it up without good reason. One hired man arrived a moment too late and found a new hired man sitting in his usual place at the table. He flatly refused to eat.

Hired men, visitors, and family all ate at the same time, at the same table. It was not unusual for two to six visitors to join us for any given meal, and often for overnight accommodations.

The breakfast menu started with gallons of coffee, pitchers of unpasteurized whole milk and cream, cereal (called "mush"), two big platters or bowls of all of the following: bacon or sausage (sometimes steak or fresh liver); fried, scrambled or soft-boiled eggs; fried potatoes; stacks of hot biscuits or pancakes; and always homemade butter and syrup. The day was planned so the men and teams would be on their way to or in the field and on the job no later than seven a.m.

The family cookbook, made of a leather-bound ledger, was passed down through generations.

Butterscotch Meringue Pie #
5 T ~~Swans Down Cake~~ Flour   1 tsp vanilla
1 C ½ brown sugar   1 baked 9 in pie shell
3 T butter   4 T sugar
1½ C milk   2 egg white stiffly beaten
2 egg yolks — well beaten   ⅛ tsp salt

Mix flour & brown sugar in top double boiler. Blend butter with mixture. Add milk, cook over hot water until thick & smooth — stir frequently. Remove from fire - add yolks & cook 10 min. Remove from fire & cool. Add vanilla. Pour in pie shell. Beat sugar & salt into egg whites & cover pie. Bake in very slow oven 12 - 18 minutes (300° 6-9 min. 335° 6-9 min

An entry in the family cookbook. This one is for Butterscotch Meringue Pie. Note that the directions include the statement, "remove from fire." This recipe is also shown typed out in the text that follows.

At eleven thirty in the morning, the crew unhitched their teams from the equipment, and filed in from the field for dinner. The teams were watered, tied in their stalls, and given their oats and hay. After the horses were taken care of, the crew washed up and waited for the dinner bell to ring at noon. Horses provided the power in those days, and men relied on them, hence horses were treated with respect.

The dinner meal was as big as breakfast. The crew was commonly served beans; roast beef or steak; sometimes a beef and vegetable stew; potatoes and gravy; homemade bread, baked daily; a vegetable or maybe two; always coffee and milk; and fruit canned by the capable hands of our mother.

We have fond memories of the magnificent, tastebud-bending aromas coming from the kitchen in those days. The smells of baking bread, pies of all kinds, and cakes to be served to the crew and family are remembered to this day. How good a big slab of freshly baked bread covered with homemade butter and homemade jam tasted to a hungry youngster just home from school or in after the chores were done.

At one o'clock it was back to the fields, going full steam until six o'clock in the evening when the crew watered, unharnessed, and fed their teams. When the men had finished their own supper, they turned their teams out to pasture for the night to get some rest and be ready for another day.

Many educational discussions and arguments took place around the dinner table. It was truly a miniature democracy. Because of displacements caused by the Depression and the Dust Bowl, many of the crew were intimately concerned with the economy and with developing world problems. Many of the younger men would later serve bravely in World War II. Disagreement was acceptable and arguments pro and con were educational to all, especially to the younger listeners who were expected to be seen and not heard. Adults were entitled to their own beliefs and were respected for them. Along with the give and take by those who entered into the discussions, we also remember fondly the good-natured bantering and teasing, usually at the cook's expense.

Like new teachers who came into the community, kitchen help never failed to attract an eligible bachelor or two. Mom was as caring and as watchful over these young ladies working in her kitchen as if they were her own daughters. Many were to become excellent cooks, and more than a few of her protégés found husbands while working on the Skinner Ranch.

Butterscotch Meringue Pie

5 Tablespoons flour   1 Teaspoon vanilla
1 Cup light brown sugar   1 baked 9 inch pie shell
3 Tablespoons butter   4 Tablespoons sugar
1 ½ Cups milk   2 egg whites stiffly beaten
2 egg yolks—well beaten   ⅛ Teaspoon salt

Mix flour and brown sugar in top double broiler. Blend butter
with mixture. Add milk, cook over hot water until thick and
smooth—stir frequently. Remove from fire—add yolks and
cook 10 minutes. Remove from fire and cool. Add vanilla.
Pour in pie shell. Beat sugar and salt into egg whites and cover
pie. Bake in *very* slow oven 12–18 minutes (300–325 degree
oven 6–9 minutes).

Skinner's Famous Jordan Valley Mustard (Ruby Skinner Gheen)

1 Tablespoon sugar   1 Tablespoon flour
1 Tablespoon dry mustard   *little bit more*
1 Tablespoon vinegar   1 Tablespoon water
                                            little bit less

Lemon Sauce
½ Cup sugar
1 Cup boiling water
1 Tablespoon corn starch
2 Tablespoons butter
1½ Tablespoons lemon juice
Pinch of salt

Mix sugar and cornstarch, add enough cold water to make a
paste, then pour in boiling water. Add butter and cook—then
add flavoring.

Ruth's Ice Box Cookies
1 Cup shortening or butter
2 Cups brown sugar
3 eggs—beaten
1 Cup nuts
3½ Cups of flour (about)
1 Tablespoon soda (sifted with flour)

Mold into loaves and let set overnight if possible. Slice and bake in a quick oven.

Sponge Cake
(Nell Parks)
4 eggs—beaten until creamy
Scant Cup of sugar
Pinch of salt
1½ Cup sifted flour
1 Teaspoon baking powder
½ Cup boiling water just before ready to put in oven.
Lemon or vanilla

Shortbread
(from Johanna's sister Jessie in Scotland)
1 Pound flour
½ Pound butter
¼ Pound sugar
1 egg

Method:
   Place butter and sugar on baking board and work together by hand. Then add egg, followed by flour into which a pinch of baking soda has been added.
   This is all worked together by hand until all floour worked well in. Then cut up in shapes. Bake in a moderate oven.

Kitchen Romances

One time, a young lady who worked in the kitchen was asked by one of the hired man to go for a car ride with him after work. Neither was familiar with the roads or the country. When it got dark, they got lost. Someone they met on the road gave them instructions on how to get home, telling them "all roads will lead to Skinner Ranch." Of course, all roads *didn't*, and they wandered around until daylight. Both were up and on the job that next morning, apologetic and humble over the somewhat scandalous hour of their return, but who had the facts to question the story they told? They left together a few weeks later, to our knowledge never to be heard from again.

The cook occupied a room in the house and was expected to be on the job by no later than five a.m. On workdays she was to have breakfast ready by six a.m. Sunday's breakfast was never later than seven a.m. Seldom would she be through cleaning up the kitchen before eight in the evening. She was expected to have meals prepared on time. With the early hours required of them, the hired women were seldom out late. Most were happy to have a job and would not jeopardize their position. Many of them remained friends of the Skinners for years and had tremendous respect for the knowledge and the treatment they received under our mother's training.

There were other kitchen romances. One involved a hired man, a Dust Bowl fugitive who came to work at the ranch. Many horses were still being used at that time, and they were important to the operation. Horses loved this guy and within a day, he would have gentled even the wildest ones and would have them eating out of his hand.

It quickly became obvious that this fellow had the same effect on the ladies. In short order he had the cook, the schoolteacher, and several ladies in the town of Jordan Valley swooning over him. One day Mom found the cook crying uncontrollably and burning all her letters from previous beaus. When Mom asked her what the problem was, she replied that she knew what kind of a guy he was, but she was leaving with him anyway, which she did. They married and years later came back for a visit—still married. She had obviously tamed him down a bit.

Another lady who was helping our mother in the kitchen during the late 1940s or early 1950s invited a hired man to go with her to her home in the Boise Valley for the weekend. On the way back to the ranch, they decided to go on to Winnemucca to get married. When they got back to the ranch neither was in any condition to be driving—or even to be walking. Though both were badly hungover, the next day they continued on the job and finished out the summer. As far as we know, that marriage worked; there were some that didn't.

On occasion, Ella Skinner's nurses had also been fair game for the hired hands. One young fellow married Ella's nurse and wrote later that the marriage didn't last and that he had joined the army. However, another of Ella's nurses married a local rancher and was a prominent member of the community for many years.

Finally—OWNERSHIP

In the Great Depression, our parents had leased the ranch for six years. During this time they kept open their standing offer to buy the property from the bondholders for thirty-eight thousand dollars. No other bids were ever submitted that exceeded that offer. Finally the chairman of the bondholders committee, M. G. Gunderson, who had been previously authorized to deal exclusively with the Skinners, accepted our parents' offer. The bondholders, being a stubborn group, drug their heels and were slow to accept the inevitable.

After nearly seven years of leasing the property to the Skinners, the sale was at last finalized in early 1938, backed by a loan program put together by The Federal Land Bank, the Production Credit Association (PCA), and The First National Bank of Oregon. Will Skinner was not allowed to be a signer on the loans or to have ownership in the ranch.

When the final papers were signed and ownership transferred to our parents there was huge relief. Something good had come from those years, though, in addition to regaining ownership. During those years of disappointment and anxiety, a powerful bond had been forged between our parents, and a "never give up the ship" attitude had prevailed. There were hard times in this decade of the Depression but they, and the community as a whole, pulled through stronger than ever.

SS

23

The Modern Outdoor Workload

In the late 1930s, the Skinner Ranch began to modernize, taking its first step in moving away from the use of horses. The first tractor arrived on the ranch—a F-30 Farmall International—accompanied by plows, discs, harrows, mowing equipment, and a hay stacker. By the early 1940s, almost every job that could be done with a team of horses could also be done with tractor-drawn equipment. While workhorses continued to be an integral part of the operation for a number of years, their use began a slow but steady decline. To this day, a few ranchers keep workhorses around for nostalgic reasons, or because they live in mountainous areas where heavy snow occurs.

I believe anybody who ever worked with a team of horses on the Skinner Ranch or any other ranch would agree it was a sad and nostalgic day when the last team of workhorses was retired in the mid-1950s. They were like friends to us, and without horses the ranch would not have existed.

There is consolation today in that no piece of equipment will ever be able to replace the saddle horse for working with cattle. That said, most ranching operations now have at least one four wheeler that will go almost anywhere a horse will go—but not quite. A four wheeler may have a horn to honk, but a buckaroo can't use it to take his dallies on that sort of horn.

The workhorse, however, has gone the way of the buggy, the buckboard, and freight wagon. It is doubtful that many ranching people operating today would know how to harness a team or hook them up to a piece of machinery. It would also be difficult to find or even to afford a harness maker, except for one who specializes in making harnesses for show horses. Times changed dramatically in the last half of the twentieth century.

A Jayhawk Stacker was used early on. Kirt Sr., Dad, is on the Jayhawk. Will is on the horse behind the stack. Uncle Bill is on the buckrake. Circa 1924.

Eventually, the stationary threshing machine gave way to the horse-drawn combine, which in turn gave way to the tractor-drawn combine, and later the self-propelled combine. Horse-drawn equipment gave way to tractor-drawn equipment, and by the mid-1940s the number of hired help required to put the hay up had been cut to about half of the previous number. Hay was now being mowed with the tractor mower. Horses were used to rake hay into windrows and to push the windrows into piles (called shocks) with a buckrake. The mower was removed from the tractor and the hay stacker put on. The stacking crew went to work and stacked the loose hay in large stacks to preserve it for cattle feed in the winter.

Today on the vast majority of ranches, including the Skinner Ranch, hay is processed using a swather. This equipment cuts the hay and puts it into a windrow. After the hay has cured sufficiently, it is baled and stacked in hay corrals where it will stay until needed for cattle feed during the winter.

Uncle Harold on a buckrake loading a shock of hay on the Jayhawk stacker in the background.

Men were lifted up and down on the stack by the derrick as is shown in this picture. One of the stackers is Joe Olsen.

John Skinner is driving Fox and Dick as they pull a slip (flat sled) with a shock of hay up to the stack.

A Jayhawk stacker is used. Kirt Sr. is on the Jayhawk. Circa 1924.

The derrick became the next way to stack hay during the late nineteen twenties and thirties. Stacks could be made higher. Kirt Skinner is on the trip rope at the bottom, left corner of the picture. One of the men on the stack is Joe Olsen.

This picture shows the net that was used to carry the hay to the top of the stack. Cap is the horse on the right—a steady worker for many years.

This picture shows a master's job of stacking hay. Stacks are smaller at the bottom and rounded on the top so that rain and snow would slide off and not soak down through the stack.

A slide is used in the haying operation. Dad (Kirt Sr.) is standing by the shock of hay. Dan is on the pull-back horse.

Dan is stacking with the Farmhand. Horse power was used exclusively before the Farmhand. After this haying has been done exclusively with machines.

Another frustrating day with the baler. Left to right: Bob, Dan, Kirt Sr., and John.

This Swather cuts and rakes hay in one operation. Dan and Bobbie.

A Swather at work.

Bob is stacking hay bales. 1963.

Bob on a tractor pulling the side-delivery rake.

Modern haying, creating the large, long, round bales.

New tractor.

The Depletion and Restoration of the Range

In the late 1880s, the mining industry had begun to falter when California banks became hesitant to continue their support of the mining industry. As the mining industry diminished, livestock that earlier had been trailed from Texas soon took over as the number one industry in the area. Along with big herds of cattle, bands of sheep were being trailed into the area from Nevada and California. The high demand for meat and wool insured good prices. In the short period of twenty to thirty years, big cattle and sheep ranching operations appeared.

As civilization moved west and the population increased, livestock raising became a major part of the economy. Newcomers homesteaded or bought land and increased their herds. It was only natural that they also take advantage of the seemingly endless supply of forage that nature provided free for their livestock.

Cattlemen who did not own property used the range year round. Sheepmen who owned multiple bands of sheep numbering from one thousand to two thousand head per band grazed them on the lower elevations in early spring, taking advantage of early growth, and moved them into higher elevations as the grass grew. In late summer and fall these bands of sheep were grazed back over the same lands to take advantage of any new growth, leaving little if any winter feed remaining for cattle. By the late 1800s overgrazing was beginning to have a detrimental affect on the amount of forage available.

Property owners believed they had the right to graze their livestock on open range near their property. Inevitably, problems arose between cattlemen and itinerant sheepmen. Even unfenced private land became fair game to some sheepmen. Anger escalated between cattlemen and sheepmen, resulting in hatred and the open warfare now known as "The Sheep Wars." Large numbers of sheep and herds of cattle were killed by the opposing factions, and many cattlemen and sheepmen fell to the guns of the opposition.

Because of their small mouths sheep could crop plants close to the ground. They were able to graze on early new growth, and were on the range well before cattle. Enormous herds of cattle also took their toll on the range, as did untold thousands of horses who ran the range year-round. Many of these were domestic horses owned by ranchers;

thousands of others were feral. Horses wintered well on the open range. They could paw through deep snow to find feed, and because they were highly mobile, they could travel long distances to water. These large herds of horses proved equally as destructive as the cattle and sheep in the deterioration of the range.

Prior to the Industrial Revolution, horses were extremely important to the economy. Horses provided the power necessary to the growing agriculture industry. In addition to transportation, horses were the main source of power required to move needed products to market centers. With the arrival of mechanization fewer and fewer horses were needed. Huge numbers of farm and ranch horses were allowed to run free year-round, and most would never be needed again. The wild herds continued to grow unchecked during this time. It rapidly became clear that the use of the range for grazing was going to require drastic changes.

The Taylor Grazing Act

In 1934, the United States Department of the Interior established the Grazing Service for the purpose of rehabilitating the range, and Congress enacted the Taylor Act in an effort to bring some sense of reason and fairness to grazing on the open range. The preamble of the Act reads, "An act to stop injury to the public grazing lands by preventing overgrazing and soil deterioration; to provide for the orderly use, improvement, and development; to stabilize the livestock industry dependent upon the public range; and for other purposes." The Grazing Service was assigned the task of rehabilitation and management of grazing lands. In 1946, the Grazing Service became known as the Bureau of Land Management (BLM), under the Department of the Interior.

The provisions of the Taylor Act established a priority system that gave preference for grazing permits to livestock owners who owned land or water rights adjacent to or near federal grazing land. History of use during the previous five years was considered, as was the ability of the livestock owners landed property to maintain the livestock during the months they were not on federal lands. That provision requiring landownership made it illegal for itinerant livestock owners who did not own land or water rights to graze their animals across public land.

The Act also established Grazing Districts; the first in Oregon was formed by a group of ranchers in Klamath Falls. The Act also provided for the creation of Advisory Boards consisting of range users and elected by their peers to give advice in the allocation of permits and management practices within the districts.

When the Jordan Valley District was formed, the elected Advisory Board representing an area from McDermitt, Nevada, to Jordan Valley included one member from Caldwell, Idaho. The names of the Advisory Board members included J. J. Ballard, McDermitt; Alex Ballantyne, Caldwell, Idaho; W. S. Bruce, Arock, Oregon; Pasco Eiguren, Arock, Oregon; Andrew Greeley, Rockville, Oregon; John Liddle, Rockville, Oregon; Sam Ross, Jordan Valley, Oregon; S. K. Skinner, Jordan Valley; and Jack Swisher, Jordan Valley.

Each District was further reduced to areas called Units. The two Units that involved the Skinner Ranch and several other ranches were designated the Cow Creek Unit and the Soldier Creek Unit. Skinner livestock had historically grazed in both of these units, and both had serious forage problems The demands for grazing exceeded the carrying capacity established by the Bureau of Land Management. Years of negotiations took place with little if any progress being made. In 1946, the Jordan District combined with the Vale District with the whole becoming known as the Vale District.

The Battle of Soldier Creek

After several years of trying to negotiate a settlement to control grazing, the Soldier Creek Unit problems became known locally as "The Battle Of Soldier Creek." In the winter of 1956, the BLM called a meeting of ranchers who had permits to graze in the Soldier Creek Unit. At the meeting, held in Jordan Valley, the BLM reviewed all grazing permits and their adjustments (reductions) to the maximum number of Animal Unit Months (AUM)—one definition being the amount of range forage required to sustain a cow and her calf for one month—allowable for each permittee. Ranchers were not willing to reduce their herds to the AUMs required by the BLM. The meeting was deadlocked. The BLM reconvened the next afternoon and evening, and again on the third afternoon and evening. The deadlock continued. The ranchers had little interest in reducing their herds to the size recommended by the BLM.

These ranchers were well aware of the condition of the range, but they felt the reduction in herd size was too harsh. It had become obvious to Dad that there was only one way to break the deadlock. He volunteered to be the first to take a two hundred and fifty AUM reduction as his part in working out a way to end the problems. His consent was followed by a chain reaction in which every permittee except one volunteered to give up a portion of their permit. Voluntary reduction resulted in the signing of the 1956 Agreement, a first for the Bureau of Land Management.

A similar situation with the Cow Creek Unit ended in a court battle and was eventually settled in the same manner as for The Soldier Creek Unit. Dad took a fifty percent reduction and in return accepted terms for a private allotment.

Because of problems experienced in these two negotiations, it became necessary to find a better way to settle range disputes. The answer, of course, rested in the ability to restore at least a portion of the production of forage. Max Lieurance, District Manager of the Vale District, worked with the advisory board to devise plans to rehabilitate large portions of the Vale District lands. Approximately ten percent of the lands in the district were treated in some manner, either by plowing and reseeding to crested wheatgrass, or by spraying to kill unwanted invasive plants and combinations of both.

Intensive range practices were also established, and with improved management, forage production has been improved greatly in some areas. Many reductions taken during those trying times have since been restored. Untreated areas have also made impressive improvements due to management practices made possible by improvement in treated areas.

In May 1984, the golden anniversary of the Taylor Act, now under the umbrella of the Department of the Interior and the Bureau of Land Management, was celebrated in Portland, Oregon, and the next day on the lawn at the Skinner Ranch in Jordan Valley, with the caterer estimating he served about four hundred and fifty meals. Many dignitaries were present including Bob Buford, National Director for the Bureau of Land Management; Marvin Klemme, the first Director of Grazing for Oregon; Bill Leavell, the current Director of Grazing for Oregon, and Max Lieurance, who had directed the development of the Vale Project.

Out on the Range and Branding

Cow Camp. Left to right: Tom Skinner, Robert McConnel. Others unidentified. 1912.

Mule team and cook wagon—driven by Uncle Tom.

Branding at Inskeep Station.

Baby calves in the old willow corral waiting to be branded.

Bob is standing over the calf on the left. Harold Skinner is on the horse roping. Bill Burr, in the foreground, is taking the branding iron back to be reheated in the barrel of hot coals. Circa 1950.

Dad (Kirt, Sr.) supporting Mom (Johanna) so that she can get a good shot with her camera.

Buckaroos (left to right): John, Tom Weybark, Walt Fisher, Dan, Kirt Jr., and Bob.

Herding cattle today is the same as it always was.

Kirt Sr. (Dad), and a shorthorn cow.

Lunch time on the range. Bob is pouring coffee for Dan. Kirt Sr. far left.

Bob and his children, Nancy, Bobby, and Sally, just before the fair. September 21, 1961.

Dan and Cathy's kids, Liz and Jocele, at the Malheur County Fair.

A Day of Rest

Whether working on the range or in the court system, whether working with the cattle or hanging the laundry, the Skinners have a tradition of adhering closely to a six-day workweek. Our mother staunchly exercised her early religious training, and Sunday was to be a day of rest. The only work allowed was that which could not be ignored. There was the irrigating that had to be done in the spring and summer months, care and feeding of the livestock in the winter, and the daily chores such as milking the cows. She held very strongly to the philosophy that if unnecessary work were done on Sunday, costly breakdowns would occur during the week. She believed men, horses, and equipment needed a day to recoup and to relax. We look back and are conflicted by this. She made considerably more work for herself, her daughters, and the cooks because Sunday dinner was made extra special for the crew, who normally did not work on Sunday.

Monday through Saturday were workdays, and everyone, including family members, was expected to set a good example and pull one's share of the load, to be productive, and to do one's job well. There were times for fun, usually in the cool of the evening after supper, and after the kitchen was cleaned up. There were footraces, water fights, "rasslin'" matches, occasional acrobatics, ball games, horseshoe games, good-natured teasing, or just sitting out on the cool lawn listening to the tales of our elders as they discussed current events as well as some of the history shared herein.

The crew took advantage of the evenings to repair their equipment and prepare it for the next day. But they too had their fun activities. A horseshoe pit was set up outside the bunkhouse door. It was a rare summer evening that you didn't hear the ring of a horseshoe against the peg, or the cheer of success when a ringer was thrown. There was a favorite waterhole in Jordan Creek for a swim in the evening to refresh oneself and to remove the dust of the day. And there was music. Some brought their radios; others brought a guitar or harmonica, a banjo or fiddle, and they made pretty good music.

Parades

Main Street Jordan Valley July 4th Parade. On horseback (left to right): Charles Loveland, Gene Loveland, Tom Remson, Fern Scoggin, Everett Jones, and Frankie Whitby. Circa late 30s or early 40s.

Hol Parks and Agnus Maher. July 4th Parade in Jordan Valley.

Watching the July 4th Parade in Jordan Valley.

Stage coach in the July 4th Parade. Dad (Kirt Sr.) is riding shotgun and Grandpa (Will) is inside. 1959 Centennial Parade.

Dan Skinner (front horse) carrying the Oregon flag, and Senator Tony Yturri in the Centennial Parade. 1959.

Mom (Johanna) ready for the Centennial Parade in Jordan Valley. 1959.

This bunkhouse (in the background), the original Clinton house, had been moved here up from Jordan Creek.

Some Shady Characters Among the Workers

Doubtless, some of the men who worked on the ranch carried shady backgrounds. With the remoteness of the area—law enforcement nearly one hundred miles away—and its roads almost impassable at times, the Jordan Valley country provided an excellent place to get lost. There was little chance of finding information on these people unless they had previously worked for a neighbor or an acquaintance. Personnel records were unheard of in those years. Through years of hiring, our parents developed a sixth sense about people. If any doubts or red flags were raised, the person was not hired. Those who came looking for work were often broke and hungry. At the Skinner Ranch they had a job, three hearty meals a day, and a place to sleep. Many were familiar with hunger pains and certainly did not want to jeopardize their chances of continued work.

It was an era of trust in one's fellow man, and it was a rare occasion in which that trust was violated. When the old E. H. Clinton home, that had been converted into a bunkhouse, was torn down in the 1960s an old, heavily rusted handgun was found beneath the floorboards. Because of its condition, it appeared to have had been hidden there many years previously. Perhaps it could tell some interesting stories, perhaps not.

One confirmed violation of trust occurred when a number of rifles, shotguns, and ammunition were stolen from a building adjacent to the ranch house. When the local Oregon State Policeman showed up to investigate, one of the hired men suddenly "got sick" and had to leave the field. After the policeman had dinner with the family and the crew, he interviewed each person. The sick man suddenly became "sicker" and said he had to leave. He was eventually arrested but had already disposed of the guns, one a prized shotgun that belonged to Dad.

On one occasion, when good help was hard to come by, Dad hired a man who brought his trailer house to live in while working on the ranch. He was an experienced ranch worker but clearly a bit strange. He wasn't threatening or aggressive, yet he had some odd quirks. For instance, he had decorated every square inch of his trailer house ceiling with chrome-plated cup hangers and towel racks. He was very proud of those decorations and wanted to show them to everybody.

A few weeks later, Dad's brother Bill, visiting from Idaho Falls, recognized this fellow and told Dad the guy had been convicted of murdering his wife, that he had wrapped and tied her up in a mattress, and rolled her body into a river in eastern Idaho. He had just recently been released from prison.

Alarmed by this revelation, and with a wife, two daughters, and a cook he was responsible for, Dad quietly informed this fellow that the work he had been hired to do was done, and let him go. The man hooked up his trailer and left. To our knowledge, he was never heard from again. He was a reasonably good worker during the month or so that he worked, and he may have done his time, but it wasn't worth the risk to keep him on the job.

Others probably were just a step ahead of the law, too, but as long as their past was unknown and they did their work well, they stayed on the job. Petty theft of tools was always a problem, and other small items would come up missing, but those problems were of little significance, and it was not uncommon to find "missing" items where they had been set down during repair work and then forgotten.

It is a tribute to the hundreds of people who worked on the ranch through the years that the majority were solid citizens, knowledgeable hard workers who took pride in their work.

SS

—Winter picture of the ranch barnyard.
Photo by Johanna Skinner.

24

Seasons and Industry

For a rancher, winter is usually the harshest, most difficult season to deal with, but there is a definite blending of one season to the next, allowing for adjustment or acclimatization. One year might bring mild winter weather, and the next winter can bring long, brutal below-zero days with ice and heavy snow. The eastern Oregon winter can start anytime between mid-October and mid-December and continues well into the spring months.

The best way to tell whether winter has arrived is to look outside. If the temperature is below freezing and fallen snow doesn't melt, there is no question—it's winter. If wind arrives with the snow, it can be brutal. When that happens, a rancher takes a look at the haystacks he put up the previous summer and the number of cattle he has to feed, and he says, "I sure hope I have enough hay in the stack to last out the winter." When the temperature falls below freezing, vegetation stops growing. Most of the growth that took place after haying will have been pretty well consumed by the cattle by the time snow flies. When that happens, the rancher has to begin feeding the hay he baled the previous summer.

In earlier years, before the baler came into use, hay was stacked loosely in large haystacks, and then fenced off to keep the cattle out. When feeding started, hay wagons pulled by a team of horses were loaded with hay at the stack and then taken out to the cattle. The hay was pitched off while the team and wagon moved in a circle. A new area was chosen almost daily in order to give the cattle a "clean plate" to eat from. The amount of hay fed to the cattle per day would amount to what they had cleaned up from the day before. If hay was left uneaten, the feeder would cut back a bit. Conversely, he may have fed a little more, if it was clear the cattle would eat more.

A nice wagon load of hay—ready to be fed to hungry cows. It is driven by Ralph Ansotegui.

In freezing weather, cattle feeders made sure the cattle could get to water. If waterholes were frozen over, the ice had to be broken in an area large enough so more than several cows could get a drink at the same time.

Cattle feeding did and still does come down to a basic science for the rancher. Cattle can withstand very cold weather as long as they are fed adequately. A cow's digestive processes generate heat. In extreme cold, cows will eat more. In moderate temperatures, they will eat less. Adequate, nutritious feed insures a high ratio of calves born to the number of mama cows in the herd, and insures that calves will be healthy and vigorous.

With modern equipment available today, there have been dramatic changes from the old days of the pitchfork. On the Skinner Ranch, round hay bales weighing fifteen hundred pounds or more are placed on a feeder tray that operates from the power take-off of a tractor. The hay is unrolled off the feeder and fed to the cattle just like it came out of the windrow.

A tractor onto which this equipment is attached today will have a cab with a heater and an air conditioner. With all the glass that surrounds the driver, the cab may get too warm on a sunny day. If so, he can turn on the air conditioner to cool off. Some would say it is almost like sitting in the living room.

But as easy as this mechanized process appears, other things are taking place while feeding the cattle, such as checking on their overall health. If a rancher locates a sick animal during feeding, he will later return on horseback to drive the sick animal back to the livestock corral to be treated.

Successful ranchers wear many hats nowadays. They have to be big equipment operators, mechanics, veterinarians, knowledgeable agronomists, experts in animal husbandry, businessmen, accountants, horse trainers, and animal nutritionists. They need to be environmentalists, be savvy about computers, and be politically aware. Today, a successful rancher's life requires far more desk-time than in years past.

Springtime

As winter wanes and a new season begins on the Skinner Ranch, feeding will be continued for the main herd along with the process of birthing calves being born to the replacement heifers. Each fall, the herd of cows is graded, and the older ones past their prime are culled and sold. Their replacements are selected from the best offspring of the herd from the previous year.

These young cows—near two years old, more or less—are now carrying a calf and will often require assistance with the birthing process. Starting in mid- to late-February, one of the Skinner crew will be out with a flashlight every two or three hours during the night to make sure all is well and no births are imminent. If a birth is indeed imminent, the cow is watched carefully. If it becomes apparent she will need assistance to help her deliver it will be provided. Some of these young cows are at a loss as to the next step required of them as a mama. In that case the calf will be encouraged to nurse, which usually turns on the motherhood switch in the cow.

The next night it will be someone else's turn to babysit. A successful birth and healthy calf make for an important adjunct to the ranch's bottom line. When the sun comes up, it is back to feeding and taking care of all the cattle.

Besides feeding and playing the OB specialist, early spring is a time to look forward to one of a rancher's busiest seasons. As soon as the frost goes out of the ground, preparation for planting will begin. The ranch crew begins working with the cattle, getting them ready to be

Taking cattle out in the spring.

turned out. New calves will be branded and marked soon after birth. On April 1 or shortly thereafter, providing it is warm enough for the grass to begin growing, the cattle are turned out on the range.

The rancher looks forward to this time of year when the cattle are out of the fields and preparation for putting up hay can begin. Ditches will be cleaned and gotten ready for irrigation. Fields will be groomed to remove and spread debris leftover from winter feeding.

When the cattle are gone, water will be turned into the ditches and every field will be irrigated at least twice before the haying starts in late June. The amount of irrigation water available depends heavily on the amount of snow that accumulates on the surrounding mountains during the winter. It is very important to cover the land once at least, and in good water years more if there is adequate water.

Summer and Fall

Due to scarcity of labor during World War II, Dad bought a J. I. Case hay baler. This introduced a brand new method of processing hay on the Skinner Ranch. The Case baler was designed and manufactured for small farms precisely because of the labor shortage, but it was an expensive piece of machinery, since metal was going to the war effort. Unfortunately, the Case baler did not have the capacity required to process the amount of hay the Skinner Ranch put up, but at that time it was the only alternative we had.

Old methods of stacking loose hay were out of the question, and would have left the hay standing in the fields. Stationary balers had been used in some places for years, with the hay being hauled by wagon to the baler. The Case baler revolutionized hay handling. It was pulled behind a tractor to pick up hay out of the windrow. This labor-saving piece of equipment required only three people to operate it, compared to older systems that used much more labor. Two people were on the baler: one poked the wires through the hay, and the one on the opposite side tied the wires. The third man drove the tractor.

The Case baler did not have the capacity for a big hay operation, so hay often laid too long in the windrows after cutting, and the quality of the hay suffered to some degree. But, we made do with it.

At this time during War II, the Skinners had started to slowly build up the cattle herd, but there were still far too few to use all the hay, so surplus hay was sold. In the bale, it was much easier and far more efficient to be transported by truck.

The best that can be said about the Case baler is that it started a significant change in haying methods, and baling is now being used exclusively to put up hay on the Skinner Ranch and most other ranches today. Balers manufactured today automatically tie the bales, so only the tractor driver is needed.

Modern haying equipment has been improved immensely. Round balers have far greater capacity than the old Case and require less labor to operate. On the other hand, round balers are very expensive. Modern machinery is engineered and manufactured for the express purposes of baling and handling and for feeding livestock more economically. Today, the majority of ranchers who feed cattle on their own property put up hay in round bales weighing upwards of fifteen hundred to eighteen hundred pounds. Hay raised for sale is baled in square bales weighing up to a ton, making it easier to transport to distant places.

It is no longer necessary or even possible to handle those large bales of hay by hand as was done with old methods. Machinery cuts and windrows the hay, and makes and stacks the bales. Special machinery is designed to feed hay to the cattle in winter. Along with the economy of less labor, hay is preserved in much better condition. The downside for the rancher is modern equipment's high initial expense and subsequent upkeep.

The most significant advantages to modern methods are the ease with which hay is put up and the much higher nutritional value of hay that is processed in prime condition. Those advantages add up to higher-quality cattle feed, and provide the consumer with a much higher-quality food product on the dinner table.

There are other advantages to the modern methods. The equipment manufactured today provides the operator with the comforts of working in the air-conditioned cab of the tractor while listening to a favorite radio station away from dust, dirt, and insects. In winter, the operator has a cozy heated cab. The rancher pays dearly for those comforts, but after so many years of braving the seasonal elements, such benefits are well deserved.

After the cattle have been turned out, new calves will be born to many of the older cows. Because cattle rustling is still a factor and mistakes can happen, a special branding takes place during the summer so these late calves can be identified. Without fail, a few animals will slip through the system and end up with a strange brand. Also, it is not unusual for a mother cow to come home without her calf. It could have gotten sick and died, or if unbranded it could have been stolen.

Autumn marks the time to gather cattle off the range and bring them back to the ranch. Older cows in the herd will have started thinking of the green grass in the fields and will be ready to head for home. It will take three or four weeks of intensive horseback work, or buckarooing, to get them all home. Some will have mixed with neighbors' cattle and will need to be separated.

Calves born in the spring will be weaned off their mamas and put into the ranch feedlot to be fed over the fall and winter and sold the next spring. Some weaner calves may also be sold in the fall.

SS

25

Education and Culture Enrich Us

Our little town is rich with the culture of diverse peoples, namely the Basque community and those who have entered the Jordan Valley as teachers from many far away places such as Ireland, Germany, and Scotland, where our mother was from. They all, and education as a whole, have figured prominently in the development of our community.

The Basques

No discussion of the livestock industry in southeastern Oregon and southwestern Idaho would be complete without inclusion of the Basques—a colorful, proud, hard-working, fun-loving group of people, many of whom have worked on the Skinner Ranch throughout the years. After arriving in America, many Basque people became employed in the livestock industry. Not only have they made a big impact on the livestock industry, they are now identified with success in every area of industry, and have added immensely to local traditions in the Jordan Valley area.

The first Basques arrived in Jordan Valley in 1889. Jose Navarro and Antonio Azcuenaga were followed by Augustin Azcuenaga in 1890. Pedro Arritola, Luis Yturraspe, and Cipriano Anacabe soon followed. They were members of the Basque ethnic group that originated in the Pyrenees Mountains between Spain and France.

Their language is unique, and they claim no allegiance to either of those countries. Because both Spain and France persecuted them, many young Basque men migrated to America in the late 1800s and early 1900s. When they prospered and became established, they sent for their families.

The Basque community entered a Jordan Valley parade to commemorate a new museum. They dressed in traditional clothing and danced. 2008.

It was not long before a thriving Basque colony claimed Jordan Valley as its home. Basque stonemasons built a Pelota Frontone, or ball court, where they played a game similar to American handball for entertainment and competition. The court, built of native stone hewn by Basque masons, still stands in the center of town and is now property of the city of Jordan Valley. It commemorates the Basque masons who built it, and is iconic to residents of Jordan Valley. It is now listed on the National Register of Historic Buildings.

John Elorriaga, past president of U.S. Bank, was born and raised in Jordan Valley. He recently donated a Basque boarding house to the town of Jordan Valley. The building was at one time owned by his parents, the late Ambrosia and Maria Elorriaga, and has been converted into a museum for the ION Heritage Council. This museum represents the connected corners of the states of Idaho, Oregon, and Nevada. Bob Skinner, Sr., is on the board of directors for this exceptional, still-expanding museum of local history.

Another gentleman of Basque ancestry, born and raised in Jordan Valley, was the late Anthony (Tony) Yturri. He was a prominent lawyer in eastern Oregon and served many years in the Oregon State Senate.

The Basques are deeply involved in the community of Jordan Valley. Since the first Basque pioneers arrived, they have successfully ventured into many professions—cattle ranching, banking, law, medicine, merchandising, and politics, to name a few. The history of the Skinner Ranch, the Jordan Valley area, and the Pacific Northwest would not be complete without mention of the significant contributions by the Basque people.

New Blood in the Community

We have discussed the education of Skinner family kids and children in the community throughout the years. The importance of their education cannot be overstated, but it brought other significant advantages to the community, too. In particular, many single ladies who came to the community to teach, eventually married into local families. A number of Skinner men made sure that a certain young female teacher did not escape. Our mother, Johanna Murray, and our aunts Edith Jones and Merle Boswell all married Skinner men. The younger generations have continued to uphold that tradition.

Merle Boswell's father brought her by car from their home in Vale, Oregon, to accept the teaching position in the little one-room country school near Danner, Oregon. He took one look at the remoteness of the area and made a strong attempt to convince her to go back to Vale with him. She didn't, of course, and in time she caught the eye of Hugh, the fourth and youngest son of Will and Ella Skinner. They were married August 20, 1930, in Vale and moved into the Homestead house, vacated when our parents moved permanently to Will and Ella's big home on the Skinner Ranch.

The fourth generation in the Skinner family has carried on the tradition of marrying visiting teachers. Our brother Dan married Catherine Ross, a ranch kid and a native of Klamath Falls, Oregon. Cathy had been teaching in the Jordan Valley School district; she and Dan were married in Klamath Falls, Oregon, on June 2, 1973.

The fifth generation took up the banner when Robert Morgan Skinner, son of Robert and Sara, married Karen McKay, a schoolteacher in the Jordan Valley School District. Karen was part of a ranching family in the Treasure Valley of eastern Oregon and was well-acquainted with ranch life. They were married in December 1973.

Both of Bob and Karen's sons have married ladies who are currently involved in the Jordan Valley schools—Tracy Sarceda married Silas, and Kelsi Johnson married Michael. Though these two women took different routes to Jordan Valley, both met their respective husbands while attending eastern Oregon State College, and have taken positions in the Jordan Valley school systems. Not only are they deeply involved in the ranching industry, but they also have become strong advocates for the education of children in the community.

A common thread runs through this family starting when Silas and Anne Jane's oldest son Will reached school age. Formal education has become increasingly more important with each generation. When Will first started school, Silas and Anne Jane saw to it that he rode horseback nearly nine miles to school and nine miles back home daily. The school operated for only two months during the summer, and some years no school was held. Several years later, Will and his sister Carrie were sent to Ohio to live with relatives for two years to attend school.

Will's total formal education amounted to those very few years. When Silas and Anne Jane moved to California in 1884, their younger children were immediately placed in schools there.

Schooling primarily consisted of the three Rs—reading, writing, and arithmetic. Few students in the rural areas moved beyond that level into higher learning, since boys in particular were working on the family farm or had become part of the labor force by the time they reached their early teens. Boys did not often progress beyond the eighth grade or high school years. Girls were given a bit more education than the boys because they often became teachers for the next generation.

Mona Skinner, youngest daughter of Silas and Anne Jane, was the first family member to attend and graduate from college. She attended The University of California in Berkeley and served as a mathematics teacher in Napa, California, for many years. Mona also taught school several years at the Skinner Ranch. Among her students in the schoolroom behind the harness shop were Kirtland, Harold, Ruby, and Verna Skinner.

It was important to Will and Ella that their older children receive basic schooling, and no less than high school for the younger members. Several of their family attended college, although none graduated.

Of the fourth, fifth, and sixth generations of Silas and Anne Jane's descendants, the vast majority are college graduates. Many hold ad-

Cow Creek School class (left to right): Dean Stitzel, Bobby Patterson, Jerry Patterson, Joanne Skinner, Mrs. Stitzel (teacher), Elaine Patterson, and Buzzy Shannon. 1945.

vanced degrees including but not limited to education, medicine, and philosophy, or are working toward those degrees. The family currently counts medical doctors, scientists, lawyers, accountants, business executives, and a number of successful ranchers in their numbers.

Early Jordan Valley Schools

The Skinner kids of my generation, and earlier, all started formal education at a one-room school in Cow Creek School District Nr. 69. Because we lived in a remote area of an isolated part of the state, seldom were there more than eight or ten students. One teacher was responsible for teaching first grade through the tenth grade, or second year of high school. Most of those teachers had no more than a two-year course in "normal school."

Only Merle Boswell, who taught for three years, and Helen Jarvis, who taught one year, were college graduates. Most were well trained, however, and dedicated. They capably steered their students through the basic foundations of reading, writing, arithmetic, spelling, etc., up to and including courses in Latin, algebra, geometry, physics, and basic calculus for the ninth- and tenth-grade students.

Most of these teachers provided students with excellent tools and a superb start on the trip through life. In a new Skinner tradition, my two oldest brothers, Bill and Bob, began attending Caldwell High School in the fall of 1935. Our parents strongly believed in exposing their children to the society of a larger school system for their last two years of high school. Bill and Bob lived with Uncle Hugh and Aunt Merle Skinner part of the first year, and the remainder of the first and second years with our Uncle Harold and Aunt Edith Skinner.

With their absence from the community, and with other families moving out of the school district at that time, there were only four students remaining to attend the little one-room country school in District 69. A schoolroom on the third floor of the Skinner home was put back into use because the four children were all Skinners, the children of Kirt and Johanna Skinner. Students that year were Silas Kirtland, Jr., eighth grade, Verna Christine, sixth grade, Daniel Herbert, fourth grade, and me, first grade. Two years later several families had moved into the district and with more students, school was again held in the more centrally located one-room school out in the sagebrush.

Following their graduation from high school in 1937, both Bill and Bob attended The College of Idaho in Caldwell, Idaho. Bob attended The College of Idaho for a year, and then decided to attend Oregon State College. He graduated with a degree in Animal Husbandry in 1941 and worked about a year with the County Agents office in Lakeview, Oregon.

Bill continued at The College Of Idaho, where he began taking flying lessons and became a member of the Civil Air Patrol. He was very near to graduating when he received an offer to go to work in Boise training army recruits to fly.

SS

26

The Years of World War II

S oon after Dad and Mom bought the ranch in 1938, disturbing news began reaching the United States from Europe. In 1939 under Adolph Hitler, Germany invaded Poland. Hitler had become dictator of Germany in the early nineteen thirties, and his apparent long-term vision was to rule the world. His armies soon overwhelmed the Central European countries, after which he declared war on Russia and Great Britain.

The United States managed to stay neutral until December 7, 1941. On that early morning, the Imperial Japanese Navy conducted a sneak attack on the United States naval base at Pearl Harbor, Hawaii. The United States immediately went to war with Japan. With Germany, Italy, and Japan aligning against the world, Germany and Italy soon also declared war on the United States.

Within a month, almost every young, able-bodied male in the Jordan Valley area was standing in line trying to join one of the military services, a phenomenon that took place in every area, town, and city in the country. The call to arms was followed in time by the draft, under which every male age eighteen or over was subject to being called up to serve. If they passed the physical examination, they were sworn in and sent to a base or camp for basic military training.

Thousands of people too old to serve joined the war effort and went to work in shipyards and other war-related industries. This had a tremendous effect on agricultural areas, leaving them without sufficient labor. Significant pressure was put on Skinner Ranch and all other ranches that required seasonal and year-round labor. Owners were essentially forced to hire either very young, inexperienced people or those who were too old or had physical disabilities that kept them from serving in the military. Our parents, Kirt and Johanna Skinner, had not yet had time to build up their cattle numbers following receivership, and therefore had been forced into raising and selling grain and hay in an effort to hold the ranch together. Both of these crops required fairly intensive labor.

The haying crew was cut from its normal ten or twelve at this time of year, to six or seven men. The tractor mower had replaced five or six horse-drawn mowers, and the summer haying crew became a family operation. Bert Palmer, son of Dad's sister Irma Palmer, drove a team of horses on a side delivery rake, and brothers Kirt, Dan, and I operated the baler.

When the haying was finished, the grain crops had to be harvested in the fall. Dad purchased a small combine, and with dry weather until October or early November, it was usually adequate to get the crop into the granary and ready for sale. But not always. During this time, Dad did most of the irrigating, starting well before the sun came up. After breakfast, he checked on his crew and irrigated in his spare time. His full day ended well after dark. During the war years, Will took significant responsibility for overseeing much of the operation.

Death of a Son

Bill, our parents' oldest son, the baby boy whom his aunts and grandmother had doted upon and spoiled, turned out to be a hard-working, bright, energetic young man. He was an exceptionally talented mechanic and musician, and when at about age two he saw his first airplane, he held out his arms to it. He was fascinated with airplanes and destined to become a pilot. He took his first ride with a barnstormer in Caldwell, Idaho, at about twelve years of age, and from that time on, airplanes were his life.

While in high school, Bill began constructing the frame for a home-built airplane. He completed the fuselage and the wings, and had carved the propeller. His plan was to mount the motor of an old motorcycle on the plane, but due to his ambition for an education, he never finished the project. The propeller Bill carefully carved and balanced to the micro ounce, is now displayed in the home of Bill's nephew, Bob Skinner, also an avid pilot.

Bill inherited his musical talents from his grandmother, Ella Skinner, and taught himself to play piano, violin, guitar, and harmonica. He found an old violin with a broken neck someone had stored in the attic.

Bill was in training to be a pilot here. Open-cockpit trainers were used then. 1939.

He carved a new neck, put horsehair in the bow, installed new strings, tuned it, and without benefit of lessons, played it at many dances and social occasions in the community. If there was music in an instrument, he found a way to make it produce. Sadly, in her declining years paralysis kept Ella from overtly responding to her protégé, but her hearing remained keen and her eyes expressive. There was never any doubt she enjoyed Bill's music.

After graduating from high school in Caldwell in 1938, Bill and our brother Bob attended The College of Idaho. Bill had been a member of a high school glee club and joined a College of Idaho glee club featured on a local radio program in Caldwell. Bill also formed a small band that included his brother Bob and entertained in high school assemblies and on the radio. In addition to normal college courses, Bill was taking flying lessons and became a member of the Civil Air Patrol in Caldwell.

Talented and ambitious, Bill was well respected by his associates. When he was about twenty-two, he bought a small Caterpillar tractor and some land-leveling and farming equipment, and then hired a man to operate it while he continued his college courses.

He had met the girl of his dreams at school, and with both approaching graduation, they had begun making wedding plans. With the onset of the war, however, those plans were set aside.

Bill had completed his flying lessons, temporarily suspended his education, and gone to work for a flying service in Boise, Idaho, where he became a flight instructor giving private flying lessons and teaching Army Air Corps recruits to fly.

In March of 1942, at age twenty-four, Bill was tragically killed when, after being given the green light to land, he and his student ran into the air turbulence of a B-17 bomber also coming in to land. They were too near the ground to recover and crashed. The student was severely injured but survived. Bill, while not yet in the service, was the second Jordan Valley man to die in the war effort. Jimmy Anderson, the son of a neighboring ranch family, was a crewman on the Navy ship *Arizona* when it was sunk December 7, 1941, by Japanese bombers in Pearl Harbor. Jimmy Corta, another young man from Jordan Valley would also give his life for his country in World War II.

The death of their firstborn son was a blow from which our parents never fully recovered. The stress and turmoil of the Depression years followed by Bill's sudden death affected their emotional stability for many years. Our parents were not unique in their sadness. Hundreds of thousands of families across the world would feel that same heartbreaking loss of a loved one before the hostilities ended.

Bob, expecting to be called into the army at any time, had quit his job in Lakeview and was at home when our brother Bill was killed. His age, his experience, and his gentle, calming nature were a godsend, to our parents and to his younger siblings. Brother Kirt was at Oregon State College in Corvallis, and our sister Chris was in high school in Caldwell. Along with me, our brother Dan and our sister Joanne were at home, too young and too scared by this tragedy to be of any significant help to our parents.

John and Bob at the hanger on the ranch. 2006.

Bob was called into the service about a month after Bill's death. Following his basic training, he was assigned to a large food supply depot in Virginia.

Family Members Who Served Valiantly in World War II

Like many others in the country, young men from the Skinner family willingly and bravely answered the call to defend their country and the citizens of the free world from the onslaught that was Germany, Italy, and Japan. Whether they served behind the lines or at the front, these men could be called on at any time to lay their lives on the line. Among those family members who were required to engage the enemy were the following young men.

Ernest Harold Skinner, son of Harold and Edith Skinner, was a second-year student at the College of Idaho in Caldwell when he received his draft notice in 1943. Ernest was an aviation cadet from September 1942 until May 1943 and was immediately commissioned as an officer and took further training at Roswell, New

Mexico, and Moses Lake, Washington, as a pilot of the mighty B-17 bomber.

He began his first tour of duty in England in November 1943 with the 447th Bombardment Group and flew twenty-five missions over Germany piloting the B-17, dodging enemy flak and German fighter planes. His B-17 bomber was named "Queen Patsy" in honor of his fiancée, Patsy Cochrane. Following this tour of duty, he was granted leave and returned to Caldwell where he and Patsy were married on June 30, 1944.

After their marriage, Ernest returned to England and flew an additional twenty-three bombing missions for a total of forty-eight missions over Germany, France, and Italy. Without exception, he and his crew were under heavy flak and attacks by enemy fighter planes while on these missions.

In addition to being an excellent pilot, Ernest was a good student. He gained a thorough knowledge of navigation and meteorology, along with general and local flying regulations. He served as Squadron Flight Operations Officer and alternated duties with higher echelon operations divisions.

Ernest was promoted to the rank of major at twenty-three, and became the youngest major in the Army Air Forces at that time. He served in the European theaters until December 6, 1945, when he reverted to inactive status. He was awarded the European Theater of Operations Ribbon, six Bronze Service Stars, the Air Medal, six Oak Leaf Clusters, and the Distinguished Flying Cross for exemplary duty.

Ernest left the service and attended Indiana University in Purdue, Indiana. He re-entered the U.S. Air Force in July 11, 1947, and completed a master's degree in aeronautical engineering at Purdue in 1948. He was assigned to be project engineer for the development of the B-52 bomber with special responsibility for cockpit design, and was designated as military personnel with Boeing on the project. The B-52 has been and continues to be a mainstay of the U. S. Air Force.

Ernest and his wife Patsy are parents of two daughters, Rebecca, born July 1, 1948, and Shirley, born March 19, 1950. Ernest died in the crash of a B-25 bomber on September 21, 1950, at Wright Patterson Field in Dayton, Ohio.

(We are indebted to John Sandmeyer, a nephew of Ernest H. Skinner, for providing the preceding information about his uncle and for information regarding his father, Steven Sandmeyer.)

Evan Gheen Jr. was the oldest son of Ruby Skinner Gheen and her husband Evan Sr. He grew up in and attended schools in Ontario, Oregon. He was in his second year at Monmouth College, in Monmouth, Illinois, when it became evident that he would become involved in the military. He enlisted in the reserve corps in hopes of retaining his college credits. He had completed his second year of college and returned to Ontario to help his father on the farm, when he received a wire to report to Salt Lake for active duty. He was sent to Tyler, Texas, for boot camp, and once there was selected with several others to report to Lafayette College in Pennsylvania. Over the period of a year, these men received a crash course in meteorology, aerial photography, and celestial navigation, and were sent to Louisiana for further training before being attached to the 84th Infantry Division.

Soon after the Invasion of Normandy, Evan found himself on a troop ship headed for England to provide replacements for soldiers lost in the D-Day invasion. The ship he was on collided with a tanker, resulting in the total loss of the tanker and its crew. The troop ship could still navigate and returned to New York for repairs. The troops were reassigned to another troop ship and embarked again for England. A week after he arrived in England, Evan was on a landing craft crossing the English Channel and landed in Normandy.

His company advanced through France, avoiding marked land mines and probing with bayonets for unmarked land mines. Within days, the company entered Aachen, Germany, and for the next month, they were in fierce combat with the German Army. There were heavy artillery shells flying everywhere, with skies filled with dogfighting planes. Each day brought slow advancement against the German Army.

In the midst of the conflagration and battle, an old man offered Evan a loaf of bread, which he shared with his fellow soldiers. In his memoirs, he told of how this act of kindness refreshed him, body and soul. The severe battle continued and by the end of the day there were only seventeen survivors in his company. All the officers in the company had been lost to the battle, and Evan ended up in command. It was December 1944 and in desperation, the German Army made this a last-ditch thrust through Belgium. It became known as the Battle of the Bulge, one of the fiercest battles ever engaged in any war.

Evan received a very serious abdominal injury when he was hit by shrapnel from a mortar shell and a shell that passed between his body and arm and buried itself up to the fins, but which thankfully did not explode. He was taken by jeep to a field hospital and then on to a hospital in Liege, Belgium, and later to a hospital in Paris. A short time later, he was transferred to a London hospital. The wing Evan was admitted to in the hospital in Liege was bombed and destroyed the night after he was sent to Paris. Evan was in fierce combat for over two and a half months from the time he arrived in Europe until he was wounded and hospitalized. During that period, the average life span for a soldier in combat was less than a week.

The town of Marche, where Evan was wounded, was the final point of advancement by the German Army in the Battle of the Bulge, and the turning point of World War II. Evan was proud that he had a part in the defeat of the German Army, in a battle that changed the course of history, and in the victory that brought an end to World War II.

Following his release from the army, Evan returned to Oregon and entered Oregon State University (OSU) in Corvallis. He lived with his sister Caroline and her husband Jeff Boyer who was also at OSU. Jeff had served with an engineering battalion in France, and while he had not been exposed to combat, he could and did relate to Evan's war memories and provided Evan with help and understanding.

Evan eventually returned to Ontario, Oregon, where he met and married Elizabeth Hartnett. They became parents to four children: Evan Pennock III, born July 9, 1950; Elizabeth Jane, born February 16, 1952; Timothy, born November 21, 1954; and Gregory Scott, born October 7, 1959.

(The preceding wartime experiences that Evan endured were related to us by his daughter, Jane Gheen Post.)

Steven Sandmeyer entered the Army Air Forces in June 1943 following an Air Force program in which he taught army personnel to fly gliders. The Air Force trained him in Mississippi and in Florida to be a mechanic on the B-24 Liberator bomber. While on leave following his training, Steve returned to Caldwell, Idaho, and married his fiancée, Eleanor Skinner, daughter of Harold and Edith Skinner, on July 21, 1944.

Steve was then sent by troop transport to the Far East theater of operations in China, Burma, and India where he was assigned to 317th

Troop Transport Squadron of the 2nd Air Force, and supervised the repair and maintenance of aircraft and monitored the mechanical functions of multi-engine aircraft in flight.

Steve flew from India over the Himalayan Mountains, known as "the Hump," delivering supplies to American and Chinese forces. He flew missions in Burma supporting Allied ground forces, sometimes behind enemy lines. The planes he was on routinely experienced Japanese antiaircraft fire, and on one occasion his plane was on the ground evacuating British soldiers when it came under fire from enemy ground forces.

When the war ended, Steve was stationed in Okinawa and served in the Occupation of Japan. He was awarded the Distinguished Flying Cross and many other decorations for his service to his country. Following his discharge from the U.S. Air Force, Steve worked as an airplane mechanic for several airlines and then took the position of Executive Pilot for The Morrison Knudsen Construction Company in Boise. He flew MK Company executives to construction sites in Alaska, Canada, the USA, and areas of South and Central America. Steve and Eleanor are the parents of two sons, Richard and John. Steve died in an airplane crash in Idaho on December 28, 1970.

Thomas G. (Tuck) Skinner, born August 16, 1917, was the oldest son of Thomas L. Skinner and his wife Violet. Following his graduation from Oregon State University in 1941 with a degree in animal husbandry, Tom was ordered to active duty as a commissioned officer in the U.S. Army. He served in the Alaska Defense Command for twenty-seven months, and in the South Pacific Theater of Operations for sixteen months where he was involved in the invasion of Peleliu. He was honorably discharged from the army with the rank of Major in Field Artillery.

Tom married Peggy Eubank on July 12, 1942. The couple had six daughters: Rae Marie, Rosanne, Mary DeMorris, Peggy Elizabeth, Sarah Ellen, and Mary Violet.

After the couple divorced, Tom married Jaci Lingle Shaver on August 6, 1969. They moved back to the Boise Valley in 1972 from Pennsylvania where Tom worked for the Department of Transportation. Tom passed away May 2, 2008, at his home in Caldwell, Idaho.

Bob home on furlough. Others from left to right: Dan, John, Mom (Johanna), and Dad (Kirt Sr.).

George Wilson, who married Mary Palmer, daughter of Irma Skinner Palmer and her husband Cecil, was a member of the U.S. Army Air Forces. He was a crew member and tail gunner on the B-17 heavy bomber. He flew many missions over Germany and the Continent during World War II. Returning from a mission, George's plane suffered heavy damage forcing the crew to bail out just as the plane reached the southern tip of the British Isles. He and his crew were rescued by local residents and returned to their base.

George and Mary returned to Spokane, Washington, where they opened a successful real estate business. George passed away in 2007. Mary survives him and lives in Portland with their daughter Patty.

Sara and Bob would marry and they, along with Dan and Cathy, would become head of the Skinner Ranch after Kirt and Johanna retired.

The War's End

Bob was called into the service about a month after Bill's death. Following his basic training, the army assigned him to a large food supply depot in Virginia, where he became acquainted with an attractive young lady named Sara Morgan, a native of Roanoke, Virginia.

After he was discharged and had returned to the ranch, Sara came to visit. Living in Oregon, few of Bob's family had been exposed to a southern drawl, and it took awhile before we quit saying *What?* and *Huh?* Sara was good-natured and in retaliation once remarked, "Y'all shuh talk funny hea'h." When Sara left to go back to Virginia we were fearful that we had chased her off, but Bob was able to entice her away from the Blue Ridge Mountains of "old Virginny" to come out West to the sagebrush country in eastern Oregon.

Left to right: Chris, Kirt Jr., and Joanne.

In the tradition of the Skinners, Bob and Sara set up housekeeping in the Skinners' big home. A bit wiser than the previous generation, however, they turned the two rooms that had at one time been the ballroom into an apartment. While this arrangement afforded them a bit more privacy as a newlywed couple, they were to be admired for their ability to cope with a grandparent, parents, and siblings— numbering from three to sometimes eight relatives or more at any given time—all of whom lived at home.

Their stress level was elevated one hundred times over following the birth of their son Robert Morgan. He instantly became the apple of the family's eye—and knew it. Any discipline from his parents was severely frowned upon by the rest of the family.

The Folks Who Fought the Home Battle

It is difficult to look back on the war years and try to remember just how the work got done. There was a small herd of cattle—too few, really, to make them pay—and they were cause for extra work. With few cattle to care for, grain and hay became our prime crops.

In those years, the summer haying crew consisted of Dad, my brothers Kirt and Dan, Dad's nephew Bert Palmer, and me. We were joined by Clifford Cline, Leonard Patterson, and Ed Lundholm, all of whom

Standing: Kirt Sr. Seated (left to right): Dan and John.

were older or family men, and two or three additional hired men, usually not healthy enough to be in the armed services, or too old or young to serve. In mid-September, Dan and Bert returned to their respective schools in Caldwell, Idaho, and Spokane, Washington, and Kirt Jr. returned to Oregon State.

To relieve the shortage of people to work on farms and ranches, the United States government brought a group of unemployed Jamaicans to the United States to aid in the harvest. These young men had been born and raised in the city of Kingston, Jamaica. One summer during the war, Dad contracted for five of these men to help stack the baled hay.

These fellows were polite and intelligent. Each had a great sense of humor, and all were the nicest young men one could ever ask for. They did, however, present problems. None had ever been near a farm or ranch, and neither did they know the difference between a pitchfork and a shovel, or even a hay bale from a cow. Moreover, they had no idea about the dangers of big farm equipment, yet every one of them wanted to drive the tractors. It was obvious they looked on their time in the states as a vacation lark and work wasn't about to get in the way of their fun.

SS

—*Will and his children. Standing (left to right): Verna, Hugh, Beata, Bill, and Irma. Seated (left to right): Harold, Ruby, Grandpa Will, Ella, and Kirt Sr. This picture was taken at Kirt's daughter's wedding (Christine and Bill Moore). 1949.*

27

SS

Search for History

As youngsters growing up on the ranch in Jordan Valley, it was necessary to drive cattle from the Skinner Ranch to the range in the spring, and back to the ranch in the fall. Most of these drives involved taking cattle very near the Ruby Ranch, earlier known as the Inskeep Station on the Skinner Toll Road. Our grandfather and father informed us that a small graveyard consisting of six graves lay very near the road, a short distance from the Ruby Ranch house and barns. These graves had been covered with small lava rocks to protect them from being trampled on by livestock, but through the years, many of the rocks had been scattered.

When Johanna, our mother, was first hired to teach Will and Ella's children at the Ruby Ranch, she would occasionally replace rocks around the edges of each grave out of respect for the deceased. If a fence had ever protected the gravesite, it had long since disappeared.

When cattle were driven by the graves, it was customary for my father or our grandfather to get ahead of the cattle and, with his horse, guard the graves to keep cattle away from them. At that time, it was known only that the graves held one of the Inskeep children, two soldiers, and a half-breed Indian. The names of the graves' occupants were unknown. Nell (Beers) Parks, the school bus driver and a member of the Beers family who owned the Ruby Ranch, informed students, one being Bob Skinner, the half-breed Indian was famous for some "unknown" reason.

The small gravesite came close to destruction in the late 1940s when the operator of a county road grader was doing maintenance on the road. Unaware of the location of the graves, the operator came very close to plowing them out. Dad, at the time a member of the Malheur County Road Maintenance Committee, was supervising the operation

Will watches over the Centennial Parade in Jordan Valley. He related a lot of family history to others, and Johanna diligently recorded his words. 1959.

and arrived just in time to divert the grader away from the graves. He subsequently moved the road farther to the west to protect them.

Johanna Skinner (right) was an avid historical researcher. Here she is at the location of the Trout Creek Station visiting with Mr. and Mrs. Gordon, the owners of the property at that time. Note the Hill Beachey barn in the background. Photo by Chris Skinner Moore.

Jean Baptiste Charbonneau, Infant Son of Sacagawea

As it turned out, in the late 1950s, a letter was directed to the Malheur County Historical Society from a gentleman named Clyde Porter in New Mexico. The county had yet to establish its historical society, and the letter was passed to Mr. Harry Sackett, the Malheur County Clerk. In the letter, Mr. Porter noted he had come across an obituary in Auburn, California, listing the death of a Jean Baptiste Charbonneau at the Inskeep Station in 1866. Mr. Porter asked if the County Historical Society had any knowledge or record of the death.

Sackett was unfamiliar with the history of the southern end of Malheur County, so he forwarded the letter to Will Skinner in Jordan Valley. Though interested, Will was by this time quite elderly so he handed the letter to his son and daughter-in-law, our parents Kirt and Johanna Skinner, for further investigation.

Dad and Mom, at this time semi-retired and both deeply interested in the history of southeastern Oregon and southwestern Idaho, and both avid historians in their own right, picked up the ball and ran with it. They researched every available record and conducted in-depth studies of any information they could find on Jean Baptiste Charbonneau. They traveled several western states and visited a number of libraries. Eventually, an obituary surfaced that had appeared in the *Owyhee Avalanche* newspaper printed in Silver City in 1866, listing a notification of the death of a Jean Baptiste Charbonneau. That information gave them more heart. Their study and their travels continued, but they were not without competition.

A person in Wyoming also discovered that a Jean Baptiste Charbonneau had been buried on the Wind River Reservation in Wyoming. His mother, also named Sacagawea, had died there at age ninety-five. This complication did not slow down the work of our parents. It was soon discovered this Jean Baptiste, son of the Wind River Sacagawea, had an entirely different personality and outlook on life, had little schooling, and was also a rounder and ne'er-do-well. He definitely was not the type of man whom Captain William Clark had given the name "Pomp" and had provided with such a fine education.

When Meriwether Lewis and William Clark began their historic trip investigating western America in early 1804, the party made their way up the Missouri River as far as a Mandan Indian camp in North Dakota. They wintered there and took on supplies and equipment for the continued trek to the west coast of the United States.

They also hired a French Canadian guide named Toussaint Charbonneau. Toussaint had recently bought and then married a young Shoshone Indian slave who had been taken captive when just a youngster, and had been raised in the Mandan Camp. Her name was Sacagawea, and she was expecting the birth of a child when she and her husband joined the expedition. The birth of this child would eventually become one of the most famous births of the nineteenth century.

The couple named the boy Jean Baptiste, and the infant accompanied the Lewis and Clark Expedition. He was carried on his mother's backboard all the way to the mouth of the Columbia River and a year later on the return trip to St. Louis, Missouri. Jean Baptiste became the apple of Captain William Clark's eye. He nicknamed the child "Pomp," and upon returning to Missouri, educated him in the best St. Louis schools. As a young adult, Pomp

Kirt and Johanna were instrumental in identifying this important grave site near the Ruby Ranch. It was of Sacagawea's son, Jean Baptiste Charbonneau.

accompanied a visiting German prince on his return to Germany. There he studied and toured Europe for six years before returning to the United States. While in Germany he became fluent in six languages.

Well-educated, at ease in most social situations, and with an adventuresome wanderlust, Jean Baptiste Charbonneau led a varied life. He was, at one time or another, a mountain man, a guide who led the Mormon Battalion from New Mexico to San Diego, a miner, a fur trapper, and an *alcalde* (similar to a mayor) of San Luis Reye, California. As an *alcalde*, he did not like the rules imposed on him in dealing with the Indian population. He resigned because he believed the Indians were being treated like slave labor. The next we know of him he had joined several other men and was headed for the mines in Montana.

After crossing the Owyhee River, Jean Baptiste Charbonneau developed pneumonia and died at the Inskeep Station. He was buried there in 1866. It is probable his grave was the first of the six graves in the tiny graveyard located about eighteen miles west of Jordan Valley. In time, it was discovered that the other graves contained the bodies of two men, cause of death unknown, and two children, one of whom belonged to the Inskeep family.

Our mother and father spearheaded the search for information on Charbonneau. With the involvement and assistance of The Oregon Historical Society and the Bureau of Land Management, it was proven beyond any doubt that the grave at Inskeep Station is that of Jean Baptiste Charbonneau, son of Sacagawea and Toussaint Charbonneau. The site was dedicated on August 6, 1971, and named as an Oregon State Park. A fence was built around the little cemetery to protect it.

Following the death of our mother in June 1972, the following letter was sent to the Editor of the *Idaho Statesman* by E. G. Chuinard, M.D., Chairman, and Irving Anderson, Member of the Oregon Lewis and Clark Trail Heritage Foundation Committee.

Ontario Argus Observer
Editor:
The members of the Oregon Lewis and Clark Heritage Foundation are saddened to learn of the passing of Mrs. Johanna Skinner of Jordan Valley. Most of our members did not know Mrs. Skinner, but we as well as most Americans everywhere have been greatly enriched by her dedicated interest and research into the life, death, and burial place of Jean Baptiste Charbonneau, son of Sacajawea. Her efforts together with those of her devoted husband, Kirt Skinner, have contributed in a major way, to the recorded history of the Oregon Country and the American West.

It was significantly to the credit of Mrs. Skinner's unusual sense of history, and her family's knowledge of the legends of Jordan Valley, that the unclaimed grave of a remarkable American resting in an obscure burial plot at the Ruby Ranch, Danner, Oregon, was found. Moreover, through the continued endeavors of the Skinner family, and vol-

unteer help from many persons, firms, and organizations together with assistance from Malheur County, the State of Oregon, and BLM, the Charbonneau gravesite has been properly preserved, marked and protected.

Those of us close to the great drama of the Lewis and Clark Expedition share in the deep feeling of satisfaction enjoyed by Johanna Skinner in realizing the fulfillment of her many years of historical research. Her special efforts, together with those of her husband, helped create a lasting mark in the saga of frontier America, for which we shall be forever grateful.

Sincerely Yours
E. G. Chuinard, M.D., Chairman
Irving Anderson, Member

Going Back to Scotland at Last

Our mother had arrived in America in 1909 at twenty years of age. In 1953, forty-four long and eventful years later, she found herself excitedly making plans to return to her native Scotland to visit family and friends. Sadly, the intervening years had decimated both. Though a number of her old friends had survived, only Johanna's sisters Jessie and Ella, along with Ella's husband and their two daughters and a son, were still living. Even so, she could barely keep her heart from leaping from her chest in excitement. She had dreamed of this day for so many years.

Travel plans did not progress smoothly, however. Jordan Valley did not yet have the convenience of phone service to homes, and to make matters worse, the coronation of the new Queen of England was scheduled to occur in 1953. Reservations for travel accommodations were difficult to arrange. Son Kirt, who was living in Portland, had access to both phones and travel services and was able to arrange passage on a luxury freighter out of San Francisco.

With travel arrangements solved, passports were applied for and received. Their luxury freighter would sail from San Francisco, California, to Antwerpe, Belgium, via Santa Barbara and the Panama Canal. Our mother's diary on the day of their departure offers only a small hint to her excitement. The wait was excruciating but at last it was time to drive to Jordan Valley to meet their bus, scheduled to depart at midnight.

The entire family escorted Mom, Dad, and our sister Joanne to Jordan Valley where they boarded the Boise Winnemucca Bus. They arrived in San Francisco the next afternoon. After spending several days with Dad's sister Beata, her husband Norman Owings, and their family in Oakland, they embarked from San Francisco, sailing out through the Golden Gate, enroute to Santa Barbara, California.

While their ship took on additional cargo in Santa Barbara, Bill and Harold Palmer, sons of Kirt's sister Irma Palmer, and Harold's wife Beverly, toured and entertained the three travelers while they awaited their ship's departure. A week later they were back on board, headed for the Panama Canal. As usual, our mother's calm exterior, belied the thrill and anticipation of going home at last.

Thirty-three days later, their ship reached Antwerpe. There they boarded a channel boat that ferried them to Dover, England, where they entrained to London. They continued by train to Glasgow and visited Mom's niece Angela and her husband Donald Weir. Angela is the daughter of Johanna's oldest sister, Ella. They spent several days with the Weir's in Glasgow before boarding another train for the north of Scotland and Mom's home village of Lairg. While in Glasgow, however, they received word that they were to bypass Lairg and go on to Kintradwell, the farm home of mom's oldest sister Ella and her family near the village of Brora, Sutherlandshire.

Their daughter, my sister Joanne Owens, contributed the rest of this chapter, describing our mother as they arrived in the north of Scotland.

ooooo

Forty-four years had gone by since she had cast her eyes on or had set foot on the soil in the Highlands of Scotland. She had a pleasant faraway look and seemed very deep in thought. Her blue eyes looking from one side window of the train to the other, she took in each view that the windows framed. A high ben (mountain) in the distance, the moors blooming with heather, contented sheep and Kiley cattle grazing on rolling green fields outlined with rock fences, and crofters' homes nestled in this pristine landscape. She appeared to be absorbing every tiny detail of this land she had longed to return to for so many years.

As the train approached her home village of Lairg and her childhood home of Drumnahaving, she obviously became a bit more restless. She was not clear why this change in travel plans had been made. Her hope had been to stop at Drumnahaving and she was disappointed in the change of plans. She remembered the train track went right by Drumnahaving on the way to Lairg and then on to Brora and her sister Ella's home.

The train came to a stop at the station in Lairg and quite without warning Mom jumped up and announced, "I'm getting off this train this minute," and she turned and left the car. Dad, surprised and scared, tried to call her back saying, "Jo, you can't do that, the train will leave without you, you simply cannot do that!" But she did, and she stepped down onto the platform. There on the platform stood her youngest sister Jessie, only a youngster of ten when our mother had left home, her arms held wide open in greeting. The sisters had not seen each other in forty-four years. There was no time for words, just for tears and a long embrace. The train conductor suddenly brought this tender moment to a halt with the announcement "All Aboard."

Back on the train tears continued to fill her eyes. She rushed to a window in our car as the train slowly moved away. This was her home, her native land, and these were tears of joy and happiness instead of longing and of loneliness as in years past during lonesome nights in a far-off land. The two sisters continued to wave until they were out of sight of each other.

As the train began to gather speed, there in the train window, was her childhood home, "There's Drumnahaving and the River Shin!" she exclaimed excitedly. Drumnahaving was now the home of her sister Jessie, whom she had just leaped from the train to embrace, and just beyond the home a short distance, the River Shin flowed deep and blue. Then came the memories, those wonderful, long-forgotten memories, rolling and tumbling through her mind, one coming on top of another. Memories of playing on the banks of the River Shin, of her carefree childhood, of her parents, her older sister, her two brothers and little sister, all dead now except for the two sisters she had come home to see at last.

Memories of childhood friends, and schoolmates, so many now gone. Of Drumnahaving ('home by the water'), constructed of rock in the year 1520, sturdy and strong, lived in and loved by the Murray clan for over four hundred years. But the train rolled right on to its destination, the home of her older sister Ella in Brora, on the banks of the North Sea. Ella was married to a gentleman named Alex Murray. The couple had two daughters, the oldest named Helen, the younger named Angela, and a son, John. It was Angela and her husband Donald Weir whom the travelers had just visited in Glasgow. Helen was married to Norman Ledingham, and they also lived on the family farm known as Kintradwell.

Mom was visibly disappointed at first that their itinerary took them beyond her family home to the town of Brora and her sister Ella's family home. Yet, the nearer the train came to the little town, the more her excitement grew. The train ride presented beautiful landscapes of northern Scotland and it became easy to understand why she had so often talked of her love of the Highlands graced by castles and fields with contented cattle and sheep. Our mother owned the enviable ability to draw on the beauty of the moment to describe it so her audience could see that same beauty.

When at last the train came to a stop at Brora Station and they stepped down onto the platform, a handsome young man dressed in a Scottish kilt stepped forward and greeted them with a heavy Scottish burr, rolling his Rs as only a Scotsman can do, and very possibly exaggerated to give Mom, who had not heard that burr for so many years, a thrill, and surely to impress Dad and Joanne. "Welcome to Scotland, I'm Norrrman, Helen's husband. I apologize; Ella couldn't come as therrre wouldna be rrroom for everyone to rrride to Kintrrradwell, but she is anxiously awaiting your arrrrival. Your luggage will be quite safe. I will immediately rrrreturrrn for it after I deliverr you folks to Kintrrradwell."

The travelers arrived at the Murray home to find Ella in the driveway waiting to greet this sister she had not seen for over forty years. Beside her stood her daughter Helen and Helen's six-year-old daughter, Joan. Joan was quite fascinated with this tall, lean rancher wearing a Stetson hat—an honest to goodness real live cowboy from Oregon's High Desert.

It was evident from the hugs and tears, that the intervening years and stored up emotions and memories were a bit overwhelming for these two sisters. Tears came fast and furious, followed by the process of becoming reacquainted and catching up on each others lives. It was very moving to observe, to watch as the years began to melt away. The Murray home overflowed hospitality, from the delicious home-cooked meal that evening to the bedrooms' wonderful view of the North Sea, so different from the views from our home on the Skinner Ranch on the high desert of Oregon.

There followed many days of travel, taking in the sights of this ancient country, from Kintradwell to the windy, rainy, and cold extreme northern tip of Scotland, not too far distant from the artic circle, then through the hinterland with its ancient castles, thatched-roof cottages, and neat farms. They attended the Highland games, including but not limited to the hammer throw, the Highland Fling dance contests, and the tossing of the caber, a test to see how far a man can throw a heavy log. They saw horse races and pony races and cattle shows, which were of great interest to Dad. Much like our American county fairs, the Highland games had something for everyone.

Back at the Murray home after our travels, we would gather in the living room to visit and talk. It would not be long before Ella's husband Alex would speak up and say "Get the booooks," and the Bibles would be passed out to each person. He would announce which passage of the Bible was to be read by him that evening while the rest followed along.

After about ten days, the travelers made plans to return to Drumnahaving and the old family home in Lairg, and what proved to be another highly emotional moment for our mother. Were there tears? Of course, there were tears! She stood very quietly for several minutes hardly moving, murmuring not a word, eyes brimming full, while she took in this beloved old home where she had been born and raised and of which she had dreamed so many dreams of returning to once again.

We were treated with the kindest hospitality and love of family during the several months of our visit to the Highlands of Scotland. Each day new memories arose. "Remember the time…?" "Do you remember the name of the girl who…?" "Whatever happened to…?" Every single day for two months our mother reveled in the love of her sisters and their families, old friends, and old haunts.

Mom's sister, Jessie, as well as the whole country of Scotland, was still suffering from the effects of World War II. Times were still hard and modern ways not yet easy to come by. Jessie, an excellent cook, was still cooking on an old pre-war wood cooking range. Our mother, who had at one time had her own doubts about cooking with electricity, decided to have a shiny new electric range installed for her sister to cook on.

Pleasant days were filled with afternoon teas and visiting friends and relatives. And sadly, each day brought closer their departure, the day they would return to the ship that would take them back to America and the high desert of Oregon, now her adopted land and also one which she loved.

SS

28

SS

The Post-World War II Years

In 1946, Jordan Valley was poised to enter a period of modernization. There was great excitement in the community. The war had ended, the economy was improving, and the Idaho Power Company had introduced electricity into the Jordan Valley area. In anticipation, our parents contracted to have the big house wired for electricity, and at the same time did a fair amount of remodeling. After twenty-nine years, it was no longer necessary to re-charge the carbide light system every month.

Along with the convenience of electricity, a full bathroom was added on the main floor and another on the second floor. That ended the long walk down the path to the outdoor facility on cold, dark nights.

A coal furnace was installed to heat the entire house, not just the living room. No longer were there intricate, naturally produced blossoms, fronds, and feathers from frozen vapor on the bedroom windows on cold winter mornings. Like ice crystals on blades of grass, these crystallized window pictures were priceless—exquisitely beautiful but temporary. But this we must say, during the years without heat in the bedrooms we did not take a great amount of time looking at those pictures. It was out of the bed, into our clothes, and down the stairs to find a hot stove.

Along with modernization, our mother bought an automatic washing machine and dryer, a refrigerator and freezer, and a very nice electric range for the kitchen. She was adamant, however, that her old wood-and-coal cooking range remain in its place. She was noted for her prowess in the kitchen and for her mouth-watering recipes. She just didn't trust the new electric cooking stove. She felt she had far more ability to control the heat with a stick of sagebrush or a lump of coal. After several months of use, she finally gave in to the convenience

Mom and Dad, and all of us! Left to right: John, Mom (Johanna), Kirt Jr., Dan, Chris, Dad (Kirt Sr.), Joanne, Bob, and Bob's wife Sara.

Bob cranking the car.

Kirt Jr. on the buck rake.

Joanne's wedding day. Standing (left to right): Chris, Kirt Jr., Bob, and Joanne. Seated (left to right): Dan, Mom, Dad, and John.

of electricity and allowed the removal of the old kitchen range. She complained, though, that her angel food cakes, for which she was quite famous, were never as light and fluffy as when they were baked in the oven of the old range.

Still lacking in the remote community was the telephone. If anyone needed to make a telephone call, it was necessary to drive thirteen miles into town to make it. If an urgent call came in for a member of the community, someone in town had to deliver the message. Installation of telephone service to all residents in 1963 brought as much or more excitement to the community as did electricity in 1946.

With the addition of electricity and the telephone, Jordan Valley, Oregon, had joined the rest of the world. It is still remote, but the remoteness is part of its attraction and charm. With today's excellent roads, automobiles, and planes most necessary services are available within an hour or less.

Ambulance and emergency care in the Jordan Valley area was established in the mid 1950s following the tragic drowning deaths of two brothers. My niece, Jocele Skinner, M.D., daughter of Dan and Cathy Skinner, supervises the medical facility in Jordan Valley and works with a Physician's Assistant in the ongoing care of minor illnesses there. Dr. Skinner works out of a rather large clinic facility in Caldwell on most days and visits the Jordan Valley clinic as time permits. On those days that she can be in residence locally she sees patients who have the more serious complaints.

A Change in Ranch Ownership

Following many years with total responsibility for the ranch operation, our parents were ready to give up active management. In 1953, they offered brothers Bob and Dan a lease proposal on the real estate and an agreement on the purchase of cattle and machinery. Although the brothers accepted, the operation continued as S.K. Skinner & Sons. Bob and Dan bought the property from our parents in 1966. Bob Jr. became a partner in 1972, soon after graduating from the College of Idaho in Caldwell, Idaho. In 1979, they incorporated the operation under the name Skinner Ranches, Inc.

With growth and expansion taking place, and a lack of grazing privileges always a limiting factor, on March 1, 1991, the Corporation pur-

Kirt and Johanna's "boys." Left to right: Bob, Kirt Jr., Dan, and John. They are watching Bob Jr. fly a toy airplane.

chased the ranch which Silas Skinner had leased in 1882 as a base for his trotting horses.

Acquiring that ranch added significantly to the Corporation's grazing privileges. It brought with it some of the highest producing native hay meadows in the Jordan Valley area. The production and value of this property have been greatly improved with the addition of an irrigation well. Further dimension and property value were enhanced in 1998, when the Corporation purchased shares in a grazing cooperative.

With mechanization relieving labor problems, emphasis was now on building up the quality and numbers of the cattle herd to the point of supporting the operation. Most of the older herd was sold due to deteriorating quality; only a few of the best remained. The purchase of two different bunches of cows in the mid-1950s had helped to put the ranch back in the cow business to some degree, but it was not fully stocked until about 1960. We bought and fed weaner calves through fall and winter, then pastured them during the summer using ranch-produced feed. The ranch had yet to reach its optimum herd size, so excess pasture, hay, and grain were sold.

Kirt and Johanna on one of their few vacations—this time they are in the Redwoods. Circa 1936.

During this period, there was continued development and improvement of the existing land. Fields were leveled to increase production and to conserve irrigation water; approximately ten miles of fence were built around the ranch's grazing allotment; and the dam in Jordan Creek that diverts water for irrigation was almost totally reconstructed from lava rock and concrete, which has greatly improved the ability to control irrigation water. It is no longer necessary to wade neck-deep into the maelstrom of Jordan Creek in late spring to pack rocks up to the dam. That is a good thing.

Our dad, with brothers Bob and Dan, operated the ranch under the name of S.K. Skinner & Sons. In about 1953 our dad and mother had started to make plans for the trip to Scotland to visit our mother's remaining family and friends, and the old Murray home where she grew up. Following many years with total responsibility of the ranch operation, our parents were ready to give up active management. They offered the brothers a lease proposal on the real estate and an agreement on the purchase of the cattle and machinery which they accepted, although the operation continued as S.K. Skinner & Sons. Eventually Bob and Dan bought the property from our parents and incorporated the operation under the name Skinner Ranches, Inc.

The Loss of a Great Historian

Our mother, Johanna, suffered a heart attack and died in 1972 at eighty-three years of age. She was and continues to be a major influence on this family. The "wee Scottish lady" also made a lasting mark on the Jordan Valley area during her active life, first as a teacher, then as the wife and helpmate to a cattle rancher, and the mother of seven children.

*—Mom. 1943. She is wearing the
pin Bob sent her from the Army.*

Johanna was an avid and well-informed historian of the surrounding area in which she lived. She had many and varied interests to occupy her mind. She loved to study the geological makeup of the land. She was fascinated with rocks, and her home hearth was formed from rocks and stones she had gathered from the world over. She knew where each one came from, and the way the forces of nature had formed it. She instilled this interest in her grandchildren to the extent that many of them, now adults, still have collections of rocks in their parents' attics.

Johanna would describe ice crystals that glistened brightly in the sun on a frosty morning as the most precious of all jewels; they were fragile, they were temporary, and even kings could not own them because, with the warming sun, they would soon fade and disappear. No amount of money could preserve them.

When she wrote, she had the enviable ability to use her words to make pictures. She could bring the reader to the exact place of her description, and they would see what she saw. She saw beauty in all things, the trees, the desert, and her beloved ocean. On a trip to the Oregon Coast, she walked across the beach holding my arm to steady herself because she said, "I want to wash my hands in the sea just one more time." It was her last.

Her death was a huge loss to her husband as well as her family and the community. While her husband and family always came first, she had a deep and abiding interest in the history of southwestern Idaho and of eastern Oregon. She will long be remembered as the first historian of Jordan Valley and the surrounding community.

Her extensive collection of historical knowledge and the diligent work she and Dad did to prove the location and the discovery of the Jean Baptiste Charbonneau gravesite near the Skinner Ranch was celebrated across the land. Following her death, Dad continued to live in their home on the ranch under the watchful eye of his sons, Bob and Dan, and their families.

The Apple Blossom Box

Hidden away by our mother in a private corner of a closet in the big house, was a box covered with apple blossom paper, square, about fourteen inches wide and long, and about four inches deep. When the big house was reduced in size and remodeled, the box was removed and again stored in a private place of honor in her new home. There it remained until after the deaths of both of our parents.

Brothers Bob and Dan and sister Joanne were present the day the box was opened in Bob's home. Bob had advised his wife Sara that it would be a good idea to have a box of Kleenex handy for the three gathered around the table. For over sixty-plus years that little box covered in apple blossom paper had held mementos of treasured moments in the life of Johanna Skinner. There were letters bearing sad messages of the death of a brother, the victim of World War I, and of the death of her parents. A cable from Scotland bore sad tidings of the death of another brother from pneumonia.

And there were letters to our Dad. Did the three present that day dare to read them? The deep feelings of intrusion into the private lives of our parents that day caused that bit of hesitation. There followed discussion of what the next step should be. Dan suggested that if our mother didn't want anyone to see these private things, she would have destroyed them long ago.

The letters were written in 1916, 1917, and 1918, with some more current. Our mother had moved to Portland for several months while making preparations for their wedding. In a letter to Dad who was in Jordan Valley, she told him about a letter she had received from her parents in Scotland, after she had informed her family of her wedding plans. There were other letters from her family in Scotland, too. There was talk of war, of sons and brothers going into the army, and there were letters of concern that their wedding plans might possibly be disrupted because of this war going on in Europe.

They had made their wedding plans for October 16, 1917. There were letters in the box written during October and November 1918, while our mother spent several months in Boise awaiting the birth of her firstborn son, William Murray Skinner. Those same letters referred to the fear and panic surrounding the flu epidemic of 1918.

There were other letters that had been exchanged between the two when Dad was in Portland on ranch business, letters written during the war years when things were the blackest, and letters written when it was almost a sure thing the ranch was lost to bankruptcy. And there were letters from Dad with words of love, hope, and appreciation, words of promise to a supportive wife, and love of family from a husband nearly overwhelmed by the negative attitude of their creditors.

Also, tucked tenderly away in a small compartment in the Apple Blossom Box, was a corsage. Dry as dust, yet still fairly well preserved. With it were two small seashells, and a postcard with a picture of Seaside, Oregon. There was also a train ticket for two from Portland, to Ontario, Oregon. It struck those who were there that day, that the bouquet placed tenderly in the box so many years ago was the bouquet she wore on her wedding dress the day they were married. Mementos of their honeymoon at Seaside, their trip back to eastern Oregon evidenced by train tickets. Was that Kleenex box necessary the day the Apple Blossom Box was opened? Yes, indeed it was.

The Life Story of Silas Kirtland Skinner, Sr.

Silas Kirtland Skinner, my father, was not a man who made a splash or put himself forward in social or formal settings. He could be tough one on one, if necessary, but was uncomfortable standing in front of a crowd. Listeners could detect a slight quaver in his voice. Seated, he could stand his ground against the finest orator. He was not loud, he seldom swore, but when he did, things usually happened.

Case in point: Dad served on a number of school boards and committees at the local, county, and state levels, one of which was the Malheur County Road Board. This board acted in an advisory capacity to the county court. In one meeting, they were debating the dispersal of tax revenues for repair and maintenance of roads in the county. Dad argued in the court that the more populated northern end of the county was unfairly receiving more than their proportionate share of funding for road maintenance, while the southern end of the county, which he represented, was receiving less.

Another member of the committee spoke up and proclaimed, "Those people who choose to live out there in the sticks in Jordan Valley don't deserve to get more money for road maintenance." That comment was a bit more than Dad could tolerate. He jumped up and gave the following three-word speech; "Well God *damn!*" He realized what he had said and was so embarrassed that he sat down. The courtroom became very quiet for a moment. The Judge broke the silence with the statement, "I'm with Kirt Skinner on this." Dad had proven that it is un-

—*Dad. 1943.*

necessary to make a long, impassioned speech to make an important point.

That true story describes Dad being quietly but deeply involved, and very effective. He was born on November 27, 1892, on the "Old Skinner Place" and was the first of nine children who would be born to Will and Ella Skinner. A short time later Harold, their second child was born and family moved to Caldwell, Idaho, where his sister Ruby was born and then later to Napa, California. Dad and Harold attended elementary school in Napa for several years, after which the family returned to Jordan Valley. Dad's formal education ended then, except for a short year in his early twenties when he attended Heald's Business College in Napa, California. In later years, our mother often said that his total school experience could be crowded into less than four years.

The limited education he received did not curtail his ability or his ambition to educate himself. He was an avid reader and taught himself to work complex mathematical problems as easily as his college-educated offspring. His handwriting was very legible and his syntax perfect. With little formal training he wrote excellent personal letters, and his handwritten business letters were cogent and to the point. He kept current with local, national, and world events through newspapers, radio, and, later, television.

He sought to expand his vocabulary by studying the dictionary for long hours during the evening after it was too dark to work outside. He was adept at completing crossword puzzles and took pride in completing them in ink. Among his many interests were his family, the successful operation of the ranch, and the local history of the country he lived in.

Dad, having grown up in the ranching business, quite naturally made cattle ranching his vocation. Following the trauma caused by the financial disaster that confronted his father, our Dad and Mother set out to bring order out of chaos. They proved to be an excellent team. There were tough and disappointing years in the beginning, and backbreaking work for both. There were long hours day in and day out, and times when the midnight oil was burned in order to keep on top of the business. There were discouraging words from bankers who didn't understand the cattle industry, and who were themselves scared of the economy. In time, these bankers realized the two people they were dealing with were honest to a fault, and that their word was their bond.

One thing stands out among many when describing this man who was our father. It is not easy to get one's arms around his qualities and the contributions he made to family, to his community, to all of Malheur County and beyond. Each page of his history reveals another kindness, another good deed done, another contribution—not necessarily in dollars, although he did that, too.

There was no big talk, no braggadocio. With his quiet and thoughtful demeanor, he gained and returned the respect of his neighbors. He had tremendous respect for the land on which they made their living, and when it eventually came time to take drastic action lest the rangeland be totally depleted for all time, Dad made the first move.

His love for his wife and his family came first. Closely following came his love and respect for his parents and his siblings. Somewhere mixed in among all of those was his tremendous love for the Skinner Ranch. He was a hard worker, on the job early and late. With the exception of the brief time when he attended school in California, he hadn't lived anywhere else, and never had any desire to. He was conditioned by the problems that had previously faced his parents, and he and our mother vowed never to allow themselves to get in that position again. Because of those experiences, he learned to be frugal and to conserve.

Yet there was another side to Kirt Skinner. He was progressive. Like most successful agricultural people, he was a strong environmentalist and a strong member of the community. He believed that what was taken from the land should be returned. He knew his future and his family's future, as well as the future of the livestock industry, depended on the intelligent husbandry of the land. He simply believed and followed the precept that it was important to make the world a better place to live.

A lifelong rancher and cattleman, he was a charter member of the Malheur Livestock Association and a member of the Oregon and National Cattlemen's Associations. He served on the Oregon Cattleman's Association Executive Board for a number of years. He was honored as "Cattleman Of The Year" and given a lifetime membership in the Malheur County Cattlemen's Association. He was a member of the first Jordan Valley District Grazing Advisory Board, and later of the Vale district, as well as serving as President of the Soldier Creek Grazing Association.

He was active in the Grange and Farm Bureau. Among the many honors he received was of being chosen Grand Marshal of the Oregon Trail Rodeo in Vale, Oregon, in 1957. He was an active supporter and served on the board of the Jordan Valley Methodist Church, and both he and our mother were charter members of the Malheur County Historical Society, and members of the Owyhee County and Idaho Historical Societies.

Dad had grown up in the ranching and cattle business. He also knew how to farm and to get the most from the land. Yet at the same time, he knew this land he lived on and nurtured was *not* farming country. Jordan Valley was cattle country. The seasons were short and the climate not conducive to annual crops. Financiers were more attuned to farming. When World War II began and agricultural workers became practically nonexistent, it became prudent for the cattle herd to be sold and for the ranch to bale and sell the hay.

Dad also had an avocation. With minimal education himself, he had a strong passion for education, not only for his own family but also for all the children in the communities in Oregon's Malheur County, in which he lived. He served on the Board of the local School District 69 at Danner, Oregon; the Jordan Valley Union High School Board; and the Malheur County School Board (Intermediate Education District) as the representative in the vast and far-flung rural corners of sparsely populated Malheur County, from the Oregon-Nevada border in the south, west to the Harney County line, then north to the extreme northwest corner of Malheur County, excluding only the more heavily populated northeastern areas of the county.

His total combined years of service to education in Malheur Country amounted to over sixty-two years when he retired. At his retirement banquet, County School Superintendent Leroy Paulsen advised those present that one of Kirt Skinner's finest hours was when he managed to overturn the Oregon State Department of Education (OSDE) on a case in which it had decided to terminate the McDermitt School District in southern Malheur County.

The small town of McDermitt straddles the Oregon-Nevada state line, and a good school existed on the Nevada side. The OSDE decided to consolidate the school on the Oregon side of McDermitt with the

Arock and the Jordan Valley Districts, both nearly a hundred miles distant from McDermitt. This was a decision made by a group of people in the distant state capital of Salem.

The members of the OSDE did not understand the distances that divide rural communities in eastern Oregon. Their unpopular decision would have required schoolchildren to commute nearly one hundred miles twice daily, or for their parents to give up employment and move closer to the schools.

With a school just across the state line in Nevada, and for many of the Oregon students just across the street, Dad proposed that the students on the Oregon side be tuitioned into the Nevada school. After a long battle, the OSDE finally gave in and allowed the transfer to Nevada. It is doubtful the members of the OSDE would require their own children make such a commute. Where decisions detrimental to children were involved, this decision by the OSDE would be the typical sort of battle Dad would take great pleasure in engaging in and winning.

It would surprise those who consider themselves to be environmentalists that Kirt Skinner loved and respected the land and was a strong and dedicated conservationist, as are most successful agricultural people. He didn't talk the husbandry of the land; he lived it daily. When the rangelands became depleted due to overuse, he was among the first to recognize that changes must be made. He was the first cattle rancher in the area to make voluntary reductions in the number of cattle he grazed on Soldier Creek grazing unit of the Bureau of Land Management. He was a charter member of the Taylor Grazing Act Advisory Board for the Jordan Valley District.

He was among the first to realize it was not only the cattle but also the many bands of itinerant sheep grazing through the area, along with the thousands of rapidly multiplying wild and domestic horses, which were overgrazing the rangelands.

Kirt Skinner was a remarkable man, and on October 16, 1917, in Portland, Oregon, he married a remarkable woman, Johanna Murray. It was a rare occurrence that an unmarried schoolteacher who came into the community, escaped marriage to a member of the community. So it was that Kirt and Johanna became husband and wife. The couple became parents to seven children—five boys and two girls. Their marriage lasted for sixty-six years over which they forged a powerful, loving, and effective partnership.

Together they turned near disaster into a successful and productive ranching operation. Each of their children was taught the principles by which their parents lived. The love of that old ranch was instilled in each and every one of their children, and it will live in our hearts till death. Even after these many passing years, we can still look back with the pride in our work ethic and in ourselves, and of the imparted knowledge that we have all called upon so many times, whether in the ranching business or other occupations.

Five years after the death of our mother on June 30, 1972, Dad married a longtime family friend in Portland, Doris Burgess, in October 1979. They made their home on the ranch in Jordan Valley until his death on September 7, 1983. Following Dad's death, Doris moved to Eugene, Oregon, to be near her daughter. Doris passed away in September 1994.

SS

29

Preserving Our Past

The care and management of the big house that Will and Ella had built had become too difficult for our parents as they were feeling the pains of age. A much smaller, more comfortable, modern home had been built for them, and they moved in 1965. In 1966, they had celebrated their fiftieth wedding anniversary in their new home with several hundred friends, relatives, and acquaintances attending from all across the western United States.

Soon after they had moved, demolition began on the top two stories of the big old home, and a great deal of the ground floor was reconstructed. It had been the center of many family and community functions from its construction to its demise. With it went fifty years of memories of fun times and sad times; of music and laughter and tears; of children grown up, married, and now gone; and a new family to fill the halls and rooms with children, music, and laughter.

The ladies who were responsible for the care and cleaning of the old monster may have remembered it quite differently. To them it meant cooking, cleaning, and housework, and the next day, more cooking, more cleaning, and more housework. It is doubtful those ladies who had the duty of keeping it presentable shed any tears. More aptly, they would have cheered. The old home had served its purpose well, but it was time for its demise.

It was about this time that many of us began to recognize that what we were observing and involved in with the big house was representative of the cycle of life. The new must—no, it *will*—replace the old, whether it be a life, a home, a business, or a family. Time marches on, and with it the dynamics of our lives.

Following their marriage in 1973, Dan and his wife Cathy were the first couple to occupy the remaining portion of the old home.

The first of their two daughters was born while they lived there. Jocele, born August 9, 1974, was followed several years later by Elizabeth, born January 25, 1978. The remaining portion of Will and Ella's big old house was not designed for a family, however, and in 1983, following the death of our dad, Dan and Cathy and their two girls moved into Dad's home.

Bob and Sara's firstborn, Bob Jr., and his wife Karen and their four youngsters were feeling the pinch for more space and the remaining portion of the old ranch house came back into play. Once again it came under the hammers and saws of re-modelers, and another comfortable and much more convenient home arose in its place. Bob and Karen moved into their own home on the ranch, near ranch headquarters, soon after their marriage. They were the first generation on the ranch not to live in the same house as their parents following their marriage. One wag has suggested that perhaps the newlyweds' parents finally wised up.

Remember Christmas in the Old House

As this chapter is being written, the Christmas season is approaching, with every newspaper doubled in size with advertisements, every television program so riddled with advertising one finds it difficult to follow the story line. People are making plans for parties and other festivities. There are Christmas trees, frantic shopping trips, and those colorful, flashy lights inside and out. Caroler's go from house to house in neighborhoods and can be heard on street corners and in the malls. Trees of all shapes, sizes, and colors stand in picture windows and yards as if to compete with nature itself. With the anticipation of gifts and family gathering, the meaning behind this day can easily be pushed to the background. For all but children, the actual arrival of Christmas Day can be anticlimactic as parents breathe a sigh of relief that the hubbub is drawing to a close.

But it wasn't always that way, at least not on the eastern edge of the Oregon high desert in the little community of Jordan Valley. We didn't have fancy electric lights at our house, and our tree didn't spend a month in the window before Christmas Day. Actually, our Christmas tree had no lights. Did we have anticipation and intrigue? Indeed we did!

Will and Ella, in all probability following Sackett family traditions, locked the double doors between the living room and the dining room of their big house shortly after Thanksgiving. In later years, our parents locked those same doors, but it really didn't make any difference who

*Santa always
made it to
the ranch on
Christmas Eve.*

was in charge; children were excluded from entering the living room for the month of December.

A child could only imagine what was going on in there. As the big day drew near, anticipation intensified and time dragged on into eternity. So, what was going on in that big living room? Today, we know there wasn't much of any Christmas activity taking place in there; that preparation was taking place in the minds of the kids.

About a week before Christmas, we would see activity. Boxes from the attic would appear in the hallway, and then were quickly moved into the living room. We would observe whispered conversations taking place. Were they staged for our benefit? Were they telling secrets about presents? As far as we were concerned, it was *for sure* something about presents. It was an exciting time for kids.

Some years, a day or two before Christmas a car would drive up to the front gate. Aunts and uncles brought their kids—our cousins were the only kids near our age that we knew—to spend Christmas with our grandparents, Will and Ella, she now in a wheelchair.

Around seven o'clock on Christmas Eve, all the kids were assembled in the dining room. An aunt, an uncle, or maybe a parent or a hired man kept the group of kids in check. Seven, or eight kids, maybe more, maybe less, were almost crazy with excitement. A tap from inside the double door signaled that all was in readiness.

When the door opened, the kids were cautioned to be very quiet. It was awesome. The room had been transformed into a wonderland. Red paper bells and red-and-white streamers crisscrossed the two big rooms. The carbide lights had been dimmed, but there in the far end by the big window in the living room stood the huge tree. There were icicles and pretty Christmas balls and sashes, and decorations of all sorts adorning the tree. No, there were no electric lights on our tree, but to us it was the most beautiful thing we had ever seen.

Our parents, grandparents, uncles, aunts, and hired men were all assembled in the darkened room. Then, "Shush, listen…Hey, did anybody hear that?" And, "There it was again!"

At that point, we heard the faint tinkle of a bell, and again a little louder before someone murmured, "Santa's reindeer!" No words adequately describe the feeling in the heart of a child or even an adult when Santa Claus appeared almost like magic in that dimly lit living room "darkened because bright lights would hurt Santa's eyes." He did not tarry; he handed a gift to each child as he called our names, wished all a Merry Christmas, and then disappeared just as he had arrived—like a ghost.

Our Christmas traditions have been modified to include the traditions of our spouses' families, as they should be, but those traditions established by our grandparents and parents have been carried forward and to a great extent still occur in many Skinner family homes today. If little ones are present there will always be great pleasure in observing the wonder and the magic of Christmas.

If They Came Back for a Visit, What Would They Think?

Silas and Anne Jane, their son Will and his wife Ella, and our parents, Will and Ella's son Kirtland and his wife Johanna, would likely be surprised and pleased if they were they to return today and observe the changes to Skinner Ranch. Of course, there would be sadness in some of the changes, mostly in the faces they would see. We believe when they looked deeper, they would see that the changes have been rather superficial. There has been a revolution in how the work is done and the power required to do it, but the land is the same, though more productive. The fields and fences are not greatly different; a home may have been built or remodeled to render it more usable; a shop altered to be more attuned to needs of today. When put into perspective, these are not major changes.

Of the three couples, Silas and Anne Jane would be most surprised to see the changes that have taken place on the land where his horses once grazed. When Silas built his toll road he could not have foreseen the full effect it would have on the early growth and development of this part of the country. The miners, stagecoach drivers, and teamsters who used his toll road had a huge hand in bringing civilization to this country. Many of them liked what they saw. They did not all stay, of course, but many did, and those who put down roots learned to love this part of America. The Skinner family is but one example of the descendants of early pioneers who still make this high desert their home.

If our great-grandfather Silas Skinner would be disturbed by anything, it would be the fences. And he would also be amazed by the fields themselves, and the lack of horses, the thousands of cattle, the cars and trucks, and the buildings. He would envy the construction equipment manufactured today that could have built his toll road in months rather than years, with nary a pick, a shovel, a span of oxen, or a drop of perspiration. He would wonder where all the horses went, and he would wonder what happened to the range forage that his horses had grazed on. *How*, he would muse, *did they become so depleted? Maybe, my son was right about clearing the land.*

Will and Ella, our grandparents, would be the most disturbed. Will would grump a bit about the newfangled ways that didn't include horses. They both would be saddened by the demise of that big house where they had raised their family and entertained the community with lavish parties—now gone, a new home in its place. They would shed a tear or two, but we believe that after consideration, they would reluctantly agree that the home they were so proud of had served its purpose and had to go.

If Ella walked around her yard today she would see some of the trees still standing where she planted them when she and Will moved into the big house ninety years ago. Of her big house, she would recognize only the back porch, which is now the entry; the kitchen; and the dining room, now converted to a living room. We doubt she would be pleased, but on reflection she would agree it is now a much more comfortable home.

Will, who dreamed and schemed and was so proud of his ranch, its fields and fences, would not see great differences, but they exist nonetheless. Some subtle, some drastic. A combination granary, shop, and equipment storage building has replaced the granary Will built and that burned down after his death. He would miss the Clinton home that his family had lived in, and which later became the bunkhouse, and the old willow corral in which thousands of cattle and horses had been worked over the years, now only a memory. He would note new ways of handling hay, a fence line moved, land now leveled and easier to irrigate, the addition of an efficient corral system for working cattle, and a sturdier dam in Jordan Creek. Mostly, we believe he would approve. He would definitely approve of the additional cattle, but like his father Silas, he would be saddened by the few horses to be seen.

There is no question that if our parents, Kirt and Johanna, were to return today, they would be very pleased. They would look with great pride on what they wrought here, but even more so, with the progress that has been accomplished in their absence. They would be especially proud of the ongoing activities and the management of the property. They would be excited and proud of the new faces that have appeared, and the families who have taken up the task of keeping the Skinner Ranch operating and producing. The new home our parents built in 1965 had planning flaws that disturbed our mother; if she walked into her home today, she would be very pleased with the remodel completed by the current occupants, the latest Silas Skinner and his wife Tracy.

Our parents would be more than pleased to hear the laughter of youngsters who play where the voices and laughter of their own children, and their children's children, are only an echo. These newer members of this now huge family are the seventh generation of Silas and Anne Jane's offspring in America. They are the future. They must take up the reins of operating their ranches and farms, of building their own chosen industries and their own chosen professions. They have the tools. They are the ones who must continue developing and improving this land we call America. May they be as strong and as steadfast as those who came before them. We, the elders in the family, are confident of their capabilities. May I brag a bit? They are from good stock.

Like every successful business, the Skinner Ranch continues to evolve and keep pace with technology. The current operators have recognized the efficiencies of improving the land and making it more productive

Four generations on the Skinner Ranch today. Left to right: Kasen, his dad Silas, Silas's dad Bob Jr., and Bob's dad Bob.

while at the same time being environmentally conscious. They have employed science in both the improvement and production of cattle, and in the husbandry of their fields and grazing lands.

As an example, the Skinner Ranch entered into an experiment with Idaho Power Company a number of years ago. The two corporations joined forces to investigate the possible use of solar energy to supply electricity for pumping water to cattle grazing on deeded rangeland. The project proved successful and was the first step into the use of solar technology—in the world—for this type of application, which is currently being employed on every continent.

Since Kirt and Johanna Skinner bought the ranch in 1938, there have been wars to deal with, years when the only help available was a skeleton crew mostly made up of those too old or young or physically disabled to serve in the U.S. military. And let's not forget the playboys from Jamaica. There have been wonderful years, mediocre years, and economic ups and downs. We were not immune to injuries along the way, and a death rocked our parents to the core. Each setback seemed to provide the impetus to make a stronger move forward.

Each generation of the family—through the one hundred and thirty years since Silas and his partner E. H. Clinton traded the toll road for property on Jordan Creek—has brought progress. That progress

Bob by the solar well.

has been slow at times but nonetheless steady. The value placed on higher education for each generation has kept pace with and has positively affected progress on this ranch and in other chosen industries and professions. It is not only in the ranching business that this now large family has excelled. Of Silas and Anne Jane Skinner's children, Mona is the only one who graduated from college (University of California, Berkeley). She taught in Jordan Valley and later in Napa, California. Ruth Norton, granddaughter of Silas and Anne Jane, daughter of Carrie (Skinner) and Lou Norton, was also a graduate of the University of California at Berkeley. For many years, she was the Dean of Women there. Her brother Daniel, another graduate of the University of California system, became Dean of the English Department at the prestigious University of Virginia. Each generation has produced increasing numbers of bachelor's, master's, and doctoral degrees.

Our father, Silas Kirtland Skinner, at a time when a minimal education in the three Rs was considered adequate, said, "That is not enough." He went about setting the original example with his involvement on many school committees and agricultural associations, including sixty-two total years of service to education and even more to his industry.

All of these men and women have continued to be active and involved, not only for the betterment of their own ranching operations, but also in the betterment of their chosen industry. They are not alone. Almost all of Will and Ella's family saw to it that their own children would be educated to the standards of the day. Some went into agriculture and related industries, others into education, law, medicine, the sciences, business, the space program, and technology of all sorts. We know of no field of enterprise that is not represented by a member of this extended family.

The Silver City Community Today

As we near the end of our story, regrettably little evidence remains of the booming mining activities or past civilization in the Owyhee Mountains, with the exception of Silver City, now nearly a ghost town. In recent years, vacationers have started buying and restoring some of the historic old miners' homes for summer use. To preserve the authenticity of the mining era, the Bureau of Land Management strictly limits renovation of the old buildings to the interiors only; exteriors must remain as near original as possible.

Walking among these ghosts of days gone by, we see the effect of time on our lives and our structures. The merchants, business owners, and citizens of Silver City walked these streets, built a toll road out of this rugged rocky land, went deep into the earth to mine its ore, and probably assumed that this city would exist forever.

The teamsters and stagecoach drivers who traveled seemingly endless trails from Sacramento, California, to the mountains of southern Idaho would find it hard to believe that today the same trip would be measured in hours rather than weeks or even months.

Preservation

History has not been kind to the original and historic names Natives and pioneers gave to their icons of the "Old West." Indians gave names to their geographical and spiritual symbols, which have largely been overridden by the white man's language. As usage changed throughout the years, or new industries arose in place of old, many historic names have been forgotten.

Silas Skinner's Toll Road still exists from Silver City, Idaho, to the Owyhee River in Oregon, though its original identity has been altered and it is no longer so-named. The Skinner Toll Road is now known as The Stage Road, and in later years, east of the approximate location of Skinner's Trout Creek Station to Silver City, the road became known as Long Ridge Road. It has fallen into disrepair to the east beyond Delamar, the location of a newer open pit mining operation that is currently abandoned.

From the approximate location of Silas and Anne Jane Skinner's Trout Creek Station near the foot of the Trout Creek Grade, west to the town of Jordan Valley, the road has been renamed Yturri Boulevard to honor Tony Yturri, now deceased, a former Oregon State Senator and a prominent member of a Jordan Valley family and of the community. We doubt Silas would mind sharing that part of his toll road with another honorable name in the community.

West of Jordan Valley, Highway 95 follows the toll road for approximately five miles and branches to the southwest on a new roadbed. The Danner Loop Road branches off Highway 95 and generally follows the old Skinner Toll Road west of Jordan Valley to the Ruby Ranch. Beyond the Ruby Ranch, location of the historic Inskeep Station, the toll road still exists as far as the Owyhee River but is now known as Emigrant Road and is largely unused, though it can be negotiated by four-wheel drive vehicles.

In the 1970s, a mining company launched an open pit mining operation near where the old town of De La Mar had once been. They widened and repaired the Skinner Toll Road between Jordan Valley and their mining operation, making it more accessible for their trucks and large equipment. Taking advantage of today's modern equipment, they abandoned the old roadbed in several places and moved it to a more convenient place for their equipment. For the most part, however, the road remains where Silas Skinner built it nearly one hundred and fifty years ago.

As years pass, much, if not all, of the history of an area will be altered by outside forces, and its original identity will be forgotten unless diligently and accurately recorded. If preserved with honesty and accuracy, history becomes a legacy left by those who came before us, for those who will come later to enjoy and build on. In every area of this great country, there have been good times, extreme hardships, wars, and financial depressions, and yet, there is a wonderful romance in stories told by the pioneers about their time. It is to our own advantage to keep their words as well as their deeds pure and alive.

We believe very strongly that the names originally given to historic places in this area, and for that matter in all historic areas, should not be changed at the whim of government agencies. With that in mind, we make a strong appeal to the Idaho Historical Society, the Owyhee County Historical Society, the Oregon Historical Society, and the Malheur County Historical Society to petition the Bureau of Land Management to restore historic names wherever they have been changed.

We make another strong appeal to the Historical Societies to fund, and for the current owners of the respective properties to allow for, the restoration of two icons on Silas Skinner's Toll Road. One is the Inskeep Station, the ruins of which are located on Ruby Ranch property near the historic gravesite of Jean Baptiste Charbonneau, and the second is The Sheep Ranch Station House near Arock, Oregon.

We Bid You Well

So ends this tale of just one of the many families in southeastern Oregon and southwest Idaho who have left their mark on the history of this part of America. If we have sparked an interest in other families to pick up the pen or to appoint someone among them to relate their own family history, we have been successful. Time marches on, and family stories need to be recorded before they are forgotten in the course of daily living.

It has been an enjoyable trip through history and to have this opportunity to become more personally acquainted with our ancestors. In our tour through the Skinner archives, we were reminded that there is another story to be told. Grandmother Ella Sackett's family arrived in America over two hundred and thirty years prior to Silas Skinner's arrival. There is only nominal mention herein of their arrival on the East Coast during colonial days, but the early Sacketts had an influential hand in the formation of this country.

We hope you, the reader, have enjoyed our story. It is unique only in that our ancestor Silas Skinner sailed the seas for about sixteen years, mined for gold, constructed an important toll road, protected himself from hostile Indians, sired seven children, and with his wife Anne Jane, raised all but one to adulthood. He then went into the racehorse business, and became a landowner and a rancher. He did all this in the short period of fifty-two years. He is the patriarch of what is now a very large, relatively close-knit, and professionally diverse family.

Every two years, the Skinner clan gathers for a family reunion. Attendance at these reunions ranges from sixty to well over a hundred, and usually there is at least a representative present, sometimes many more, from each branch of the Skinner family tree. The 2007 reunion was held in Napa, California, where we had the opportunity to visit Silas and Anne Jane's horse ranch. The 2009 reunion will be in Washington's Tri-Cities area. Check your ancestry; if you are kin, you are welcome.

—*Toast given by Silas Kirtland Skinner (Dad) on his nineteenth birthday.*

Here's to the past,
and the years that have fled.
Here's to the years
that are lying ahead.
But better by far,
we each will confess,
here is to now,
which is all we possess.

The Promise Continues

Appendix I

SS

Kirt and Johanna's Kids

William Murray Skinner, deceased.
  Bill was born in Boise, Idaho, October 31, 1918, and was the first of seven children who would be born to Kirt and Johanna Skinner. He was also the first of thirty-one grandchildren of Will and Ella Skinner. Bill's interests were not necessarily in cattle and horses, but in things mechanical, yet he also was a very capable ranch worker. In his early twenties he purchased some land and farm equipment and went into land-leveling, and contracted farm work in the area, along with his continued college courses.

While attending the College of Idaho, he became interested in flying and eventually, with the probability of World War II beginning, he was hired by a flying service in Boise, Idaho to give flying lessons to Army Air Corps personnel and also to private students.

His life was cut short in an accident that occurred at Gowen Field in Boise on March 31, 1943 when he and his student were engulfed in the air turbulence of a B-17 bomber—both planes had been given the green light to land.

Bill on tractor.

Robert Harold Skinner

Robert was born June 26, 1920. A graduate of the School of Agriculture at Oregon State College (OSU), Bob entered the army and was stationed in Virginia. There he met his future wife, Sara Morgan, a native of Roanoke, Virginia. Soon after his discharge they were married on November 9, 1946 and settled on the Skinner ranch. A remodeling of the old ballroom in the big house served as an apartment for their first home. In 1953 with a growing family and needing additional space the "Homestead House" was moved nearer to ranch headquarters, where, with several additions, it still serves as their home.

In addition to co-managing the ranch operation with his brother Dan, Bob has an impressive history of serving his community and the ranching industry. He has served forty-two combined years on the Jordan Valley High School Board, and the Malheur County and Oregon School Reorganization Committees. Acting in the Advisory Council to the Dean of Agriculture at OSU was an interesting and enjoyable experience. He has been an active member of the county, state and national Cattlemen's Associations and served a term as president of Oregon and Malheur Co. Associations, and the Board of Directors of the National Group. He was one of the Oregon representatives to the national Public Lands Council for many years. He was a charter member and director of the Jordan Valley Methodist Church. With prodding, he will acknowledge that he is the recipient of a number of honors and awards for his involvement in the community and for his leadership ability.

Three children were born to the couple: Robert Morgan, born May 22, 1950; Nancy, born September 11, 1952; and Sally, born March 1, 1956.

Robert (Bob Jr.), now the general manager of the Skinner Ranch, married Karen McKay. They have four children: (1) Robin, born February 12, 1975, married Michael Eiguren, a local rancher—they have four boys, Nicholas Pascual, Kirk Morgan, Burch Michael, and Ross Sackett; (2)Kimberly, born June 26, 1975, married Morgan Johnsrud, and currently lives in Jordan Valley with their two boys Grayden Silas and Bode Morgan; (3) Silas, born August 12, 1977, married Tracy Sarceda. They have three children, Kasen, Regann, and Cort; and (4) Michael, born May 13, 1982, married Kelsi Johnson—they have a son named Jayden Patrick. Silas and Michael, and their families, work and live on the ranch. They help manage the Skinner ranching operation in Jordan Valley.

Nancy, married Ray Melville. Nancy graduated from The College of Idaho majoring in education. She taught school, became an administrator, and program coordinator in the California school system. She and Ray have two sons: Jeff, born June 27, 1979, married Shawna; and Adam was born November 24, 1981.

Sally graduated from The College of Idaho majoring in education. She is a school principal in the Boise School district. She has two children: Christopher Sherman, born March 1, 1984; and Sara Jo Sherman, born March 9, 1987.

Standing (left to right): Sally, Ray Melvill, Nancy, Bob Sr., Bob Jr., and Karen. Seated: Sara.

Silas Kirtland Skinner, deceased.

Kirt Jr., born on August 28, 1922, married Naida Weybark in Portland in 1957. Much like the rest of his siblings, he worked with his parents on the ranch. He graduated from Oregon State, majoring in Agriculture, with an emphasis on Animal Husbandry. In 1943 he joined the army and about a year later was given a medical discharge. He returned to Oregon State and worked on the ranch during the summer months. He worked for a short time for the County Agent in Benton County and then joined Van Waters and Rogers, an agricultural chemical company in Portland. Several years later he became employed with Dow Chemical Company in their Agricultural Chemical division. He was promoted from sales to become a district sales manager and finally personnel manager. He and his wife moved to Kirkland, Washington in 1961, where they adopted twins, a boy they named William, and a girl they named Barbara.

Kirt retired from Dow Chemical in 1983. The family moved to Bend, Oregon, and with both Kirt and Naida being avid golfers, they joined and became active in the Bend Country Club, fully enjoying a life of retirement in popular Central Oregon.

Kirt passed away in August 1995. Naida is now remarried to Ed Schmidt, a pleasant gentlemen and transplant from New York. Ed, is also an avid golfer, who has discovered the beauty of the West, especially Central Oregon.

Kirt and Naida's son, **Bill**, born April 9, 1961, passed away on January 10, 2007. Their daughter, **Barbara**, born April 9, 1961, lives in Michigan and is employed by Wolverine World Inc. as Global Production Director. Barbara has two daughters, Stephanie, born

Left: Kirt Jr. and Naida's wedding picture. Above: Barbara and Bill.

2/13/1981, married Moses Fetters. They have a daughter, Amaya, born April 19, 2008. They continue to live in Michigan. Barbara's daughter, Karrah, born November 10, 1987, recently moved to the Northwest and currently lives in the Seattle area.

Christine Skinner Moore

Christine was born July 3, 1924, and after her early years on the Skinner Ranch, she received a Bachelor of Science degree in 1946 from Oregon State College. Interested in journalism, she wrote for the Barometer, the campus newspaper, and decided journalism would be an interesting career. She was hired by the *Ontario Argus*, an Eastern Oregon biweekly newspaper in Ontario. A merger united the *Ontario Argus* with the *Eastern Oregon Observer* to become the *Ontario Argus Observer*. She was named Managing Editor several years later, a position she held for many years. She also freelanced for a number of agricultural and livestock publications.

Chris married C. William Moore Sr. of Ontario, Oregon, August 29, 1949. In addition to her journalistic work, she and her husband owned and operated a ranch and raised Registered Hereford Cattle for a number of years. Later the couple moved into Ontario, closer to their work. There are few civic organizations in eastern Oregon and the City of Ontario that Chris has not been a member of and actively supported with special projects. As a charter member and past president of the Malheur County Historical society, she has contributed immensely to the collected history of southeastern Oregon and southwest Idaho, and is considered an expert on the Oregon Trail as it passed through Idaho and Oregon. Much of her work has been incorporated into and appears in this writing.

In early 2007, her husband Bill developed health problems and passed away. Following her retirement from the *Oregon Argus Observer*, Chris and her late husband had an enjoyable time investigating and writing about historical events and points of interest in Eastern Oregon and Southwestern Idaho. Chris continues to live in the family home in Ontario and keeps busy doing freelance writing and working in her garden.

Five children were born into Chris and Bill's family: Theodore Kirtland (Tik), born December 1, 1950; Leah, born March 4, 1953; William, born September 16, 1955; Johanna, born April 10, 1960; and Robert, born February 6, 1964.

Theodore (Tik) married Marilyn Mohr. They have two children: (1) Jennifer, born July 25, 1979. Jennifer married Marc Slatter—they have three children, Lindsey, Colton, and John Weston; and (2) Randall, born July 9, 1982, who married Jami Meath—they have one child, Theodore Joshua, born June 29, 2008.

Leah married Robert Churchill. They have three children: (1) Karen, born March 3, 1977, married Joel Garcia—they have three children: Maria, Alexandra, and Sofia; (2) Robert, born September 4, 1981; and Karey, born February 24, 1989.

William married Nancy Ingle. They have two children: (1) Nathaniel, born April 28, 1982, married Cassie Masterson—they have two children: Macy and Krece; and (2) Sara, born June 14, 1984, married Barrie Downey.

Johanna married Michael O'Rourke. They have four children: (1) Nicole, born February 2, 1984; (2) Tamara, born August 18, 1985; (3) Bryna, born March 4, 1987; and Jake, born August 31, 1991.

Robert married Kerri Cathey. They have two children: (1) Michael, born October 5, 1991; and (2) Savannah, born July 19, 1996

Standing (left to right): Johanna, Bill Jr., Tik, and Bob. Seated (left to right): Leah, Bill Sr., Chris.

Daniel H. Skinner

Dan, born August 12, 1926, worked on the ranch for several years and, while recuperating from an injury to his hand, he decided to attend Oregon State College. After about a year, he returned to the ranch in Jordan Valley and joined his dad and brother Bob on the ranch.

Dan was drafted into the army in 1950 and after basic training, served as an artillery instructor. After he was released from active duty he returned to the ranch.

He was the first to introduce the airplane to the ranch operation and it soon became an important piece of equipment. He built a landing strip near ranch headquarters and, in 1965, after he received his license, purchased a small airplane.

A farm accident grounded Dan from flying, but his introduction of an airplane for ranch use is as important today as tractors, hay balers and other equipment. Dan's nephew, Bob Jr. flies a Cessna airplane to accomplish jobs in hours that it would take days otherwise. The air strip Dan built is not only a great asset to the ranch, but has on a number of occasions provided a safe haven for pilots who have found themselves in trouble because of weather or malfunctioning equipment. Dan also put the strip to good use teaching many of his nieces and nephews how to drive safely.

Dan married Cathy Ross, a high school science teacher in June 1973, and set up housekeeping in the remodeled portion of Will and Ella's big home. Now, both retired, Dan and Cathy live in Caldwell, Idaho. He occupies his time with his grandkids, his yard, tournament horse-shoes, and meets with his high school classmates for dinner monthly. Dan has also become ambassador to his family, friends and neighbors from Jordan Valley who have the misfortune of spending time in a Caldwell or Boise Hospital.

Dan and Cathy are parents to two daughters: Jocele, born August 19, 1974, and Elizabeth, born January 25, 1978.

Jocele married George Decker. Jocele is a highly respected physician in Caldwell, Idaho. She also serves as a physician a few days a month at the Jordan Valley Health Clinic. She and George have two children: (1) Katie, born June 21, 2005; and (2) Jack, born February 28, 2007.

Elizabeth married Steve Lavigne. Liz is a Surgical Nurse in Silverton Hospital in Silverton, Oregon. She and Steve have two children: (1) Daniel, born January 10, 2006; and (2) James, born March 2009.

Left: Cathy and Dan. Right (left to right): Liz and Jocele.

John S. Skinner

I was born April 10, 1929. The first twenty-four years of my life were involved with working on the Skinner Ranch in Jordan Valley. I attended Oregon State College (now OSU) for two years, and graduated with a Business Degree from the College of Idaho. In September 1952, I married Carole McGuire, a young lady from Twin Falls, Idaho, soon followed by two years of Army service during the Korean conflict.

Following my release from the Army, I worked in several areas of business management including retail, food products, and health care, from which I retired. We currently live in Salem, Oregon.

Carole and I have four children: Michael, born February 18, 1954; Rebecca Jo, born November 9, 1955; Daniel, born July 1, 1959; and Diana Kay, born January 31, 1964.

Michael married Katherine Meyer. Two children were born to the couple: (1) James Arthur, born August 31, 1986, and (2) Michelle Johanna, born September 26, 1988. Following the couple's divorce, Mike married Sheryl Warner. They live in Kirkland, Washington.

Rebecca Jo married Arthur Witkowski. They are parents to two boys: (1) Mitchell John was born December 12, 1982, and (2) Mark Daniel was born January 4, 1991. They also live in Kirkland, Washington.

Daniel married Tammy Green. They are parents to three boys: (1) Cody Christian, born September 17, 1989; (2) Colton Daniel, born June 12, 1993; and (3) Brice Delous, born October 30, 1994. The couple divorced, and Dan later married Marie Capellano. Marie's daughter Linzy, was born December 4, 1995. Dan and Marie and their famility live in Nampa, Idaho.

Diana Kay married David Unruh. Three boys have been born into the family: (1) Travis Glen, born September 18, 1988; (2) Trevor Daniel, born June 13, 1991; and (3) Tanner John, born March 9, 1996. The Unruh's live in Salem, Oregon.

Left to right: Becky, Mike, Carole, John, Dan, and Diana.

Johanna (Joanne) Skinner Owens

Joanne was born on November 22, 1932. She was the second daughter and seventh and last child born to Kirt and Johanna Skinner. Several years before Joanne started school, the District hired Virginia Fleming, from Warrenton, Oregon, to teach. A close relationship developed between the two. Miss Fleming called her "Shadow" as Joanne seldom left her side. This friendship has lasted over 70 years. Miss Fleming became Joanne's first grade teacher and from the first day she attended that one room school in the sagebrush, her plan was to emulate her teacher.

After attending the one room school for ten years, Joanne enrolled at Caldwell High School and graduated in 1950. That fall she enrolled in the College of Idaho, majoring in Elementary Education. She started her teaching career in first grade at Cole School in Boise, Idaho with thirty-six students. She also taught in Culver, Bend, and Sherwood.

Joanne married Duane Owens and they made their home in Bend. In 1968 Duane was hired by Portland Community College to teach in the Physical Education Department. They built a home in Sherwood and continue to live there.

Joanne developed a Ranching Unit while teaching in Sherwood. Bob and Sara were invited to visit Hopkins School. Bob authentically dressed in a western hat, leather chaps, boots and spurs. The students quickly named him "Cowboy Bob." He patiently answered thousand of questions from the curious students giving them a snapshot of ranch life. Bob brought a saddle for the students to sit on. He had bridles, saddle blankets, branding irons, a "lass" rope and a rawhide reata (rope) among the displays. Sara was in charge of Indian artifacts and jewelry made by Indians, and loaned to the Skinners by an Indian couple employed on the ranch. During the days the Skinners spent with Hopkins' students the Second Grades took a field trip to the "Then and Now Cowboy Museum" in Portland. Another event was the Hopkins Spring Concert. In music class the students learned and sang western songs and "Cowboy Bob" led them in singing, "Home on the Range."

Joanne is an active member of the Sherwood United Methodist church. She takes a memoirs class and enjoys recording family stories. She is a strong historian in her own right and has taken a major role along with brother Bob in sorting and filing thousands of pages of family history that have accumulated over the last 150 years. Their work and dedication has resulted in this writing.

Joanne and Duane's family includes five children, all of which reside in Oregon. Martin, born 1958; Billie Jo, born 1960; Alison, born 1961; and Wesley, born 1969.

Andrea Gay, born 1957, is vice-pricipal of La Grande High School,.

She married Doug Waldrop and they have two children: Carrie, born in 1983, and Bill, born in 1985. Carrie married Joseph Sloan in 2009.

Marty, born 1983, is a Purchasing Agent for a cable company in Wilsonville, Oregon.

Billie Jo is an instructor at Blue Mountain Community College. She married Paul Burns, and they have three children: Brock Joseph, born 1990; Joseph Callow, born 1992; and Bailey Johanna, born 1994.

Alison owns a Flower Shop in Sherwood and married Jeffrey Alan Bertalotto, and they have two children: Jacob, born 1992, and Jessica Clarice, born 1996..

Wesley, born 1996, is principal of Sherman County High School.

Now retired, Joanne enjoys traveling around the United States with her husband Duane.

Standing, left to right: Alison, Andrea, Marty, Billie Jo, and Wes. Seated: Duane and Joanne.

Appendix II

SS

The Family Tree in America

The number to the left of each entry indicates the generation that entry belongs to within that family line.

Skinner Generation 1

1 Silas Skinner was born June, 1834 in Andreas, Isle of Man and died April 12, 1886 in Napa, California. He married Ann Jane Callow February 24, 1870 in Kirk Andreas, Isle of Man. Ann Jane was born January 1846 in Parish Andreas, Isle of Man. (For Ann Jane's ancestors see page 56 above). They are considered to be the first generation in America. To them were born seven children, the second generation: William Silas, born May 8, 1871 in Ruby City, Idaho; Catherine (Carrie), born 1873 in Trout Creek, Jordan Valley, Oregon; Annabel, born 1875 in Ruby City, Idaho; Thomas Lewis, born 1877 in Jordan Valley, Oregon; Horatio (Ray), born 1879 in Jordan Valley, Oregon; Sara Ellen, born 1881 in Jordan Valley, Oregon; and Mona, born 1883 in Jordan Valley, Oregon.

Skinner Generation 2
The Family of William Silas Skinner

Son of Silas & Anne Jane

2 William Silas Skinner (Will) was born May 8, 1871 in Ruby City, Idaho. He died March 3, 1960 in Jordan Valley, Oregon. He married Ella Sackett November 11, 1891 in Napa Valley, California. Ella was born June 21, 1868 in Napa, California and died October 17, 1941 in Jordan Valley, Oregon. (For Ella's ancestors see The Family of Thomas Sackett below). Nine children were added to the family, the third generation: Silas Kirtland Sr., Thomas Harold, Ruby Aileen, Verna Claire, Nancy Irma, William Callow, Ella Marjorie, Anna Beatrice (Beata), and Hugh Sackett.

Skinner Generation 3
The Family of Silas Kirtland Skinner Sr. (Kirt—Dad)
Son of Will and Ella Skinner

3 Silas Kirtland Skinner Sr. (Kirt) was born November 27, 1892 in Jordan Valley, died September, 1983. He married Johanna (Hanna) Murray on October 16, 1917 in Portland, Oregon. Johanna was one of seven children born to John and Christina (McKenzie) Murray, the others being Ella, Robert, Alexander, Christina, Dianna, and Jessie. Johanna was born November 14, 1889, in Scotland, and died in June of 1972. Seven children were born to the family, the fourth generation: William Murray (Bill), born October 10, 1918, died in March, 1942; Robert Harold (Bob), Silas Kirtland Jr., Verna Christine (Chris), Daniel Herbert (Dan), John Sackett, and Jessie Johanna (Joanne). (See below for more on the fourth generation in this family).

Skinner Generation 3
The Family of Thomas Harold Skinner
Son of Will and Ella Skinner

3 Thomas Harold, born March 3, 1894 in Jordan Valley, and died October 1970. He married Edith Elizabeth Jones in 1919 in Jordan Valley, Oregon. Three Children were added to the family in Jordan Valley: Eleanor Irma, Ernest Harold, and Esther.

4. Eleanor Irma Skinner, b. 3/10/1920 in Jordan Valley, OR. She married Steven Sandmeyer in 1944 in Caldwell, Idaho. They had two children: (5) Richard Skinner, b. 12/14/1946; and (5) John Stephen, b. 1/13/1950. Eleanor would later marry Francis Serviss in 1986 in Boise, Idaho.

4. Ernest Harold Skinner, b. 7/11/1922 in Jordan Valley, OR; d. 9/21/1950 at Wright-Patterson Air Force Base in Ohio. He married Patricia Cochrane in 1944 in Caldwell, Idaho. They added two fifth generation children to the family, Rebecca and Shirley: (5) Rebecca Susan Skinner Spofford, b. 7/1/1948 in Layfayette, Indiana. She married Mark William Hoffman 9/6/1969 in Boise, ID. They had two children: (6) Sarah Elizabeth, b. 10/8/1972 in Idaho Falls, ID; and (6) Mark Stephan b. 1/7/1976 in Honolulu, HI. (5) Shirley Jean Skinner Spofford, b. 3/19/1950 in Fairborn, Ohio. She married William George Lee-Warner 9/12/1970 in Corvallis, OR. They had five children: (6) Joshua Michael, b. 4/4/1973 in Orange, CA; (6) Suzannah Joy, b. 6/14/1975 in Portland, OR; (6) Rebecca Faith, b. 9/19/1978 in Portland, OR; (6) Jonathon David, b. 8/26/1980; and (6) Abigail Hope, b. 4/17/1983.

4. Esther Elizabeth Skinner, was b. 2/28/1929 in Jordan Valley. She married Vernon Donald Emmel in 1951 in Caldwell, ID. They had five children: (5) Thomas Charles Emmel, b. 7/29/1952 in Caldwell, ID. He married Thea McManus in 8/2/1980 in Baltimore MD. They had two children in Baltimore MD: (6) David Donald, b. 6/13/1984; and (6) Rachel Lauren, b. 10/21/1985.

(5) Patricia Susan Emmel, b. 7/1/1954 in Hillsboro, OR. She married Jeffrey Michael Swarts 4/26/1980 in Wooster, OH. They had three children: (6) Gabriel P., b. 10/30/1980 in Brooklyn, NY; (6) Benjamin Michael, b. 5/24/1982 in Wooster, OH; and (6) Brian Douglas, b. 6/28/1984 in Ravenna, OH. (5) Kathryn Elizabeth Emmel, b. 10/14/1955 in Hillsboro, OR. She married Mark Steven Holcomb 6/24/1978 in Caldwell, ID. They had two children born in San Diego, California: (6) Megan Elizabeth, b. 5/9/1984; and (6) Keri Lyn, b. 2/13/1987. (5) Mary Esther Emmel, b.3/21/1959 in San Jose, CA. She married Malcolm Arthur Cooper 7/31/1982 in Napa, CA. Their children: (6) Lindsey Marie, b. 10/27/1987 in New London, CT; and (6) Kirsten Leigh, b. 1/14/1990, New London, CT. (5) John Ernest Emmel, b. 1/17/1958, San Jose, California.

Skinner Generation 3
The Family of Ruby Eileen Skinner Gheen
Daughter of Will and Ella Skinner

3 Ruby Eileen Skinner was born February 4, 1896 in Caldwell Idaho. She married Evan Pennock Gheen in 1919 in Berkley, California. Four children were added to the family:

4. Ella Caroline Gheen, b. 5/29/1921, Jordan Valley, OR. She married Jeff Boyer,1942, in Portland, OR. They had four children: (5) Jefferson Chelcey, b. 11/11/1943, Ontario, OR; He married Mary Love Pool 6/17/1969 in Portland, OR. Their children: (6) Joshua Evan, b. 3/22/1972, married Jennifer; and (6) Chelcy Eliza, b.12/16/1976, married Stutzman. (5) Michael Evan, b. 8/6/1946, Ontario, OR; (5) Ruby Cathleen, b. 9/17/1947, Corvallis, OR, married Brian Day 4/19/1968, and later married Michael Anthony Amen 5/19/1973 in Oregon City, OR. Child of Ruby and Brian: (6) Hagen Anthony, b. 10/29/1970. Children of Ruby and Michael: (6) Adrian John, b. 8/17/197-, His child: (7) Emily Amen, b. unknown. (6) Hagen Amen, b. Unknown. Her child: (7) Emily Amen, b. unknown.(5) John Scott, b. 9/2/1948, North Bend, OR. Married Maria Katchis in Portland, OR. Their child: (6) John Michael, b. 1/7/1978.

4. Evan Pennock Gheen Jr, b. 11/10/1923, Jordan Valley, OR, d. 1/30/1993 in Caldwell, ID. Married to Mary Katherine Prahl Millbook, 1977; married to Mary Brown Swigert, 1987. The children of Evan and Katherine: (5) Evan Pennock III, b. 7/9/1950, Ontario, OR, married Michelle Louise Mitchell 4/28/1978. Their children: (6) Nathan Timothy, b. 2/3/1980, married Maria Silva 9/17/2005. Their children: (7) Spencer Neal, b. 5/9/1982 and (7) Jordan Mitchell, b. 1/21/1985. (6) Spencer Neal, b. 5/7/1982; and (6) Jordan Mitchell, b. 1/21/1985. (5) Elizabeth Jane, b. 2/16/1952, Portland, OR, married John Wesley Post 12/10/1973 in Ontario, OR. Their children: (6) Amy Elizabeth, b. 12/15/1982; and (6) Daniel John, b. 3/5/1986. (5) Timothy, b. 11/21/1954, Portland, OR, married Shelly Ann Mart, later Terri Cole 6/21/1978 in Weiser, ID, and on 5/6/1987 Shelly Ann. Children of Timothy and Shelly: (6) Shawn Timothy, b. 11/20/1985 and (6)

Shayler Beau, b. 1/31/1987. Children of Timothy and Terri: (6) Janelle O'Neil, b. 8/5/1980 and married Daniel Glover. Their children: (7) Brenna O'Neil Gheen, b. 6/4/2003, and (7) Julie Irene Gheen, b. 8/12/1982. (6) Julie, b. 8/12/1982. (5) Gregory Scott, b. 10/7/1959, Ontario, OR, married Diane Carole Kusha 11/11/1982. Their children: (6) Adrienne Megan, b. 5/12/1985 and (6) Jessica Michelle, b. 1/13/1987.

4. Aileen Beatrice Gheen, b. 4/2/1925, Kennett Square, PA, d. 1/13/1992, in Vale, OR. Married John (Jack) T. Marquis, 8/24/1947 in Ontario, OR. Their children: (5) Katherine Aileen, b. 5/30/1948, married Carl Judy 8/24/1968. Their children: (6) John Carl, b. 8/7/1969, married Shannon Schlothauer; (6) Tanya, b. 12/8/1971, married Bryan Lanspery; and (6) William Charles, b. 7/16/1973, married Gwen. Their children: (7) Cayla Marie, b. 2/18/1998 and (7) William Charles II, b. 6/2/2003. (5) Marilyn Beatrice, b. 4/15/1953; married E. Paul Scott, 3/17/1991, Ontario, OR; (5) Carol Ann, b. 6/27/1958, married David Moran, 8/21/1993, Ontario, OR.

4. Edward Callow Gheen, b. 6/24/1933 in Berkeley, CA. Married in Ontario, OR Cheryl Mansfield, 6/29/1968; Denise Hardin, 8/22/1976; Sherri in1999. Children of Edward and Cheryl: (5) Rashelle Lynn, b. 12/3/1969, married Kelly Mack. Their child: (6) Eric Joshua, b. 2/25/2000; (5) Shannon Renae, b. 2/21/1971, married Philip Smith. Their child: (6) Braden Philip, b. 8/6/2007. (5) Cassie Janelle, b. 12/16/1999. Child of Edward and Denise: (5) William Scott, b. 5/9/1983; who married Synthia. Child of Edward and Sherri: (5) Cassie Janelle, b. 12/16/1999.

Skinner Generation 3
The Family of Verna Claire Skinner

Daughter of Will and Ella Skinner

3 Verna Claire Skinner was born September 25, 1897 in Napa, California, and died May 5, 1991 in Ontario, Oregon. She married Elvin Wiley Van Matre October 16, 1932 in Berkeley, California, son of Willis Van Matre and Sarah Hunnel. They had two children:

4. Janet Claire, b. 12/8/1936, Ontario, OR. Married Fred Sower 9/10/1961 in Fruitland, ID, son of Vere Sower and Freda Brown. Their children: (5) Carmen, b. 6/14/1964, who married Jeff Hall, 11/22/1992, and have three children: (6) Forrest, b. 5/22/1997, (6) Tristean, b. 7/24/2000, and (6) Nina, b. 7/24/2000. (5) Angie, b. 8/3/1967 (who married Brian Chamblee).

4. Ernest Wiley, b. 11/7/1939, Ontario, OR. He married Juliie Pence 1/16/1971 in Payette, Idaho. Their children: (5) Zachary Franklin, b. 3/18/1973, Ontario, OR and (5) Nathan Wiley, b. 12/27/1974, Ontario, OR.

Skinner Generation 3
The Family of Nancy Irma Skinner
Daughter of Will and Ella Skinner

3 Nancy Irma Skinner was born October 26, 1898 in Napa, California and died in February, 1985 in Spokane, Washington. She married Bert Cecil Palmer Sr., 1923, son of Fred Palmer. To them five children were born:

4. Mary Palmer, b. 5/1/1924 in Jordan Valley, OR. She married George W. Wilson Sr, 1944 in Spokane, WA. Their children: (5) George W., b.4/24/1947, Spokane, WA who married Sheila, and later, Rebecca. His child: (6) Rebecca Jr. (5) Stephen M. b. 6/3/1948, Spokane, WA, married Christine Gehrett. Their children: (6) Gabriel J., b. 3/27/1972 in Seattle, WA, married Anna. Their children: (7) Alexander, b. 2003. (7) Maxillion, b. unknown. (6) Samuel G., b. 11/3/1973). (5) Patti L., b. 1/1/1951.

4. Bert C. Palmer Jr., b. 5/24/1926 in Jordan Valley, OR, and died 12/26/1997 in Spokane, WA. He married Shirley Reinhardt, 1947; Lori Tuschy, 12/2/1967. The children of Bert and Shirley: (5) Kathleen, b. 11/29/1945, who married Eric Woolett, and later, Steve Cooper. Children of Kathleen and Eric: (6) Amy, b. 12/31/1982 and (6) Brett, b. 10/9/1984. Child of Kathleen and Steve: (6) Robin, b. 3/10/1974 married Louis Blackburn. Their children: (7) Kayla, b. 9/7/1994 (7) Jessica, b. 8/8/1996, and (7) Steven, b. 1/11/1999. (5) Bert C. III, b. 1/11/1951 and married Tami Moore. Their Children: (6) Jennie, b. 1/17/1989 and (6) Joel, b. 3/28/1991. (5) Gail, b. 5/11/1953. Her child: (6) Adam, b. 7/28/1981. (5) Michael William, b. 10/24/1956. Married Stacy Main. Their children: (6) Cameron, b. 5/24/1989, (6) Bergen, b. 12/8/1992, and (6) Madisen, b. 10/26/1994.

4. Frances Palmer, b. 5/4/1928 in Jordan Valley, OR. She married Philip Cook, 6/2/1951 and Jim Lanyon, 11/1/1971. The children of Frances and Philip: (5) Deborah J. b. 7/22/1952, married Duane Walker 1974. Their children: (6) Travis and (6) Nickolus. (5) Sandra M., b. 5/3/1954, married Paul Fors, 1978. Their children: (6) Dustin, b. 1979, (6) Andrew, b. 1981, (6) Brett, b. 1983, and (6) Emily. (5) Michele F., b. 7/18/1956, married Michael Roban, 1984. Their children: (6) James, b. 1978. (6) Amy, b. 1980. (5) Sherri L., b. 3/5/1963, married Kevin Rotchford, and later, Karl Young. Children of Sherri and Kevin: (6) Shelby, and (6) Cody. Child of Sherri and Karl: (6) Cody Young.

4. William F. Palmer, b. 10/25/1929 in Jordan Valley, OR. He married Jeanine Luella Cummings 6/2/1954 in Huntington Park, CA. Their children: (5) William F., b. 4/23/1960; married Peggy Ann Sebring. (5) Laurie Jeanine, b. 3/22/1964.

4. Harold Palmer, b. 3/4/1931 in Jordan Valley, OR. Married Beverly Porter, 1950 in Los Angeles, CA. Their children: (5) Gregory, b. 1951; (5) Pamela Sue, b. 1952; married Lou Lantieri; (5) Jeffrey, b. 1954 and married Sherrie Currier, 1981. Their children: (6) Renee, b.5/7/1981, married Roland Addison. Their children: (7) Quest, b. 5/3/2002, (7) Cadence Beverly, b. 4/26/2004, and (7) Ryder, b. 2/15/2008. (6) Cole, b. 6/28/1987. (5) Nancy, b. 1956, married Cliff May, and later, Michael de Marinis, 1979. Children of Nancy and Michael: (6) Michael, b. 1979

and (6) Kyle, b. 1983. (5)Amy Louise, b. 5/22/1962, married Joseph Skrzymowski. Their children: (6) Amanda, b. 10/17/1988. (6) Jennifer, b. 9/2/1988. (5) Theresa, married Steve Symons.Their children: (6) Nicholis, b. 8/11/1992 and (6) Megan, b. 9/2/1996.

Skinner Generation 3
The Family of William Callow Skinner
Son of Will and Ella Skinner

3 William Callow Skinner born August 5, 1901, died August 5, 1982, in Idaho Falls, Idaho, and married Edna Mae Metheson April 8, 1928, in Boise, Idaho.

Skinner Generation 3
The Family of Ella Marjorie Skinner
Daughter of Will and Ella Skinner

3 Ella Marjorie Skinner was born January 12, 1903 in Jordan Valley, Oregon, and died 1998 in Portland, Oregon. She married Clifford Norman Carlsen Sr. June 21, 1926 in Jordan Valley, Oregon, son of Elias Carlson and Carrie Lee. Their four children:

4. Clifford N. Carlsen Jr., b. 3/16/1927 in Kent, WA; d. 3/5/1998 in Portland, OR. Married Doris Cooper 6/21/1952 in Menlo Park CA, daughter of Edwin Cooper and Edna Herrington. Their children: (5) Laura Edria, b. 3/1/1957, Vancouver, WA and married Luis Hernandez 9/8/1990 in Portland, OR. Their children: (6) Carlos, b. 1/23/1991, d. 2/1/1991 (6) Andres, b. 2/3/1992 in Mexico City, Mexico, and (6) Julia, b. 1/14/1994 in Mexico City, Mexico. (5) Jane Cooper, b. 3/3/1958, in Vancouver, WA and married John Eric Estrem 8/15/1987 in Portland, OR. Their children: (6) Anina Jane, b.3/17/1988 in San Francisco, CA and (6) Samuel John, b. 9/14/1989, San Francisco, CA. (5) Clifford N. III, b. 4/26/1960, Portland, OR, married Lisa Cathleen Zuniga 9/10/1993 in San Francisco, CA. Their children: (6) Maria Leigh, b. 2/28/1997, San Francisco, CA, (6) Clifford Norman IV, b. 1/13/1999, and (6) Paul Elia, b. 11/25/2002. (5) Amy Lee, b. 11/11/1965, Portland, OR, married Kevin Richard Kohnstamm 7/1/1995 in Portland, OR. Their children: (6) Cooper George, b.6/29/1997, Portland, OR, (6) Otis Carlsen, b. 12/21/2000 and (6) Richard Alexander, b. 9/22/2002.

4. Marjorie June Carlsen, b. 7/6/1928 in Corvallis, OR. She married Robert Chandler; Bill Kilkenny; Robert Alan Sederstrom 8/9/1953 in Portland, OR, son of Oscar Sederstrom and Alice Dahlberg. The children of Marjorie and Robert: (5) Susan Ella, b. 5/10/1954, Portland, OR, married Donald Grover in Salem, OR. Their child: (6) Elizabeth Ella, b. 5/23/1984, Washington, D.C. (5) Sally Ann, B. 9/11/1955, Portland, OR, married Forrest Rogers 8/12/1989 in Salem, OR. Their children: (6) Marjorie Grace, b. 12/1998, (6) Susan Ella, b. 2/17/2000, and (6) Anna Lee, b. 2/26/2001. (5) Robert Alan, b. 3/6/1957, Portland, OR, married Karen Lee Craton 8/17/1985 in Hood River, OR. Their children: (6)

Donn Robert, b. 11/15/1988, Kent, WA, (6) Adam Alan, b. 5/14/1991, WA, and (6) Ryan Andrew, b. 1/18/1994, OR. (5) Kirt Carlsen, b. 8/2/1959, Portland OR. Married Jill Holzhouser 6/9/1990. Their children: (6) Katherine Ann, b. 6/19/1992, and (6) Julia, b. 8/24/1994.

4. Ella Lee Carlsen, b. 9/24/1929 in Jordan Valley, OR. She married George Webster Ross Jr. 12/27/1949 in Portland, OR. Their children: (5) George Webster Ross III, b. 5/11/1955, Coos Bay, OR, married Betty Peachey. Their children: (6) Lindsey Ella, b. 6/5/1987, LA. (6) Alison Peachy, b. 3/10/1990, CA. (6) George Webster, b. 9/9/1992, HI. (5) Thomas William, b. 2/5/1959, Everett, WA, and married Frances Marie McGranahan. Their children: (6) Ryan Thomas, b. 12/5/1984, OR, (6) William Elliot, b. 9/23/1986, OR, and (6) Benjamin Curtis, b. 8/14/1990, AR. (5) Mary Ella, b. 1/19/1964, Crossett, AR, and married Ronald Wayne Young 9/26/1998. Their children: (6) Ross Willem, b. 1/30/2000, and (6) Ella Lee, b. 1/25/2004.

4. Joanne Marie Carlsen, b. 5/13/1931 in Vader, WA. She married Kenneth Martinson 7/19/1952 in Portland, OR. Their children: (5) Steven Dewaine, b. 8/27/56, Portland, OR, married Lynnel Porter. Their children: (6) Stevi Annette, b. 8/27/1990. (6) Thais Lynnel, b. 8/27/1990. (5) Michael Lee, b. 3/5/1958, married Jennie Wagner 1984. Their children: (6) Joanne Marie, b. 8/26/1986, and (6) Shadow Stephen, b. 4/14/1992. (5) Daniel Kenneth, b. 9/13/1959, Portland, OR, married Jody Schnackenburg. Their child: (6) Tanner Daniel, b. 1/17/1985. (5) Timothy Craig, b. 7/28/1961, married April McAllister. Their child: (6) Timothy Craig, b. 2/1/1985. His child: (7) Daughter Martinson. (5) Sarah Joanne, b. 3/1/1966, Portland, OR, married Rob Carpenter 9/20/1997 in Portland, OR. Their children: (6) Eric, b. 11/11/1988, and (6) Austen James, b. 12/10/1998.

Skinner Generation 3
The Family of Anna Beatrice Skinner (Beata)

Daughter of Will and Ella Skinner

3 Anna Beatrice Skinner was born March 26, 1907 in Jordan Valley, Oregon, and died about 1977 in Ontario, Oregon. She married Norman Henry Owings, 1927, in Boise, Idaho, son of William Owings and Anna Trebow. Born to them were:

4. Beatrice Owings, b. 1928 in Camas, WA. She married Silas K. Simpson 1953 in Oakland, CA. Their children: (5) Cynthia, b. 7/24/1955, Berkley, CA, married Randall Thelen, and later, William M. See. Child of Cynthia and William: (6) William See III, b. 1987. (5) Melissa, b. 10/3/1957, Seattle, WA, married Harold Chavous, and later, Jeff Cahill, 1984. Child of Melissa and Harold: (6) Alex, b. 6/30/1995. Child of Melissa and Jeff: (6) Kirt, b. 8/1985. (5) Silas K. III, b. 2/20/1959, Seattle, WA, married Sharon Kohler 1992 in Atlanta, GA. Their children: (6) Taylor, b. 5/3/1993, (6) Katie, b. 10/10/1997, and (6) Haley, b. 1999.

4. Richard Norman Owings, b. 2/14/1932 in Caldwell, Idaho. He married Louise Kathryn Mencarini 12/8/1956 in Lodi, CA, daughter of Dan Mencarini and Theresa Bressani. Their children: (5) David Richard, b. 2/4/1958, Berkley, CA, married Karen Lee Blakken 5/28/1983 in Mercer Island, WA. Their children: (6) Jeffrey David, b. 6/18/1987, Bellevue, WA, (6) Amy Corrine, b. 10/17/1993, Bellevue, WA and (6) Robert Mackenzie, b. 6/19/1995, Bellevue, WA. (5) Diane Elizabeth, b. 4/29/1961, Salinas, CA. (5) Lisa Lorraine, b. 8/8/1962, Lodi, CA, married Michael Eugene Langston 11/30/1985 in Mercer Island, WA. Their children: (6) Madison Eva, b4/26/1989, and (6) Terese Kathryn, b. 2/2/1991.

4. Laurence Edgar Owings, b.1940, Boise, ID, died 1959 in Berkeley, CA.

Skinner Generation 3
The Family of Hugh Sackett Skinner
Son of Will and Ella Skinner

3 Hugh Sackett Skinner was born January 5, 1909 in Jordan Valley, Oregon, and died October 20, 1962 in Lapine, Oregon. He married Merle Boswell on August 20, 1930 in Vale, Oregon. Their children are:

4. Suzanne Frances Skinner, b. 7/24/1931 in Ontario, OR. She married Kenneth Dwain Fairchild 11/19/1950 in Redmond, OR. Their children: (5) Scott Marlo, b. 9/29/1951, Redmond, OR, married Cindy Diane Donnelly 4/5/1980 in Reno, NV. Their children: (6) Brian Scott, b. 5/10/1982, Bend OR, and (6) Brett Milo, b. 3/15/1984, Bend, OR. (5) Kristi Ann, b. 5/2/1953, Redmond, OR, married Bruce Lehman Dunlap 6/8/1974 in Powell Butte, OR. Their children: (6) Tyler Joseph, b. 9/22/1980, Portland, OR and (6) Kelsey Elizabeth, b. 9/29/1982, Portland, OR. (5) Sharon Kay, b. 3/5/1957, Prineville, OR. She married David George Manning 9/1/1978 in Cottage Grove, OR; and later, William Thomas Waller 7/30/1982 in Victoria, B.C. The children of Sharon and David: (6) Merriah Sierra, b. 1/22/1977 and (6) Sundance, b. 11/23/1978. The child of Sharon and William: (6) Sky Thomas, b. 3/26/1987, Victoria, B.C. (5) Karen Gay, b. 3/5/1957, married Joseph Paul Gaber 10/24/1972 in Redmond, OR, and later, David Morse Roberts 12/22/1980 in Eugene, OR. The children of Karen and David: (6) Paul Jason Gaber Roberts, b. 11/1/1972, Tacoma, WA, married Samantha, and later, Kandy 6/3/1991 in Eugene, OR. Children of Paul and Samantha: (7) Monica Jean, b. 12/26/2003, and (7) Jacob Paul, b. 6/14/2005. The children of Paul and Kandy: (7) Tasha Kristine, b. 7/31/1991, Eugene, OR. (7) Tanita Shanice, b. 11/26/1992, Eugene, OR. (6) Danielle Suzanne Gaber Roberts, b. 11/19/1974, Tacoma, WA, married Paul Hoffman. Their child: (7) Dakota Bear, b. 5/30/1996, Baker City, OR. (6) Grace Anne Roberts, b. 10/23/1985, Roseville, CA, m. Andrew Carver 12/2005. (5) Shelly Rene, b. 9/15/1964, Redmond, OR, married Scott Wayne Knutz 3/19/1983 in Powell Butte, OR. Their children: (6) Tucker Howard, b. 11/12/1984, Redmond, OR, and (6) Kayla Kristine, b. 12/18/1988, Portland, OR.

4. Darlene Skinner, b. 11/24/1932 in Vale, Oregon. She married Richard Edward Zarozinski 9/4/1955 in Portland, OR. Their children: (5) Maureen Michele, b. 1/31/1957, Portland, OR, married Tim Ivan Mast 4/25/1987 in Portland, OR. Their child: (6) Carter Charles, b. 4/4/1990. (5) John Edward, b. 10/29/1958, Lakeview, OR, married Emily Ann Scott 5/10/1985 in Silverton, OR. Their children: (6) Chelsey Michelle, b. 11/12/1987, Bend OR, and (6) John William, b. 5/9/1990, Bend,OR. (5) William Stanton, b. 6/12/1960, Lakeview, OR, married Carma Gay Bekebrede 7/14/1984 in Klamath Falls, OR. Their child: (6) Chazz Kindrick, b. 11/16/1992, Yuma, AZ. (5) Robert Kent, b. 7/24/62, Lakeview, OR, married Nancy Lynn Gordon 9/22/1990 in Cannon Beach, OR. Their children: (6) Rudolph Edward, b. 8/4/1993, Klamath Falls, OR, (6) Nikolai Alexander, b. 11/18/1994, and (6) Arianna Elizabeth, b. 8/7/1997.

4. Kirtland Hugh Skinner, b. 8/3/1935 in Caldwell, Idaho. He married Tonya Wolf, 1954, and later, Annette Peterson 9/12/1979 in Carson City, Nevada. The children of Kirtland and Tonya are: (5) Michael Kirtland, b. 5/12/1956, and married Roberta Ann McMaster 9/6/1975. Their children: (6) Jason Kirtland, b. 6/22/1977, m. Stephanie Elizabeth Schrantz 7/10/2004. (6) Shanna Elizabeth, b. 11/20/1981, m. Matt Brewer 7/7/2007. (5) Ricky Dean, b. 3/9/58, married Cheryl Underwood 8/3/1996. Their child: (6) Candance Loiuse, b. 1/23/1991. (5) Jeffrey Lee, b. 11/19/1960, married Teresa Harral 5/21/1983, in Bend, OR. Their children: (6) Asa Lucas, b. 7/8/1999, and (6) Beau, b. 11/1/2000. (5) Donald Duane, b. 8/28/1962, married Julie Cleveland Otis 10/22/1994. Their children: (6) Nicholas Congdon, b. 12/23/1989, (6) Marree Congdon, b. 1/23/1992, (6) David James, b. 4/19/1995, and (6) Heidi Love, b. 3/27/1997. (5) Mark Allen, b. 8/21/1964, married Dawn Aery. Their children: (6) Logan Daniel, b. 3/26/1992 and (6) Paige Alena, b. 11/1/1999.

Skinner Generation 2
The Family of Catherine "Carrie" Skinner
Daughter of Silas and Ann Jane

2 Catherine "Carrie" Skinner was born February 18, 1873 in Trout Creek Station, Owyhee County, Indiana, and died 1970 in Berkley, California. She married Lou J. Norton in Napa, California. Their children:

3. Daniel Silas, born in Berkeley, California and married Catherine.

3. Ruth Dorothea, born in Berkeley, California and married J.B. Donnelly.

Skinner Generation 2
The Family of Annabel Skinner
Daughter of Silas and Ann Jane

2 Annabel Skinner was born February 19, 1875 in Trout Creek Station, Owyhee County, Indiana, and died October 7, 1913 in Isle of Man, Great

Britain. She married Robert Quine Hampton August 7, 1913 on the Isle of Man, son of Joseph Hampton and Elizabeth Callow. Their only child:

(3) Anne Elizabeth, was born January 10, 1919 and died November, 2001 at Bexhill on Sea, England. She married Anthony Humphreys on May 30, 1953 on the Isle of Man. Their children: (4) Sarah Elizabeth, born April 2, 1954, at Birkenhead, England, and (4) Robert John, born September 24, 1955, Birkenhead, England, who married Sara Margaretha Dobbs 5/7/1986 in London, England. Their children: (5) Peter Conway, b. 11/25/1988, England; (5) Alexander Michael, b. 11/30/1990, England; and (5) Anna Brigit Corinne, b. 1/11/93, Tulsa, OK.

Skinner Generation 2
The Family of Thomas Lewis Skinner
Son of Silas & Anne Jane

2 Thomas Lewis Skinner was born in 1877 in Jordan Valley, Oregon. He married Violet Glover in 1916 in Jordan Valley, Oregon. Four children were added to the family: Thomas George (Tuck), Gardner William, James Timothy, and Rae.

3. Thomas George (Tuck) was born March 16, 1917 in Jordan Valley, Oregon. He worked as real estate appraiser for many years. Tuck married Peggy Eubanks in 1942 (now deceased). He later married Jacquelyn Lingle Shaver (Jaci) in 1969 and lived in Caldwell, Idaho. To Tuck and Peggy were born six children: 4.Rae Marie Skinner (Mimi), b. 5/14/1944. She married Dean Richard Reynolds in 1964. They had three children: (5) Kecia Marie Reynolds, b. 9/6/1965; (5) Marc Jason Reynolds, b. 2/28/1967; and (5) Scott Alexander Reynolds, b. 9/8/1972. 4. Roseanne Skinner (Sanne) was b. 8/21/1946. She married Patrick Eugene Moran 2/18/1978. They had two children: (5) Patrick Cavanaugh Moran, b. 11/13/1984; and (5) Harry Cavanaugh Moran, b. 9/1/1987. 4. Mary Demorris Skinner (Tuni), b. 11/16/1947. 4. Peggy Elizabeth Skinner (Nikki), b. 4/19/1949. 4. Sarah Ellen Skinner (Sally), b. 1/17/1951. She married Gary Arthur Greener 4/15/1978. They had two children: (5) Katie Michelle, b. 8/13/1981; and (5) McKenzie Elizabeth Greener, b. 11/16/1984. 4. Mary Violet Skinner (Neno), born March 8, 1953.

3. Gardner William Skinner was born 1919 in Jordan Valley, Oregon. He worked as a sales executive in Boise, Idaho. Gardner married Virginia Juanita Yriondo of Boise in 1943. Both are now deceased. Several members of Gardner and Virginia's family are currently proprietors of Skinners Rockhouse, a popular stopping place in Jordan Valley, Oregon. Six children were born to the couple: 4. Gardner William Skinner, Jr. b. 11/28/1944. He married Barbara Wade. They had four children: (5) Gardner William III, b.8/25/1965, married Janice Lynn Grant. (Gardner later married Jeanette Naomi Hanson Zahm in 1982.) Their children: (6) Jordan Lynn, b. 6/11/1996 and (6) Sarah Jane, b. 6/19/1999. (5) Mathew Arthur, b.6/21/1968. (5) Daniel Joseph, b.9/8/1970, married Heather Gay Kirk

6/25/1999. Their children: (6) Isaac Hayden, b. 11/28/2000 and (6) Emelia Violet, b. 4/13/2004. (5) Carrie Ann, b.1/9/1974. 4. Stephen Lewis Skinner, b. 5/28/1946. He married Yvette Powell and they had two children: (Stephen later married Kristine Helen Steglich in 1987.) (5) Zachary Hughes, b. 10/15/1977 in Boise, ID and Nichole Schallenberger. Their child: (6) Jackson James, b. 8/27/2008. (5) Flynn David, b.4/9/1981, married Beth May. Their child: (6) Evianne Elaire, b. 10/7/2008. 4. Richard Glover Skinner, b. 11/25/1948, married Joy Leigh Palmer on June 7, 1980, and later married Mardi Tensen Butcher on July 5, 2002. 4. Elizabeth Juana b. 10/25/1949. She married Neil Pincock Moss in 1974. They had two children: (5) Heather Shea Moss, b. 2/13/1977, married James Wallace Hicks 10/20/2001. Their children: (6) Riley James, b. 9/5/2003, (6) Grayson Wallace, b. 9/5/2003, and (6) Alexandra Shea, b. 12/29/2007. (5) Rebecca Anne Moss, b. 5/21/1978, married William Rosse Parsons 11/12/2005. Their child: (6) Audrey Grace, b. 12/7/2007. 4. David Rupert Skinner b. 1/12/1953. He married Patricia Jane Cleary 6/9/1979. They had four children: (5) Laura Elizabeth, b. 6/24/1982; (5) Jacob David, b. 1/13/88; (5) Kathryn Cleary, b. 3/23/1991; and (5) Benito Gardner, b. 11/3/1993. 4. Jonathon Andrew Skinner, b. 8/30/1966. He married Kristina Marie Iglesias 6/13/1992. Their children: (5) Andrew Isaac, b. 4/22/1994; (5)Timothy William, b. 3/19/1997; and (5) Jack Gardner, b. 1/6/2002.

3.James Timothy Skinner, b. 11/12/1921. He married Marsha Ann Baker, September 3, 1943. Jim is now deceased. Six children were born to the couple: 4. James Timothy Skinner, Jr., b. 10/5/1944. He married Beatrice and they had four children: (5) Cameron William, b. 5/1/1970, married Kathryn Sirr and had a child, name unknown. (5) Allison Shea, b. 4/12/1972; (5) Nathaniel Glover, b. 11/22/1975; and (5) Casandera, b. 11/22/1975, married John White and had a son: (6) Jacob Conlon White, b. 6/9/1997. 4. Marilyn Kay Skinner, b.4/30/1946, married Robert Lanier, and had three children: (5) Mathew Eggers, b. 3/8/1976; (5) Tyler Foute, b. 5/19/1981; and (5) Carly Foute, b. 9/7/1982. 4. Barbara Ann Skinner, b. 5/25/1947, married Mr. Allen and had two children: (5) Michael Ernst, b. 8/19/1967; and (5) Gerald Allen, b. 5/10/1973. 4. Keith Joseph Skinner, b. 1/18/1952, married Denise, and had three children: (5) Olivia, b.1/18/1976; (5) Breanna, b. 3/28/1977; and (5) Joseph Ryan, b. 3/10/1978. 4. Thomas Patton Skinner b. 2/3/1957, married Cindy Hallinan, and had a child: (5) Lauren Rae, b.11/26/1990. 4. Robert Marcus Skinner b. 9/15/1965, married Pam. Their three children: (5) David Windsor, b. 3/29/1993; (5) James Edward, b. 2/5/1995; and (5) Anne, b. 1997.

3.Rae Skinner was born in 1922. She attended Marylhurst College in Lake Oswego, Oregon and joined the Holy Names Convent. She taught in a number of Catholic Elementary and High Schools in Oregon. Rae is now retired and lives in the retirement community on the grounds of Marylhurst.

Skinner Generation 4
The Family of Robert Harold Skinner (Bob)
Son of Silas Kirtland Sr. and Johanna

4 Robert Harold Skinner (Bob), was born June 26, 1920. He married Sara Morgan November 9, 1946 in Roanoke, Virginia. Three children were added to the family in Ontario, Oregon: Robert Morgan, Nancy Jane, and Sally Ann.

(5) Robert Morgan Skinner b. 5/22/1950 in Ontario, OR. He married Karen McKay about 1973 in Vale, OR. Four children were added to the family: (6) Robbin, 2/12/1975 in Caldwell, ID, who married Michael Eiguren in 11/29/1996. Their children: (7) Nicolas Morgan, b. 4/5/1997 (7) Kirk Pascual, b. 4/14/2000, (7) Birch Michael, b. 9/4/2003, and (7) Ross Sckett, b. 10/28/2008. (6) Kimberly, b. 6/26/1976 in Caldwell, ID, married Morgan Johnsrud 7/10/2004 in Jordan Valley, OR on the Skinner Ranch. Their children: (7) Greyden Silas, b. 4/14/2005, and (7) Bode Morgan, b. 12/20/2006. (6) Silas, b. 8/12/1977 in Caldwell, ID, who married Tracy Sarceda in 1998 in Ontario, OR. They have three children: (7) Kasen, b.3/2/1999 (7) Regann, b. 9/15/2000 and (7) Cort, 12/19/2001. (6) Michael, b. 5/13/1981 in Caldwell, ID, who married Kelsi Johnson 11/11/2006 in Butte, MT, have a son: (7) Jayden Patrick, b. 10/21/2008.

(5) Nancy Jane Skinner, b.9/11/1952 in Ontario, OR. She married Ray Melville. They have two children: (6) Jeff, b. 6/27/1979; and (6) Adam, b. 11/24/1981.

(5) Sally Ann Skinner, b. 3/1/1956 in Ontario, OR. She married David Sherman in Boise, ID. They have two children: (6) Cristopher, b. 3/21/1984; and (6) Sara Jo, b. 3/9/1987.

Skinner Generation 4
The Family of Silas Kirtland Skinner Jr. (Kirt)
Son of Silas Kirtland Sr. and Johanna

4 Silas Kirtland Skinner Jr. (Kirt) was born August 26, 1922, died August 1995, and married Naida Weybark in 1957 in Portland, Oregon. Their children:

5. Barbara Skinner, b. 4/9/1961 in Seattle, WA. She married Brad Browning. They have two children: (6) Stephanie, b. 2/13/1981, married Moses Fetters 6/9/2007 in East Lansing, MI. Their child: (7) Amaya Christine, b. 4/19/2008. (6) Karrah, b. 11/10/1987.

5. William Skinner, b. 4/9/1961 in Seattle, WA; died January 10, 2007, CA.

Skinner Generation 4
The Family of Verna Christine Skinner Moore (Chris)
Daughter of Silas Kirtland Sr. and Johanna

4 Verna Christine Skinner (Chris) was born 1925 in Jordan Valley, Oregon. She married Charles William Moore in 1949 in Jordan Valley. They have five children:

(5) Theodore Kirtland, b. 12/1/1950 was born in 1959 in Ontario, OR. He married Marilyn Jean Mohr. They have two children: (6) Jennifer Jean, b. 7/25/1979, in Ontario, OR, married Marc Slatter 6/24/2000 in Ontario, OR. Their children: (7) Lindsay Jean, b. 10/2/2000, (7) Colton Dean, b. 10/30/2002, and (7) John Weston Theo, b. 3/27/2004. (6) Theodore Randall, b.7/9/1982, in Ontario, OR, married Jami Meath 8/10/2007 in Baker City, OR. Their child: (7) Theodore Joshua, b. 6/29/2008.

(5) Leah Christine, b. 3/4/1953 and married Robert Churchill in Citrus Heights, CA. They have three children: (6) Karen Michelle, b. 3/3/1977, in Carmichael, CA. She married Joel Garcia 7/9/1999 in Sacramento, CA. Their children: (7) Maria Christine, b. 3/27/2000, (7) Alexander Tirso, b. 4/15/2003, and (7) Sofia Luna, b. 5/2/2005. (6) Bobby Joseph, b. 9/4/1981; and (6) Karey Anne, b. 2/24/1989.

(5) William Thomas, b.9/16/1955 in Ontario, OR. He married Nancy Ingle in Ontario. They have two children: (6) Nathanial Thomas, b. 4/28/1982 in Ontario, OR, and married Cassie 6/27/2003 in Ontario, OR. Their children: (7) Macey Mckenna, b. 4/18/2005 and (7) Krece William, b. 2/21/2008. (6) Sara Anne, b. 6/14/1984.

(5) Johanna Mary, b. 4/10/1960 and married Michael O'Rourke in Ontario, OR. They have four children: (6) Nicole Christine, b. 2/2/1984; (6) Tamara Renee, b. 8/18/1985; (6) Bryna Johanna, b. 3/14/1987; and (6) Jake Michael, b. 8/31/1991.

(5) Robert Paul, b. 2/6/1964 in Ontario, OR. He married Kerri Cathey, 7/29/1988 in Boseman, MT. They have two children: (6) Michael Paul, b. 10/5/1990; and (6) Savannah Elizabeth, b. 7/19/1996.

Skinner Generation 4
The Family of Daniel Herbert Skinner (Dan)

Son of Silas Kirtland Sr. and Johanna

4 Daniel Herbert Skinner (Dan) was born August 12, 1926. He married Catherine Ross in 1973 in Klamath Falls, Oregon. They have two children born in Nampa, Idaho:

(5) Jocele Ann, b. 8/9/1974, married George Decker in Nampa, ID, 10/2004. Their children: (6) Katie, b. 6/21/2005; and (6) Jack Edward, b. 2/28/2007.

(5) Elizabeth Megan, b. 1/25/1978, married Steven La Vigne 8/21/2004 in Silverton, OR. Their children: (6) Daniel Edward, b. 1/10/2006; and (6) James Thomas, b. 3/2009.

Skinner Generation 4
The Family of John Sackett Skinner

Son of Silas Kirtland Sr. and Johanna

4 John Sackett Skinner was born in 1929 in Jordan Valley, Oregon. He married Carole McGuire in 1952 in Twin Falls, Idaho. They have four children:

(5) Michael John, b. 2/18/1954 in Twin Falls, ID. He married Katherine Meyers 8/1/1981 in Cleveland, OH. He married Sheryl Warner 7/16/2005 in Kirkland, WA. The children of Michael and Katherine: (6) James Arthur, b. 8/31/1986 in Detroit, MI; and (6) Michelle Johanna, b. 9/15/1988 in San Francisco, CA. The children of Michael and Sheryl: (6) Scott Warner and (6) Sara Warner.

(5) Rebecca Jo, b. 11/9/1955 in Twin Falls, ID. She married Arthur Witkowski 11/4/1978 in Salem, OR. They have two children born in Kirkland, Washington: (6) Mitchell John, b. 12/12/1982; and (6) Mark Daniel, b. 1/4/1991.

(5) Daniel Delous, b. 7/1/1959 in Twin Falls, ID. He married Tamara Green in Boise, Idaho. They had three children: (6) Cody Christian, b. 9/17/1989; (6) Colton Daniel, b. 6/23/1993 in Nampa, ID; and (6) Brice Delous, b. 10/30/1994 in Nampa, ID.

Daniel married Marie Capellano 10/4/2001. Their child: (6) Linzy Marie, b. 12/4/1995.

(5) Diana Kay, b. 1/31/1964 in Caldwell, ID. She married David Unruh 3/30/1985 in Salem, OR. They have three children born in Salem, OR: (6) Travis Glenn, 9/18/1988; (6) Trevor Michael, b. 6/13/1991; and (6) Tanner John, b. 3/9/1996.

Skinner Generation 4
The Family of Jessie Johanna Skinner Owens (Joanne)
Daughter of Silas Kirtland Sr. and Johanna

4 Jessie Johanna Skinner Owens (Joanne) was born November 22, 1932. She married Sanford Duane Owens, in Redmond, Oregon. They have five children:

(5) Andrea Gay Owens, b. 5/10/1957 in Canyon City, OR. She married Douglas Duane Waldrop. They have two children: (6) Carrie Lynne, b. 11/18/1983; and (6) William Douglas, b. 10/31/1985.

(5) Martin Murray Owens, b. 10/23/1958 in Redmond, OR.

(5) Billie Jo Owens, b. 3/18/1960 in Redmond, Oregon. She married Paul Anthony Burns 12/17/1988 in Sherwood, OR. They have three children: (6) Brockel Joseph, b. 5/14/1990 in Pasco, WA; (6) Joseph Callow, b. 9/2/1992 in Pasco, WA; and (6) Bailey Johanna, b. 10/26/1994 in Pasco, WA.

(5)Tamara Alison Owens, b. 12/3/1961 in Redmond, OR. She married Jeffery Alan Bertolotto 8/13/1988 in Sherwood, OR. Their children: (6) Jacob Ronald, b. 1/5/1992 in Portland, OR; and (6) Jessica Clarice, b. 12/5/1996, Tualatin, OR.

(5) Wesley Duane Owens, b. 3/22/1969 in Redmond, Oregon.

ooooo

The Family of Thomas Sackett

1 Thomas Sackett was born in 1530 in England. He died March 1596 in Isle of Thanet. He was married in 1555 in England. Four children were born to the family: Thomas, born in 1557 and died in November 1615 in Birchington; Anne, born 1560; Mildred, born 1562 in Isle of Thanet, and married Daniel Ruffe in 1596; and George, born 1565 in Isle of Thanet, and married Katherine Thompson in 1590.

2 Thomas Sackett was born in 1557 and died in November 1615 in Birchington. He married Martha Strowde in 1582 in St. Peter, Isle of Thanet. Nine children were born to the family in the Isle of Thanet: Johann, born 1582, later married Hugh Write; John, born 1586 and died 1677 in St Lawrence in Thanet; Martha, born 1588; Sara, born 1591, died in 1634, and married Richard Mockett February 6, 1614 in Birchington; Thomas, born 1593 and died 1619 in Thanet; Simon, born November 1595 and died October 1635 in Newtown, Massachusetts; William, born 1598; Henry, born 1601 and died in 1665; and Elizabeth, born 1604 and married Nicholas Stephens in 1625 in Thanet.

3 Simon Sackett was born in November 1595 and died October 1635. He married Elizabeth Boyman November 2, 1618. They had three children: Christianna, born July 1620 in Margate and married Thomas Tanner in 1641; Elizabeth, born April 1623 in Thanet and died in England; Martha, born in June 1625. Simon's first wife, Elizabeth, died February 27, 1626. He then married Isabel

Pearce August 6, 1627. They had two children: Simon, born 1630 in England and died July 9, 1659 in Springfield, Massachusetts. He married Sarah Bloomfield in 1652 in Springfield; and John, born 1632 in Newtown, Massachusetts and died October 8, 1719

4 John Sackett was born in 1632 in Newtown, Massachusetts and died October 8, 1719. He married Abigail Hannum, daughter of William Hannum and Honor Capen. Nine children were born to the family: John, born November 4, 1660 in Northhampton, Massachusetts; William, born April 20, 1662; Abigail, born December 1, 1663 and died July 3, 1683; Mary, born 1665 and died November 19, 1667; Hannah, born March 7, 1669; Mary, born June 1672; Samuel, born September 16, 1674; Elizabeth, born May 27, 1677; and Abigail, born 1683. John would marry again to Sarah Stewart.

5 John Sackett was born November 4 1660 in Northhampton, Massachusetts and died in 1745. He married Deborah Filley December 1, 1686. Six children were born to the family: John, born March 3, 1688; Abigail, born October 16, 1690; Daniel, born August 14, 1693; David, born July 7, 1696; Benjamin, born October, 31, 1698; and Deborah, born November 16, 1701. Later John would marry again to Mahitable Danks. Five more children were added to the family: Isaac, born February 14, 1703; Ezra, born 1704; Israel, born March 6, 1706; Eliakim, born March 12, 1712 in Westfield, Massachusetts and died in 1764 in the same town; Mary, born March 5, 1715.

6 Eliakim Sackett was born March 12, 1712 in Westfield Massachusetts and died there in 1764. He married Bethseda Fowler July 5, 1738. Bethseda was born in 1717 to Samuel Fowler and Maria Root. Ten children were born to the family: Eliakim Jr., born November 1739 and died August 26, 1758; Rhoda, born December 21, 1740 and married Josiah Ashley; Mercy, born November 25, 1742 and married Oliver Weller; Justice, born October 14, 1745; Stephen, born May 23, 1748, died 1830, and married Eunice Ross; Ezra, born November 15, 1750, died 1834, and married Lydia Lovering February 14, 1779; Pliny, born May 24, 1753; Eunice, born February 19, 1756; Sarah, born August 29, 1758 and married Elna Hoyt; and Molly, born November 1761.

7 Pliny Sackett was born May 24, 1753. He married Elizabeth Kellogg April 1780. Three children were added to the family: Royal; Pliny, died 1853; and Electra.

8 Pliny Sackett died in 1853—his birth date is unknown. He married Nancy Barlett in 1814. Nancy was the daughter of Chirstopher Barlett. She died in 1841. Six children were added to the family: Israel, born 1815, died 1848, and married Hannah Aldridge; Isaac, born 1817 and died 1856; Samuel, born 1819 and died 1838; Maryette, born 1821 and married Hiram Roodrich who was born 1823; Chauncy, born 1826 and died 1890; and Kirtland, born April 10, 1831 in Boston Center, Erie County, New York. He died October 23, 1908 in Napa, California.

9 Kirtland Sackett was born April 10, 1831 in Boston Center, Erie County, New York. He died October 23, 1908 in Napa, California. He married Nancy Henery November 5, 1861 in Napa, California. Nancy was born April 3, 1836. She was the daughter of Samuel Henery. Eight children were added to the family: Hattie Edith, born August 13, 1862; Lena, born October 23, 1863 and died October 24, 1863; George Kirtland, born May 27, 1866; Ella, born June 21, 1868 in Napa, California, died October 17, 1941 in Jordan Valley, Oregon, and married William Silas Skinner November 11, 1891 (see Ella's entry into the Skinner line at generation 8); Mary Jane, born December 4, 1864 and died March 24, 1869; Samuel, born March 31, 1870; Charles Pickie, born February 25, 1872; and Margaret, born July 11, 1875, married William Imrie.

10 Ella Sackett, was born June 21, 1868 in Napa, California, and died October 17, 1941 in Jordan Valley, Oregon. She married William Silas Skinner November 11, 1891. They went on to have nine children. (See The Family of Ewan Skinner above).

10 Margaret Sackett (Ella's sister) was born July 11, 1875 and married William Imrie. He was an insurance executive in Napa California. Their children included: Wallace Kirtland, married Elizabeth; Margaret Lavelle, married George Lane; and Janet Elizabeth, married William Barlow.

11 Janet Elizabeth Imrie and William Barlow were parents of two children, Diana Leigh Barlow and Steven Imrie Barlow. The Imries and Will and Ella Skinner became very close and visited often in each other's homes. The Imries were avid hunters and for many years hunted each fall on the Skinner Ranch.